Real-Life X-Files

REAL-LIFE
X-FILES

investigating
the paranormal

JOE NICKELL

THE UNIVERSITY PRESS OF KENTUCKY

Publication of this volume was made possible in part
by a grant from the National Endowment for the Humanities.

Editorial and Sales Offices: The University Press of Kentucky
663 South Limestone Street, Lexington, Kentucky 40508–4008

05 04 03 02 01   5 4 3 2 1

Library of Congress Cataloging-in-Publication Data

Nickell, Joe.
    Real-life X-files : investigating the paranormal / Joe Nickell.
        p.   cm.
    Includes bibliographical references and index.
    ISBN 0-8131-2210-4 (hardcover : alk. paper)
    1. Parapsychology—Case studies. I. Title.
    BF1031 .N52 2001
    133—dc21   2001003408

This book is printed on acid-free recycled paper meeting
the requirements of the American National Standard
for Permanence in Paper for Printed Library Materials.

Manufactured in the United States of America.

Contents

Acknowledgments

I am grateful to colleagues at the Center for Inquiry in Amherst, New York, for help in various ways, including research assistance. They include Tim Binga, Director of the Center for Inquiry Libraries; Kevin Christopher, Public Relations Director of the Committee for the Scientific Investigation of Claims of the Paranormal (CSICOP); Barry Karr, Executive Director of CSICOP; Tom Flynn, Director of Inquiry Media Productions; Kendrick Frazier, Editor of *Skeptical Inquirer* magazine; Benjamin Radford, Managing Editor of *Skeptical Inquirer*; and Ranjit Sandhu, Research Associate of the Center for Inquiry, who also prepared the manuscript. Specific production assistance also came from Lisa A. Hutter, Art Director, and Paul Loynes, Production, as well as staff member Allison Cossett, former *Skeptical Inquirer* Art Director Chris (Kuzniarek) Karr, Matt Nisbet, and Etienne Ríos.

I am deeply indebted to Robert A. Baker, Emeritus Professor of Psychology, University of Kentucky, and John F. Fischer, forensic analyst (retired) at the Orange County, Florida, Sheriff's Department crime laboratory, who have been invaluable over the years as fellow investigators, coauthors, and friends.

I am also indebted to fellow CSICOP Executive Council members James E. Alcock, Barry Beyerstein, Thomas Casten, Kendrick Frazier, Martin Gardner, Ray Hyman, Lawrence Jones, Philip J. Klass, Lee Nisbet, Amardeo Sarma, Béla Scheiber, and Paul Kurtz, Chairman of CSICOP.

In addition to individuals mentioned in the text I am also grateful to the following: S.L. Carson, Silver Spring, Maryland; Barbara Henry, Perry, New York, Public Library; Buffalo and Erie County, New York, Public

Library; the late J. Porter Henry Jr., Cincinnati, Ohio; Mike Hutchinson, South West Essex, England; Tammy Miller, Chamber of Commerce, Perry, New York; New York State Library, Inter-Library Loan Department; Tom Pickett, Department of Physics, University of Southern Indiana; Herbert Schapiro, Tucson, Arizona; and Beth Wilson, Howard County Library, Columbia, Maryland.

Introduction

Strange mysteries—UFO and haunted-house reports, claims of spontaneous human combustion and weeping icons, and even more bizarre enigmas—continue to fascinate. We call them *paranormal* because they are beyond the normal range of nature and human experience. It is a broad term that includes not only the "supernatural" but also such reported anomalies as the Loch Ness monster and extraterrestrials, which—if they exist—could be quite natural creatures.

I have investigated such alleged phenomena for thirty years. I joke that I've been in more haunted houses than Casper and have even caught a few "ghosts." I have gone undercover to attend table-tipping séances, obtained police warrants against a mediumistic purveyor of fake spirit pictures, exposed bogus "x-ray clairvoyants," tested dowsers, interviewed UFO eyewitnesses and alien "abductees," examined "weeping" icons, and much, much more.

Whenever possible, I have taken a hands-on approach in my investigations. I have visited relevant sites (like England's crop-circle fields and the shrine of Santiago in northern Spain), experimented to recreate phenomena (such as the liquefying blood of Saint Januarius and the giant Nazca ground drawings of Peru), challenged psychic and other claimants, and devised innovative strategies to investigate strange mysteries.

I have risked lawsuits and charges of trespass, inflicted "stigmata" on myself with a knife, flown in a hot-air balloon over a "monster"-inhabited lake, walked across a twenty-five-foot bed of fiery coals—even appeared twice on *The Jerry Springer Show* and lived to tell about it.

My interest in the paranormal grew with my involvement in magic, a childhood interest rekindled in 1969 while I was employed as a young—and restless—advertising writer. I soon worked as a carnival pitchman, then began to perform professionally as a stage magician. Subsequently, to develop my investigative skills, I became an operative for a world-famous private detective agency, going undercover to investigate arson, grand theft, and other crimes. Still later, after stints as a blackjack dealer, museum exhibit designer, riverboat manager, newspaper stringer, armed guard, stuntman trainee and movie extra, among other roles, I returned to the University of Kentucky to teach technical writing and obtain a Ph.D. in English (with an emphasis on literary investigation and folklore). I studied hoaxes, frauds, and forgeries, as well as myths and mysteries of all types.

With my hands-on investigative approach, I sought to avoid the pitfall of so many who encounter paranormal claims as either "believers" or "debunkers"—that is, with their minds already made up. I decry both a credulous and a close-minded approach, holding that mysteries should neither be fostered nor dismissed but rather carefully investigated with a view toward solving them.

Investigation is predicated on a rational, scientific approach. Therefore, since proving a negative is difficult (often impossible), the burden of proof must fall on whomever advances a claim. In addition, the maxim that "extraordinary claims require extraordinary proof" must apply, meaning that evidence must be commensurate with the extent of a claim. The principle of "Occam's razor" also applies; it holds that the simplest tenable explanation—the one requiring the fewest assumptions—is to be preferred as most likely correct.

I have attempted to follow these principles in the studies and adventures that follow, representing some of my most interesting and challenging cases. They are taken from the pages of *Skeptical Inquirer* and *Skeptical Briefs*, the magazine and newsletter, respectively, of the Committee for the Scientific Investigation of Claims of the Paranormal (CSICOP). I became CSICOP's Senior Research Fellow in 1995 and soon launched an "Investigative Files" column, as well as producing other articles, reviews, and news analyses.

I hope readers will find them as engaging as I have. To be sure, the solving of a mystery can bring disappointment, but there is compensation in the knowledge gained, because—as I have discovered over the years—learning the truth about the paranormal ultimately teaches us about ourselves.

Now turn the page: as Sherlock Holmes would say, "The game is afoot!"

3

Chapter 1

The Case of the Petrified Girl

Raised in the hills of eastern Kentucky, I grew up with the legend of the "petrified girl." Set in the little farming village of Ezel, near my hometown in Morgan County, the story evokes religious accounts of "incorruptible" corpses as well as ghoulish tales of the "undead."

Late in the last century—one account says "in 1880," another "the 1880s," still another "around 1900"—workmen were moving graves from the old Ezel burying ground to a new cemetery site. In some accounts, the reason for the relocation is not recalled, but most state it was due to a typhoid epidemic that stemmed from the graveyard's pollution of local wells. In the course of the disinterments, the men uncovered the grave of a young girl. Some vague accounts have neither name nor age for her, while others reach near agreement that she was "a 17-year-old daughter of a Mr. and Mrs. Wheeler" or more specifically "Minnie Wheeler, a seventeen-year-old girl."

When her casket was reached, it was reportedly too heavy to be lifted. But more men and ropes were obtained, and a hole was drilled in the coffin to let water out. Finally the still-heavy casket was lifted out of the grave and opened, whereupon the girl was discovered to have been petrified; even her clothing, says one narrative, had turned to stone (Nickell 1994). (See figure 1.1.)

Supposedly—some say because of fears the grave would be robbed and the body exhibited in a sideshow—the girl's body was reburied in an unmarked grave, the location of which was thereafter kept a secret. However, one versified account claims that the fears were actually realized: "To this day, her body had never been found, / Because her brother

Figure 1.1. A relocated cemetery in Ezel, Kentucky, supposedly holds among its secrets a "petrified girl," believed buried among these graves. (Photo by Joe Nickell)

George sold her stone body for many crowns / to a museum for display; she brought in crowds. / People viewed her with awe in disbelief with frowns" (Plumlee 1993).

Documentation

Involving aspects of folklore analysis, historical and paranormal research, forensic pathology, and other disciplines, my investigation began with the collection of various narratives and personal interviews, then progressed to a search through the death notices in the *Hazel Green Herald*. There was no "Minnie Wheeler" listed, but there was this entry in the Wednesday, October 7, 1885, issue: "Miss Nannie Wheeler, daughter of J.W. Wheeler, of Grassy, died of flux [unnatural discharge] on last Thursday, and was buried at Ezel on Friday. Miss Wheeler was about 17 years of age." ("Last Thursday" would have meant that she died on October 1, 1885.) Federal census records revealed that "Nannie" was actually Nancy

A. and that among her five siblings was a younger brother, George W. The matching surnames and the similarity of given names ("Nannie" easily being garbled into "Minnie"), together with other parallel details, including the same age and a brother George, persuaded me I had found my quarry. The burial at Ezel was an especially corroborative fact, and so (I would soon learn) was the time period in question.

Further searching through back issues of the *Herald* turned up the following report, dated February 17, 1888: "The people of Ezel, feeling that the location of the grave yard [*sic*] has had much to do with the epidemic of sickness, on Wednesday commenced to remove those who are there buried to a more suitable place. We understand fifty graves will be required to accommodate the coffins removed." The following issue reported: "Ezel, Feb. 20 . . . A beautiful site has been procured for the public grave yard at this place, and the work of transferring the dead from the old to new grave yard has begun, and will continue until all are moved."

I expected next to see a report on the discovery of Nannie's "petrified" body, but in one of the most disappointing moments in my career as an investigator, I learned there was a gap in the record—missing issues of the newspaper during the relevant period. I was therefore forced to rely on hand-me-down narratives. Although, as I have already indicated, these are quite variable as to details, the *effect* of the discovery comes through quite clearly. But was Nannie's body really *petrified*?

Petrifaction?

On the one hand, the water that was reportedly drained from the coffin could be an indication that conditions were right for petrifaction. That occurs when groundwater containing dissolved mineral salts infiltrates buried organic material, replacing the decaying matter with the minerals while preserving the shape and even the cellular structure of the original material ("Petrifaction" 1986).

On the other hand, true petrifaction in the case of a coffin burial would be exceedingly unlikely. Several "petrified" people have been out-right hoaxes, including the Forest City Man, shown at the World's Columbian Exposition in Chicago in 1893; the Pine River Man (made of water-lime, sand, and gravel) "discovered" in 1876; the Colorado Man (faked for P.T. Barnum at a cost of $2,000); and others, including the notorious Cardiff Giant (unearthed at Cardiff, New York, in 1869) (MacDougall 1958, 23–24; Stein 1993, 13–14, 145).

Often, bodies are said to be petrified when observers are simply astonished to find them in a surprising state of preservation. For example, there is a persistent legend that the corpse of Abraham Lincoln was "petrified" and indeed had "turned to stone" when it was observed in a well-preserved state while his body was on tour after his assassination in 1865, as well as upon reburials in 1886 and 1901. On the latter occasion, his corpse was described as resembling "a statue of himself lying there." In fact, the body had been expertly embalmed and had been kept in an airtight coffin (Lewis 1929).

I researched another Morgan County case that occurred in 1921 when the body of a woman who had died elsewhere was brought home by train. Those who touched her well-preserved body said it felt "hard," and several thought it was "petrified," although the railway company physician explained that the body was simply embalmed—something the rural folk were relatively unfamiliar with (Nickell 1994).

In the case of young Nancy Wheeler, the excessive weight of her coffin could well have been due to its having been waterlogged (as in fact described) and/or due to the story's exaggeration over time. But what about the unusual preservation itself? It is extremely unlikely that her body was embalmed, yet after nearly thirty months it had remained free, or apparently free, of decomposition.

Although comparatively rare, there are numerous reports of "incorruptible" corpses. In more than one instance, investigation has shown that the body had in fact been embalmed. In many other cases, the body is actually mummified—i.e., desiccated—a condition that can occur naturally under certain conditions (such as being kept in sandy soil or in a dry tomb or catacombs; it can also be induced by embalming). Several supposedly "incorruptible" bodies of Catholic saints are revealingly described as "having brown, dry skin with the texture of leather," or being "darkened and wrinkled with age," even "completely mummified" (Cruz 1977). Some of the corpses on display in glass coffins have had to be extensively repaired—for example, being treated with resin and braced with wire, and even, like Saint Bernadette of Lourdes, having the exposed face covered with a wax mask (Cruz 1977; Nickell 1993, 85–93).

But what about cases in which the corpse had not been kept in dry conditions but rather was found intact despite perpetually wet conditions? As forensic pathologists and anthropologists know, a body that has been submerged in water or in wet soil for a long time may form a soaplike substance called *adipocere,* which may develop in the outer layer of fat after three months or more (Spitz 1993, 38). It is estimated to become "complete in adult bodies" after "a year to a year and a half" (Gonzales et al. 1954, 68). Adipocere was once thought to be caused by the body's fat turning literally into soap; actually it is due to the decomposition of the fat into insoluble salts of fatty acids, producing a yellowish-white substance popularly known as "grave wax." It usually forms in the face and buttocks but may affect any part of the body. Depending on the subsequent conditions, the body may eventually take on the leathery effect of mummification, or may in time decompose completely (Ubelaker and Scammell 1992; Geberth 1993). (Many of the "incorruptible" bodies of saints are only temporarily preserved and are later found to be reduced to skeletons [Nickell 1993]).

In certain European (e.g., Slavic) and other countries, the discovery of a preserved corpse may provoke a bizarre response. Some people believe such preservation means the person is one of the "undead," so they may drive a wooden stake through the corpse's heart and then burn the body to end the imagined ghoulish activities of the "vampire" (Wilson and Wilson 1992).

Most likely, adipocere produced the "petrified" appearance of Nannie Wheeler's corpse, which was reportedly unearthed in conditions of excessive saturation from groundwater. Certainly her body does appear to have been well preserved—some say as beautiful as she had been in life, with her hands still clutching her hat. However, the time between burial and disinterment had been less than two and a half years, and there have been instances of excellent preservation over much longer periods—even without apparent embalming.

An 1896 Massachusetts case may likewise be explained by adipocere formation. Reportedly, a woman's body, being relocated to another cemetery, was found to be "petrified." If it is true that (after several months) "the flowers on her breast *seemed as fresh* as on the day of her burial" (emphasis added), that is more consistent with their having been kept under cool, wet conditions than with a claim of petrifaction, since flowers that were actually petrified would have looked like stone. Significantly, there was "a spring which boiled up nearby" (Whalen 1981).

As to the story about Nannie's body being placed on display, that is probably untrue, being absent from all but one account. It was apparently based on someone having seen a body in a museum (reportedly in Cincinnati) that was thought to resemble the teenager.

It is an irony that the young lady has come to be better known for her repose in death than for her all-too-brief life, but such is the effect that mystery can have.

References

Cruz, Joan Carroll. 1977. *The Incorruptibles.* Rockford, Ill.: Tan.

Geberth, Vernon J. 1993. *Practical Homicide Investigation.* Boca Raton, Fla.: CRC Press, 571–72.

Gonzales, Thomas A. et al. 1954 *Legal Medicine,* second ed. New York: Appleton-Century-Crofts.

Lewis, Lloyd. 1929. *Myths After Lincoln.* Reprinted Gloucester, Mass.: Peter Smith, 1973, 259–89.

MacDougall, Curtis D. 1958. *Hoaxes.* New York: Dover.

Nickell, Joe. 1993. *Looking for a Miracle.* Buffalo, N.Y.: Prometheus.

———. 1994. Historical sketches: petrified girl, *Licking Valley (Kentucky) Courier,* Nov. 3. (Except as otherwise noted, information on this case is taken from this source, which provides more detailed documentation.)

"Petrifaction." 1986. *Encyclopedia Americana.*

Plumlee, Mary Irene. 1993. "The Major Accent," in Poem puts accent on Ezel at century's turn, *Licking Valley Courier,* Jan. 14.

Spitz, Werner U., ed. 1993. *Spitz and Fisher's Medicolegal Investigation of Death,* 3rd ed. Springfield, Ill.: Charles C. Thomas.

Stein, Gordon. 1993. *Encyclopedia of Hoaxes.* Detroit: Gale Research.

Ubelaker, Douglas, and Henry Scammell. 1992. *Bones: A Forensic Detective's Casebook.* New York: HarperCollins, 150–51.

Whalen, Dwight. 1981. Petrified women, *Fate,* July.

Wilson, Colin, and Damon Wilson. 1992. *Unsolved Mysteries Past and Present.* Chicago: Contemporary, 368–400.

Chapter 2

The Devil's Footprints

The case of "The Devil's Footprints" is a classic of the "unsolved" genre, having been featured in Rupert T. Gould's *Oddities: A Book of Unexplained Facts* (1928, 1964); Frank Edwards's *Stranger than Science* (1959); C.B. Colby's *Strangely Enough* (1971); Rupert Furneaux's *The World's Most Intriguing True Mysteries* (1977); Martin Ebon's *The World's Greatest Unsolved Mysteries* (1981); and many other anthologies and compendia of the unexplained. The fullest account, complete with the original source material, is given by Mike Dash in *Fortean Studies* (1994).

Colby tells the story in concise form:

There was no denying the footprints in the snow on the morning of February 9, 1855. The odd tracks appeared in several towns in South Devon, England. Residents of Lympstone, Exmouth, Topsham, Dawlish, and Teignmouth all reported the same thing. During the night some weird and uncanny creature had raced in a straight line through these towns, covering a hundred miles and more and leaving behind the tracks nobody could identify.

Each track, about 4 inches in length and $2^3/4$ in width, was exactly 8 inches apart. They were roughly shaped like a hoofprint and were promptly christened "The Devil's Footprints" by all who saw them. Even the conservative *London Times* printed a report of the footprints in the snow. . . .

Going straight across country, the tracks never swerved. They were found upon the top of 14-foot walls and they crossed the roofs of barns and houses, went up and over snow-covered piles of hay and even appeared on the tops of wagons which had been left out all night.

It was as if the creature had leaped up or down, for the tracks showed no apparent change of pace or speed. In many places it was reported

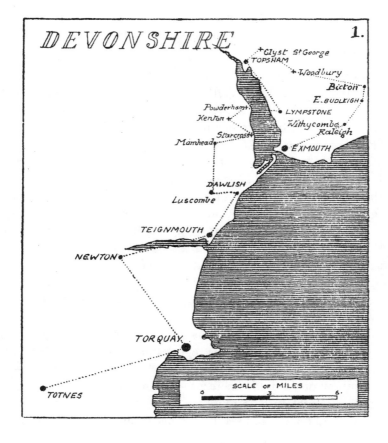

Figure 2.1. Map showing the Devonshire, England, localities in which the "Devil's Footprints" were observed in early February 1855. Contrary to some reports, the trail did not extend in a straight line but zigzagged as shown.

that the snow had been "branded" away or melted from the ground where the "feet" had touched. . . .

Over the hundred-mile course, the distance between the tracks never varied from the regular 8 inches, yet how could anyone or anything travel that far in a single night without varying its stride?

Too many people saw the tracks for it to have been a joke or a local phenomenon. In some instances the prints vanished at the edge of unfrozen ponds or rivers, and appeared again exactly in line on the opposite side, to race away in that straight and mysterious flight across the sleeping countryside. And in all that distance, no one saw it, no one heard it. Only the tracks remained as evidence of the creature's passing.[See figure 2.1.]

Some sources, like Edwards (1959), incorrectly give the date as February 7, 1855, the confusion resulting from early reports mentioning the night of the eighth. By the seventeenth, the story had reached the national newspapers, which published correspondents' accounts through mid-March. Experts from the Zoological Gardens in Regent's Park and from the British Museum were silent, but others offered theories that postulated everything from an escaped kangaroo to birds, rats, cats, foxes, and other creatures. No kangaroo was on the loose, but the naturalist Sir Richard Owen (1855) claimed the solution to the mystery was a badger, based on his interpretation of published drawings and descriptions of some of the tracks. But like those of others, Owen's solution failed to account for all of the reported factors. As one writer noted, a badger could not have "jumped a fourteen-foot wall or squeezed through a six-inch drain pipe, let alone have left clear marks on the sill of a second-storey window!" (Brown 1982)

So what is the solution? It begins with the acknowledgment that "no one explanation will cover all the reported factors" (Brown 1982). But that statement is meant to imply some further, unknown source—perhaps, as many of the mid-nineteenth-century rural South Devon folk thought, the Devil himself. Suppose, however, we postulate that the various reports are manifestations of what psychologists call *contagion*—a term I like to define by an example: in 1978, in Holland, a media alert regarding a small panda that had escaped from a zoo in Rotterdam resulted in some one hundred panda sightings made all over the country; yet as it turned out, the panda had been killed by a train a few yards from the zoo and obviously no one had seen the rare animal (Van Kampen 1979). How do we explain the many sightings? The answer is contagion—an idea or concept that is spread by suggestion, somewhat analogous to a contagious disease. In other words, people's anticipations can lead them to misinterpret what they have actually seen. One person perceives out of the corner of his or her eye a dark shape crossing a yard; thus, a dog becomes a "panda." Someone driving in the countryside sees a rustling in some bushes, and so what is actually a native wild animal triggers another "panda" sighting. Soon, hoaxers will get in on the act and phone

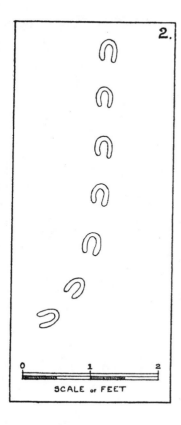

Figure 2.2. A sketch of the strange tracks that appeared in the *Illustrated London News,* February 24, 1855.

in bogus reports. Not surprisingly, contagion is easily recognizable in many paranormal events such as certain UFO and monster "flaps" (Nickell 1995).

Just as there were many sightings attributed to a single panda on the loose in the case in Holland, many factors must surely have been involved during that brief period of near hysteria in February of 1855 in South Devon. In fact, although Furneaux (1977) continued to treat the case as a mystery, he briefly suggested the basic explanation of the case:

> On 8 February there had been a slight thaw; more snow fell that night and a freezing wind got up at dawn, enlarging and distorting, perhaps, the prints of hundreds of badgers, otters, rats and cats.
>
> The prints were discovered over a wide area and they were observed by hundreds of people. No one observer tracked them all. Everyone needed to rely on the reports of others. The stories told agreed as to

14

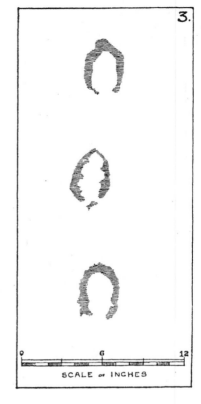

Figure 2.3. Another sketch, portraying "hoofmarks," published in the *Illustrated London News,* March 3, 1855.

size and shape, because everyone tried to fit his or her observations into the general pattern.

On this last point, however, Furneaux is partially in error. Many of the early descriptions were clearly contradictory, thus helping establish that there were indeed multiple creatures involved. Some drawings showed hoofmarks that were "plainly made by a pony-shoe" (Brown 1982), while others described tracks that were "cloven." Some reported "claws" and "toes" in the tracks (Brown 1982; Furneaux 1977). (See figures 2.2 and 2.3.)

By no means did all correspondents report tracks of exactly the same size and spacing. For example, the account published in *The Times* (London) of February 16, 1855, stated that the tracks varied from 1 1/2 to 2 1/2 inches in width, and while their spacing was "generally" eight inches (Gould 1928, 1964), other sources represented the stride as up to twice that distance (Dash 1994). Nor were the tracks in a straight, unbroken line, as shown by various sources, including a dossier kept in a parish church by the Reverend H.T. Ellacombe, who had been vicar in 1855. Says Brown (1982): "He made careful drawings of the tracks and had found that the marks were *not* continuous, but appeared sporadically, e.g. suddenly in the middle of a field, with a flurry surrounding them, as though made by a large ice-laden bird struggling to take off. It was noticed in the estuary that many of the birds seeking water were liable to become frozen into the water, as has happened in some more recent frosts this century. So birds with ice on their feet seem part of the solution, but not all." Moreover, Gould dismissed as "in the last degree unlikely" that any one person had followed the tracks continuously for the alleged one hundred or more miles.

As for Colby's (1971) claim that "the tracks never swerved," that is simply not true. First of all, there is *The Times* report: "The creature seems to have approached the doors of several houses and then to have retreated." Indeed, Dash (1994) correctly notes: "Contemporaries reported meandering lines of prints crisscrossing gardens and churchyards," and a map of the area shows the large-scale zigzagging that is necessary to connect all the villages where the tracks were reported (Gould 1928, 1964).

The notion of the unswerving line seems to have originated from accounts that mention the tracks appearing in a straight line, with one print directly in front of the next. And various animals, such as the donkey, fox, and cat, for example, can leave trails that resemble a single line of imprints. As well, rabbits, hares, rats, and squirrels can leave hopping tracks that not only appear in a straight line, but with their four feet held together, "can form a pattern similar to a hoofmark" (Dash 1994). In any case, one newspaper reported that the tracks were "alternate of each other like the steps of a man and would be included between two parallel lines six inches apart" (Knight 1950).

I believe we can rule out hoaxed tracks like those Brown (1982) mentions at Woodbury, which he says "were obviously manufactured by practical jokers with a hot shoe, since they were said at the time to look like this, the shoe pressed cleanly down to the ground as if made by a hot iron." Surely an iron would not have remained hot for the production of many tracks, thus making the supposed method impractical; and the description seems consistent only with the effect of melting and refreezing that took place. However, there is ample evidence, in addition to the

15

variety of track descriptions, that multiple creatures were involved. A number of cats, for instance, were responsible for many of the tracks in one village, as was explained in 1923 by a woman who had been a young girl there in 1855. As Furneaux (1977) relates:

> She recalled that the footprints were all over the town of Dawlish where her father was Vicar. He and his curates, she said, carefully examined the tracks which ran from the Vicarage to the vestry door, and came to the conclusion that they had been made by the paw-marks of many cats which had been partly washed away by the slight thaw, and expanded into the shape resembling hoofmarks by the early-morning frost. An explanation which, she says, was vehemently rejected by the townspeople who preferred to think they had been visited by the Devil himself. A widespread conviction which the Vicar of Lympstone, the Rev. Musgrave, also found himself unable to dislodge.

In the village of Torquay, a man followed a line of tracks leading from his garden to a tree stump, beneath which he discovered the putative track-maker: a large toad! Gordon Stein (1985) has made a very good case for Devonshire foxes making many of the tracks, although he conceded they would have had difficulty scaling fourteen-foot walls or walking on roofs. He suggests that swans might be responsible in the latter instances, except that their footprints do not match those reported. But can we not expect that tracks on roofs, and no doubt in many other out-of-the way locations, were seen at a distance, which would have left their exact appearance to the imagination?—a collective imagination it would seem.

Clearly, as most writers on the topic agree, no one creature—not even a paranormal one—left all the reported "Devil's Footprints." As Stein (1985) points out, "When no explanation will exactly fit, either we need an additional explanation, or else some of the 'facts' may need to be discarded as weak." I suggest that we need both: we have seen that many of the alleged facts are indeed weak, and only the concept of contagion seems capable of explaining the overall case.

References

Brown, Theo. 1982. *Devon Ghosts.* Norwich, England: Jarrold Colour, 47–53.
Colby, C.B. 1971. *Strangely Enough.* New York: Scholastic, 174–75.

Dash, Mike, ed. 1994. In *Fortean Studies,* vol. 1, ed. by Steve Moore. London: John Brown, 71–151.

Dingwall, Eric J. Cited in "The Devil's Footprints," in Ebon 1981, 102–06.

Ebon, Martin, ed. 1981. *The World's Greatest Unsolved Mysteries.* New York: Signet.

Edwards, Frank. 1959. *Stranger Than Science.* New York: Ace.

Furneaux, Rupert. 1977. *The World's Most Intriguing True Mysteries.* New York: Arc.

Gould, Rupert T. 1928. (Reprinted 1964.) *Oddities: A Book of Unexplained Facts,* 3rd ed. New York: Bell, 9–22.

Knight, W.F. Jackson. 1950. Cited in Dash 1994, 107–09.

Nickell, Joe. 1995. *Entities: Angels, Spirits, Demons, and Other Alien Beings.* Amherst, N.Y.:Prometheus. (See index entries for contagion, "copycat" effect, and hysteria.)

Owen, Richard. 1855. Letter to editor, *Illustrated London News,* March 3, quoted in Gould 1928, 16–17.

Stein, Gordon. 1985. The devil's footprints, *Fate,* Aug., 88–95.

Van Kampen, Hans. 1979. The case of the lost panda, *Skeptical Inquirer* 4(1) (fall): 48–50.

Chapter 3

Magicians Among the Spirits

They have become legendary in the history of spiritualism and continue to spark interest and controversy. The question persists: were the Davenport Brothers "probably the greatest mediums of their kind that the world has ever seen," as Sherlock Holmes's creator Sir Arthur Conan Doyle wrote (1926, 226), or was magician Harry Houdini (1924, 26) correct in reporting that he had facts "more than sufficient to disprove their having, or even claiming, spiritualistic power"? My research into the recently discovered Davenport scrapbook sheds new light on these claims and the fierce disagreement they provoked between Doyle and Houdini.

The Davenports made their debut as mediums in 1854, six years after two schoolgirls, Maggie and Katie Fox, launched modern spiritualism at Hydesville, New York. No doubt the two Buffalo newsboys—thirteen-year-old William Henry Harrison Davenport (b. February 1, 1841) and his fifteen-year-old brother Ira Erastus (b. September 17, 1839)—had heard how the Fox sisters seemed to communicate with ghosts by means of mysterious rapping noises. The boys' father, Ira D. Davenport, was the first to relate the strange happenings. Dishes and cutlery danced about the family's kitchen table and young Ira—when alone—sometimes claimed the spirits had whisked him to distant spots. At household séances, the boys demonstrated their flying ability. As magician John Mulholland explained in his *Beware Familiar Spirits* (1938, 51), "That is, at the beginning of the séance Ira Erastus would be sitting on a chair at one side of the room, and when the lights were turned up after it was over, the chair and boy would be on the other side of the room." Because this transpired in the dark, credulous spectators simply assumed the youth had flown.

At the séances, the spirits supposedly also rapped out messages in the by-then-familiar way, but soon advanced to "automatic writing" (Bowers n.d., 155), which was supposedly produced by spirits guiding the entranced subject's hand. Then the brothers' spirit guide, "George Brown," found he could speak through Ira when the youth was in a "trance state" (Mulholland 1938, 49–50). Another spirit entity was "John King," who decided the boys should take their spirit demonstrations on the road.

In the halls and theaters rented by their father at the direction of "John King," the Davenport Boys (as they were originally called) began to give demonstrations of "spiritual manifestations." To show that they were not physically responsible for the phenomena, they were tied to chairs placed behind a curtain. Later the curtain was replaced by a specially designed "spirit cabinet" (Mulholland 1938, 52). This resembled a huge armoire with built-in benches on either side to which the boys were secured by lengths of rope (Jay 1987, 229; Houdini 1924, 21).

On the floor of the cabinet were placed musical instruments such as violins, guitars, concertinas, and tambourines. Then the doors were shut and the lights turned down. Soon, the instruments were heard to play, and phantom hands were seen to wave eerily through small diamond-shaped windows in the cabinet doors. When the gas lights were turned up and the cabinet opened, the Davenport boys were still securely tied. Spectators were divided over the manifestations; some believed, while others scoffed—or worse—and still others were simply mystified (Mulholland 1938, 53–54).

In time the boys traveled throughout the United States and, as they matured, called themselves the Davenport Brothers. In 1864 they sailed for England, where they "took the literati and public of London by storm" (Dawes 1979, 87) and performed throughout Europe. "Les Frères Davenport" attracted a full house in Paris and went on to Berlin, Vienna, St. Petersburg, and elsewhere. On their return from abroad, a Boston handbill proclaimed that "The World-Renowned Davenport Brothers will appear after a most extraordinary and successful tour of four years in Europe, in their unique and startling wonders, mysterious displays, and unaccountable manifestations" (Christopher 1962, 101).

On July 1, 1877, while the brothers were on tour in Australia, William Davenport, who had long been in ill health, died. Years later when Harry Houdini (1874–1926) was in Australia, he visited William's grave and, finding it in poor condition, had the stonework repaired and flowers planted. On the same trip, Houdini met William M. Fay, who had once performed with Ira and William as the "Davenport Brothers and Fay." Houdini subsequently wrote to Ira at his home in Mayville, New York, and arranged to meet him at the train depot there. Ira took Houdini home and introduced him to his wife (a Belgian woman whom he had met in Paris) and the couple's daughter. Apparently in part because he was moved by Houdini's thoughtfulness in tending to his brother's grave, Ira shared with him a lifetime of secrets (Houdini 1924, 17–25).

Ira spoke to Houdini as one magician to another, even revealing how he and his brother had extricated themselves from their bonds in order to produce the "spirit" effects. Houdini stated, "Ira Davenport positively disclaimed Spiritualistic power in his talk with me, saying repeatedly that he and his brother never claimed to be mediums or pretended their work to be Spiritualistic" (Houdini 1924, 26). Ira did admit that in order to spare their feelings, they never confessed the truth to their believing parents. Years after Ira's death (on July 8, 1911), Houdini included a chapter on the Davenports and Ira's revelations in his *Magician Among the Spirits* (1924, 17–37). Houdini included a facsimile of a letter from Ira claiming in regard to the brothers' performances that "We never in public affirmed our Belief in spiritualism" (28).

By this time, Houdini's friendship with Arthur Conan Doyle (1859–1930) was irreparably strained. Houdini had been debunking some of the very mediums Doyle had endorsed, and the latter had written to him: "Our relations are certainly curious and likely to become more so, for as long as you attack what *I know* from experience to be true I have no alternative but to attack you in turn. How long a private friendship can survive such an ordeal I do not know, but at least I did not create the situation." Houdini did not help matters by publishing this and other excerpts from Sir Arthur's letters (Houdini 1924, 164). Subsequently, in his *History of Spiritualism* (1926, I: 228), Doyle continued to debate Houdini: "It is to be remarked that the Davenports themselves, as contrasted with their friends and travelling companions, never claimed any preternatural origin for their results." But Doyle noted that Ira's statement to Houdini only said the brothers had never "in public" affirmed belief in spiritualism, implying that *in private* Ira was indeed a spiritualist.

Doyle went on to say that "As Mr. Houdini has seemed to question whether the Davenports themselves ever asserted that they were Spiritualists," the matter was clarified by a letter they had written in 1868 to *The*

Banner of Light, the leading American spiritualist journal. Regarding the claim they were not spiritualists, the brothers wrote: "It is singular that any individual, sceptic or Spiritualist, could believe such statements after fourteen years of the most bitter persecution and violent opposition, culminating in the riots of Liverpool, Huddersfield, and Leeds, where our lives were placed in imminent peril by the fury of brutal mobs, our property destroyed, and where we suffered a loss of seventy-five thousand dollars, and all because *we would not renounce Spiritualism*, and declare ourselves jugglers, when threatened by the mob, and urged to do so. In conclusion, we have only to say that we denounce all such statements as falsehoods" (quoted in Doyle 1926, II: 302).

Concerning Houdini's claim that Ira Davenport had admitted that his results were due to trickery, Doyle (1926, 228–29) said that "Houdini has himself stuffed so many errors of fact into his book . . . and has shown such extraordinary bias on the whole question, that his statement carried no weight. The letter which he produces makes no such admission."

Doyle insisted that the Davenports "were never exposed, nor even adequately imitated." As to the latter, he specifically mentioned the claims of British conjurer John Nevil Maskelyne (1839–1917), who produced a spook show in imitation of the Davenports but billed it honestly as magical entertainment (Doyle 1930, 23; Mulholland 1938, 65–66). Doyle railed at magicians who said the brothers were tricksters, although he was himself ignorant of legerdemain and baffled by the simplest tricks. He refused to accept the evidence that the Davenports were merely entertainers, later writing, "There can be no question at all, to anyone who has really weighed the facts, that Ira Davenport was a true medium" (Doyle 1930, 45). With an astonishing lapse of both logic and good sense, Doyle cited "the evidence of thousands of witnesses" as if so many people could not be fooled—a patent absurdity. He also argued that the brothers, if they were truly conjurers, could have so announced themselves and by performing tricks as such "have won fame and fortune" (Doyle 1930, 45)— a dubious notion since they probably gained far more attention by their spiritualist pretense.

Astonishingly, Doyle even suggested that Houdini himself might have had mediumistic powers! Terming Houdini "the greatest medium-baiter of modern times," Doyle (1930, 1) suggested he might also have been "the greatest physical medium of modern times." At least, he said, he was "very sure that the explanations of his fellow-conjurers" as to how Houdini effected his sensational escapes "do not always meet the case" (26). (Doyle failed to understand that magicians often deliberately give incomplete explanations of tricks, and that Houdini and others often had more than one way of accomplishing an effect.)

That bizarre notion aside, the question remains: were the Davenport brothers indeed spiritualists rather than mere "jugglers"—a dichotomy Doyle advanced (1926, II: 302)? Or is that a false dichotomy, a limited choice between two views, with the truth lying elsewhere? A scrapbook that has recently surfaced helps to settle this continuing controversy.

I first saw the scrapbook on one of my visits to Lily Dale Assembly, the "World's Largest Center for the Religion of Spiritualism" (as the entrance sign proclaims). I was taking some colleagues on a tour, and in the museum I spied the scrapbook in a display case. Its pages were open to a clipping heralding the "Davenport Boys" and annotated "Bangor Me. 1858." Seeing my interest, Curator Joyce LaJudice announced that I was looking at the Davenport Brothers' own scrapbook and very graciously removed it from the case for me to peruse. "You know, Joe," she said, "I wouldn't let just anyone look at that." It had recently been discovered in a storage area and recognized as a significant find. I was unable to give it more than a cursory look at the time but later made arrangements to study it at length. I was extended every courtesy in this, being provided a special work area and permission to fully examine and photograph the pages, which I did as part of a three-day stay at Lily Dale, August 7–9, 1998.

My first task was to authenticate the scrapbook.[1] Several flourished signatures—"Ira Erastus Davenport," "I. Erastus Davenport," and "Ira E. Davenport," with addresses of Buffalo and Chicago (the latter dated "1861")—are found throughout the pages. These compare favorably (making allowances for variations over time) with the "Ira E. Davenport" signature on the January 19, 1909, letter to Houdini (previously mentioned). There are also apparent signatures of his brother—"Wm. Davenport" and "Mr. William Davenport"—although I had no known specimens for comparison. The scrapbook may have been shared by the brothers, but it appears to have been kept mostly by Ira and, after William's death in 1877, became solely Ira's while falling largely into disuse. The most recent clipping is from the "New York 'Dramatic Mirror,'" dated August 20, 1910; it features a picture of and brief article about actress Zelie Davenport, Ira's daughter, who was "well known as a leading woman" and who came from "an old theatrical family"—an interesting characterization of the Davenport Brothers.

Most significantly, the scrapbook contains evidence in favor of both Doyle's and Houdini's views. First, there are several indications that Ira Davenport was indeed an avowed spiritualist. For example, there is the obituary of his infant son and first wife who died in childbirth. Headed "Passed to Spirit Life" (and datelined "Adrian [Michigan], June 29, 1863"), it was very likely written by Ira. It said of his unnamed but "accomplished and beautiful wife"[2]: "Possessing a highly refined and cultivated mind and fully realizing the importance of the great truths of spiritualism, she exercised an elevated influence over her husband in properly directing his energies and mediumistic powers, for the advancement of the facts of immortality." The scrapbook also contains some clippings of sentimental verse, one asking "Is Life Eternal" and answering in the affirmative, another telling a dead lover that "You will be my guardian here."

More evidential are penciled "spirit" writings that appear on some of the early pages. These writings are scrawled, smeared, overwritten, stained, and otherwise difficult to read. There seems little of interest, but one phrase declares, "connected with/with [*sic*] spirit manifesting." The writing may be an early form of Ira's handwriting. It is very likely from the 1850s, at which time Ira was practicing "automatic" writing (Bowers n.d., 155).

In addition, there is a suggestive annotation that Ira signed with his initials. It follows a brief, undated clipping about the Davenport Brothers' impending trial at Centerville, Indiana. The charge was unstated but may have been "showing without a license," which (as demonstrated by another clipping) they were charged with at Ionia, Michigan, in September 1860. To the Indiana journalist's sarcastic comment, "the spirits will help them out of their difficulties, of course," Ira responded by writing, "And they did. I.E.D." The comment is ambiguous. Taken literally it suggests that Ira believed he received spirit aid. Or he might have meant that spirits became a mitigating religious issue, which actually happened at Ionia; spiritualists there testified "that the demonstrations given by the Davenport boys were some of the methods which Spiritualists use for disseminating their religious belief."

The Ionia trial provides still additional evidence that bears on Ira's relationship to spiritualism. The brothers had given what one journalist disparaged as "an exhibition of their skill in hemp handling" (i.e. rope tricks) on each of eight successive evenings at a spiritualist assemblage held at nearby Lyons. The article mentioned that "the Spiritualists which number many of our most substantial citizens, felt much aggrieved because of the prosecution." The Davenport Brothers' participation in the "Lyons Spiritual Convention" suggests they were—or were pretending to be—practicing spiritualists.

A clipping from the *Brighton Herald* (England) of December 17, 1864, confirms what is known from other sources, that the Davenport Brothers were accompanied during the early part of their overseas tour by the Reverend J.B. Ferguson, a Presbyterian who became an ardent and eloquent proponent of spirit manifestations and who served as a lecturer with the Davenports' show. By all accounts he had a "minister's simple faith" in the genuineness of the brothers' mediumship (Mulholland 1938, 56, 62). Doyle's insistence that the Davenports were actually spiritualists was based in part on Ferguson. Doyle stated that if Ira claimed otherwise, then he was "not only a liar, but a blasphemer as he went around with Mr. Ferguson, a clergyman, and mixed it all up with religion" (quoted in Houdini 1924, 148).

Even the fact that the scrapbook was discovered at Lily Dale, where it had obviously been for many years, is highly suggestive of Ira's ties to spiritualism. In fact, at an 1885 spiritualist "Camp Meeting" of the Cassadaga Lake Free Association (which became the Lily Dale Assembly in 1906 [LaJudice and Vogt 1984]), Ira Davenport was one of two featured "physical mediums" (those who produced physical phenomena). In reporting on the event, *The Banner of Light* (August 29, 1885) stated that Ira's "fame in this phase of mediumship is world wide." Ira may have had even further involvement in Lily Dale; he lived in the same county, Chautauqua, only a few miles from the scenic spiritualist village.

All of this evidence from the scrapbook indicates that Ira Davenport identified himself as a spiritualist, as Doyle insisted. (So did Ira's obituary in the July 9, 1911, *New York Times*, which specifically referred to him as a "spiritualist." And his tombstone has a religious, compatibly spiritualistic, message, depicting a rising sun with the words, "There never was night that had no morn.")

On the other hand, it is Houdini whom the scrapbook vindicates regarding the Davenport Brothers' demonstrations. In clipping after clipping there is evidence that supports his claim that—as he said Ira admitted to him—the brothers secretly performed the "spirit" effects by slipping free of their bonds. For example, according to an unidentified clipping, circa 1857–1858:

> [A] printer of this city visited the boys and taking along a little printer's ink, after seeing that the boys were firmly tied, placed it on the neck of the violin. He placed quite a quantity there, and the result was that soon the spirit "John" ["John King"], called through the old tin trumpet for a light, as he had been daubing the boys all over with *paint*! When the light was brought it was found that one of the boys, sure enough, had his shoulder pretty well besmeared. Of course the manager stoutly contended that it was placed there by the spirit, but our printer friend was of the opinion that "John" was rather an ignorant spirit if he did not know *printers ink* from paint!

The newspaper continued, saying of the Davenports' performance, "The whole thing is a trick; but it is a clever one."

A similar exposé occurred in Indiana in 1863, as reported in the May 22 issue of the *Richmond (Indiana) Palladium* in an article titled, "The Celebrated Davenport Boys Brought to Grief." A Dr. Henry Davis "applied oil of kreosote [sic] to the handle of the [violin] bow, and as soon as the musical part of the manifestations was over, the hands of the 'mediums' were examined and the odor of the oil was found quite perceptible on the right hand" of one of the brothers. It was therefore he, said the paper, "who had been making the 'spirit music' with which the audience had been edified," and the brothers were thus "convicted . . . of that part of the swindle." They refused to be tested further, whereupon "a crowd of one or two hundred persons rushed upon the stage" and demanded a refund from the Davenports. "Their box, horns, violins, banjoes, etc., were pretty roughly kicked about the stage." When patrons were promised a refund from the ticket office but found it closed, "A large crowd now assembled in the street and demanded to know the whereabouts of the swindlers." Peace was only restored by an appeal to law and order. The brothers and their two associates were arrested and charged with "obtaining money under false pretenses." After posting bond, "the swindlers," said the paper, were "turned loose to prosecute still further their nefarious thieving operations."

Another clipping reported that at the previously mentioned 1860 trial at Ionia, Michigan, a committeeman had been placed with the brothers in the spirit cabinet. He testified that in the dark, "he secured between his knees one of the instruments the spirits were said to play on, and . . . after jerking it several times and finding it fast, one of them [the brothers] said in a low voice, 'don't hold it so fast.'" As well, "several witnesses testified to what appeared to them signs of humbuggery" which were "such that darkness was required to do them in."

Two clippings (one from the *Detroit Free Press*, the other from the *Clearwater [Michigan] Democratic Union*) describe a revealing exposé of November 1860. On a Sunday afternoon, the brothers gave one of their exhibitions where, as usual, "permission was given for any person who wished to do so to examine the 'boys' and satisfy themselves that there was no deception about the matter." Thereupon (continued the *Free Press*), "One or two persons took advantage of the permission given, and commencing the search, discovered some of their implements of trade concealed in the boot of one of the performers." The brothers announced that no further searching would be permitted, but when the searchers persisted, "a general *melee* ensued, during which one of the Davenports drew a bowie-knife or dirk and threatened to kill any person who should lay hands on him." This ended the exhibition and resulted in charges being placed against the brothers. "The one arrested for assault," reported the *Democratic Union*, was subsequently acquitted, after which "the whole were tried" for "exhibiting on the Sabbath" and convicted. Rather than pay a $25 fine each, they elected to serve a thirty-day jail term.

Still another scrapbook clipping (unidentified but dated March 24, 1865) tells how two aggressive English skeptics, a Mr. Hulley and Mr. Cummins, "took an active part . . . in baffling the spiritualistic pretensions of the Brothers." Details are not given in this particular article, although in similar instances reported elsewhere (McHargue 1972, 131–33), the Davenports were stymied when they were tied especially securely. As a result, several persons sought to recover their five-shilling admission fee on the grounds that the brothers failed to perform what their sponsors had promised in their advertisements.

Taken as a whole, the evidence of the scrapbook does indicate that Ira Davenport was a practicing spiritualist, or at least pretended to be, although he and his brother used trickery to accomplish the effects they attributed to spirits. Clearly they were career deceivers who (according to Ira's obituary) "made a fortune of $600,000" before William's untimely death and Ira's subsequent retirement. In his old age, Ira's qualms about their dishonesty probably prompted him to make some atonement by confessing their secrets to Houdini while, at the same time, trying to present their actions in the most favorable light.

References

Bowers, Edwin F. [n.d.] *The Phenomena of the Séance-Room.* London: Rider.

Christopher, Milbourne. 1962. *Panorama of Magic.* New York: Dover.

Dawes, Edwin A. 1979. *The Great Illusionists.* Secaucus, N.J.: Chartwell.

Doyle, Arthur Conan, 1926. *The History of Spiritualism*, vols. I and II. Reprinted New York: Arno, 1975.

———. 1930. *The Edge of the Unknown.* Reprinted Alexandria, Va.: Time-Life, n.d.

Houdini, Harry. 1924. *A Magician Among the Spirits.* New York: Harper & Brothers.

Jay, Ricky. 1987. *Learned Pigs & Fireproof Women.* London: Robert Hale.

LaJudice, Joyce, and Paula M. Vogt. 1984. *Lily Dale: Proud Beginnings,* n.p. [Lily Dale, N.Y.], 5, 27–28.

McHargue, Georgess. 1972. *Facts, Frauds, and Phantasms.* New York: Doubleday.

Mulholland, John. 1938. *Beware Familiar Spirits.* Reprinted New York: Charles Scribner's Sons, 1979.

Nickell, Joe. 1990. *Pen, Ink and Evidence: A Study of Writing and Writing Materials for the Penman, Collector and Document Detective.* Lexington: Univ. Press of Kentucky.

———. 1996. *Detecting Forgery: Forensic Investigation of Documents.* Lexington: Univ. Press of Kentucky.

———. 1999. *Crime Science: Methods of Forensic Detection.* Lexington: Univ. Press of Kentucky.

Chapter 4

The Specter of Spontaneous Human Combustion

Like Count Dracula, the mythical specter of "spontaneous human combustion" (SHC) refuses to die. The latest book to fan the flames of belief, so to speak, is *Ablaze!* by Larry E. Arnold. The dust jacket blurb states that the author "redirected a background in mechanical and electrical engineering to explore the Unconventional." Indeed, Arnold is a Pennsylvania school bus driver who has written a truly bizarre book—one that takes seriously such pseudoscientific nonsense as poltergeists and ley lines (362–66), and that suggests that the Shroud of Turin's image was produced by "flash photolysis" from a body transformed by SHC "into a higher energy state" (463).

As if he were a trained physicist on par with any Nobel laureate, Arnold blithely posits a subatomic "pyrotron" as the mechanism for SHC (99–106), and he casually opines that "extreme stress could be the trigger that sets a human being ablaze" (163). In the many cases in which the alleged SHC victim had been a careless cigarette smoker or in which the victim's body was found lying on a hearth, Arnold dodges the issue of spontaneous human combustion by invoking "preternatural combustibility," an imagined state in which a body's cells reach a heightened susceptibility to ignition by an outside spark. To understand Arnold's approach, we can look at a few of his major examples—those cases which are treated at chapter length in *Ablaze!*

The Death of Dr. Bentley

Arnold leads off with the 1966 case of Dr. John Irving Bentley, who was consumed by fire in the bathroom of his home in Coudersport, Pennsylvania. About all that was left of him—in recognizable form—was his lower leg, which had burned off at the knee; it was lying at the edge of a hole about two and a half by four feet that had burned into the basement.

Spontaneous human combustion? Actually, the infirm ninety-year-old physician had a habit of dropping matches and hot ashes from his pipe upon his robes, which were spotted with burns from earlier occasions. He also kept wooden matches in both pockets of his day robe—a situation that could transform an ember into a fatal blaze. Apparently waking to find his clothing on fire, Dr. Bentley made his way into the bathroom with the aid of his aluminum walker—probably at an accelerated pace—where he vainly attempted to extinguish the flames. Broken remains of what was evidently a water pitcher were found in the toilet. Once the victim fell on the floor, his burning clothing could ignite the flammable linoleum; beneath that was hardwood flooring and wooden beams—wood for a funeral pyre. Cool air drawn from the basement in what is known as the "chimney effect" could have kept the fire burning hotly (Arnold 1995, 1–12; Nickell and Fischer 1984).

The "Cinder Woman"

In chapter six of his book, Arnold relates the fiery death of a widow, Mary Reeser, who perished in her efficiency apartment in St. Petersburg, Florida, in 1951. This classic case of SHC has long been known as the "cinder woman" mystery. Except for a slippered foot, Mrs. Reeser's body was largely destroyed, along with the overstuffed chair in which she had sat and an adjacent end table and lamp (except for the latter's metal core). The rest of the apartment suffered little damage. "Nor," adds Arnold, "did the carpet beyond her incinerated chair show signs of fire damage!" (76)

In fact, the floors and walls of Mrs. Reeser's apartment were of concrete. When last seen by her physician son, Mrs. Reeser had been sitting in the big chair, wearing flammable nightclothes and smoking a cigarette—after having taken two Seconal sleeping pills and stating her intention of taking two more. The official police report concluded that "Once the body became ignited, almost complete destruction occurred from the destruction of its own fatty tissues." (Mrs. Reeser was a "plump" woman, and a quantity of "grease"—obviously, fatty residue from her body—was left at the spot where the immolation occurred.) As the fat liquefied in the fire, it could have been absorbed into the chair stuffing to fuel still more fire to attack still more of the body. (We will discuss the "candle effect" more fully later on.) (Arnold 1995, 73–91; Nickell and Fischer 1984)

SHC Survivor?

In chapter 15, Arnold relates the case of Jack Angel, who told him "an incredible incendiary tale." Angel stated that in mid-November 1974, while he was a self-employed traveling salesman, he awoke in his motor home in Savannah, Georgia, to find that he had a severely burned hand (which later had to be amputated), plus a "hell of a hole" in his chest and other burns—in the groin area, and on the legs and back "in spots!" Angel claimed one of his doctors said he had not been burned externally but rather internally, and he claimed to be a survivor of spontaneous human combustion. Interestingly, his clothing had not been burned, and there were no signs of burning in his motor home.

Unfortunately, when Arnold and I appeared on a Canadian television show to debate SHC, Arnold was unaware of an earlier story about the injuries that Angel had told—in court. I revealed it on the show for the first time (courtesy of fellow investigator Phil Klass), thus publicly humiliating Arnold, who has ever since been trying to rationalize away the evidence.

As it happens, a 1975 civil-action suit filed by Angel's attorney in Fulton County Superior Court tells how Angel (the plaintiff) was in his motor home, and "while Plaintiff was in the process of taking a shower, the water suddenly stopped flowing from the shower plumbing." In attempting to learn why there was insufficient water pressure, Angel "exited said motor home and attempted to inspect the hot water heater. In making said inspection, the pressure valve on the hot water heater released and as a result, scalding hot water under tremendous pressure was sprayed upon plaintiff." The complaint claimed that the defendant, the manufacturer of the motor home, was negligent both in the design of the heater and valve and in failing to provide adequate warning of the damage. The suit was later transferred to federal court, where it was eventually dismissed for costs paid by the defendant.

Arnold attempted to rebut this evidence—for example, by quoting some motor home mechanics—but it does not seem that he gave them the full facts in soliciting their statements. We did not, for instance, postulate "a bad valve" (as Arnold quoted the servicemen as stating in *Fate* magazine). Indeed, Arnold has repeatedly dodged—even outright omitted—powerful corroborative evidence, such as the water pump's drive belt being off, the water pump's drive pulley being loose, and the water heater's safety relief valve being in the open position! In our investigative report, John Fischer and I listed more than a dozen additional corroborative factors, including the unburned clothes, which were especially consistent with scalding. We even included the opinions of two doctors whom Arnold cites as having diagnosed "electrical burns" as if their opinions—which were again apparently based on incomplete information—were more harmful to our position than his (Arnold 1995, 227–36; Nickell with Fischer 1992).

Exploding Body?

Arnold's next major case is that of Helen Conway, who perished in 1964 in Delaware County, Pennsylvania. Except for her legs, her body was largely destroyed along with the upholstered chair in which she sat in her bedroom. The destruction took place in only twenty-one minutes (according to the fire marshal), although Arnold uses "commonsense deduction" (and an assumption or two) to wheedle the time down to just six minutes (which becomes "a few seconds" in the caption to a photograph). Arnold asserts that Mrs. Conway's body "exploded."

In fact, Mrs. Conway was an infirm woman, who according to the fire marshal was also "reported to have been a heavy smoker with careless smoking habits." He added: "Cigarette burn marks were evident about the bedroom." (Isn't it curious how people who are careless with fire are those who attract "spontaneous human combustion"?)

Apparently, the fire took less time to destroy Mrs. Conway's torso than it did the body of Mary Reeser, but it may have begun at the base of the seated body and burned straight upward, fed by flammable upholstery and the fat in the torso, and may have thus been a much more intense fire—not unlike grease fires, which all who cook are familiar with. Indeed, in searching through the dense smoke for the victim, an assistant chief sank his hand "into something greasy" that proved to be the woman's remains.

As to the bits of scattered debris that Arnold cites as evidence of "Spontaneous Human Explosion," that could have been caused by the chair's heavy right arm having fallen across the body at one point and thus scattering some bits of debris. Another possibility stems from the fact that the assistant fire marshal stated, "There wasn't debris scattered all over" (384), even though bits of debris are indeed shown in photos of the scene (illus. facing 212): in other words, the scattering may not have originally been present at the scene but could have been due to splashback from the firemen's high-pressure spray that was used to extinguish nearby flames. It is important to note that it is only Arnold—and not the fire officials, who actually blamed the fire on a dropped cigarette—who claimed the body exploded. (Arnold 1995, 378–92)

The Mott Case

The fifth and last of Arnold's chapter-length cases is that of a fifty-eight-year-old retired fireman named George Mott. He died in 1986 in the bedroom of his home outside Crown Point, New York. His body was largely consumed along with the mattress of the bed on which he had lain. A leg, an implausibly reported shrunken skull, and pieces of the rib cage were all that remained that were recognizably human. Arnold insists that there was no credible source for the ignition.

Whether or not we agree with Arnold's dismissal of the theories of two fire investigators—first, that an electric arc shot out of an outlet and ignited Mott's clothing, and second, that an "undetected" gas leak had been responsible—there are other possibilities. Mott was a man who formerly drank alcohol and smoked heavily. The day before he died he had been depressed over his illnesses, which included respiratory problems and high blood pressure. What if, as could easily happen in such a state of mind, he became fatalistic and, shrugging off the consequences, opted for the enjoyment of a cigarette? This possibility gains credence from the fact that he was not wearing his oxygen mask, although he was in bed and his oxygen-enricher unit was running. On top of the unit, next to the mask, was an otherwise puzzling cannister of "barn burner" matches, yet there was no stove or other device in the room they would be used for. (At least Arnold does not mention a stove or other device being in the room. If there was, then we have another possible explanation for the fire, and there are additional potential explanations in any case—each more likely than SHC.) (Arnold 1995, 393–411)

Arnold cites the Mott case as a quintessential one of SHC, based on the process of elimination. He does not allow SHC to be eliminated, however, although there is no single instance that proves its existence and no known mechanism by which it could occur. And so he often dismisses what he feels is unlikely in favor of that which the best scientific evidence indicates is impossible. Such thinking has been called "straining at a gnat and swallowing a camel."

In fact, Arnold's process-of-elimination approach here as elsewhere is based on a logical fallacy called "arguing from ignorance." As the great nineteenth-century scientist Justus von Liebig explained, "The opinion that a man can burn of himself is not founded on a knowledge of the circumstances of the death, but on the reverse of knowledge—on complete ignorance of all the causes or conditions which preceded the accident and caused it." (Liebig 1851)

In his relentless drive to foster any sort of mystery, in this and other cases, Arnold raises many attendant questions. For example, he wonders why extremities, such as a victim's leg, and nearby combustibles are not burned. The answer is that fire tends to burn upward; it burns laterally (sideways) with some difficulty. Anyone with camping experience has seen a log that was laid across a campfire reduced to ashes by the following morning while the butt ends of the log remain intact. Thus, outside the circle that burned through the carpet covering the concrete floor of Mary Reeser's apartment was found her slippered foot, because Mrs. Reeser had a stiff leg that she extended when she sat. Beyond the circle, some newspapers did not ignite, while a lamp and table within it did burn. Similarly, Dr. Bentley's intact lower leg extended outside the edge of the hole that burned through his bathroom floor.

Beyond this matter of proximity, Arnold cites other examples of fire's "selectivity" that puzzle him. For example, in the Mott case, he wonders why matches near the burning bed did not ignite while objects in other rooms suffered severe heat damage. The answer is one of elevation: heat rises. In Mrs. Reeser's apartment, due to the accumulation of hot gases, soot had blackened the ceiling and walls above an almost level line some three and a half feet above the floor, there being negligible heat damage below the smoke line but significant damage above it; e.g., plastic electrical switches had melted. Thus, in George Mott's house, reports Arnold, "On the counter directly beneath the melted towel holder sits an unopened roll of Bounty towels, upright. Ironically, it and its plastic wrapping were undamaged except for a glazed film on the top!" (398)

Other factors relevant to heat-damage "selectivity" include the objects' composition, density, confinement (e.g., in a cupboard), placement on a surface that either radiates or retains heat, or its placement relative to convective currents, cinders carried aloft, etc., etc.

"Preternatural Combustibility"

While acknowledging that there is often a source for the ignition of the body, Arnold points to the sometimes extreme destruction—of the torso especially—as evidence, if not of SHC, then preternatural combustibility, the imagined heightening of the body's flammability. In the nineteenth century, alcohol consumption was thought to cause increased flammability, but we now know that its only effect is in making people more careless with fire and less effective in responding to it. (Nickell and Fischer 1984)

Arnold and other SHC advocates are quick to suggest that bodies are difficult to burn (which is true under certain circumstances). According to popular writer Vincent Gaddis, "the notion that fluid-saturated fatty tissues, ignited by an outside flame, will burn and produce enough heat to destroy the rest of the body is nonsense" (Gaddis 1967). Actually, the reference to "fluid-saturated" tissues is correct but misleading in Gaddis's attempt to suggest that the great amount of water would retard burning. In fact, the argument works more strongly *against* the concept of SHC, there being no known means by which such fluid-saturated tissue could self-ignite. On the other hand, it is a fact that human fatty tissue will burn, the water it contains being boiled off ahead of the advancing fire.

Referring specifically to claims of SHC (and favorably citing the research done by John F. Fischer and me), a standard forensic text, *Kirk's Fire Investigation*, states:

> Most significantly, there are almost always furnishings, bedding, or carpets involved. Such materials would not only provide a continuous source of fuel but also promote a slow, smoldering fire and a layer of insulation around any fire once ignited. With this combination of features, the investigator can appreciate the basics—fuel, in the form of clothing or bedding as first ignition, and then furnishings as well as the body to feed later stages; an ignition source—smoking materials or heating appliances; and finally, the dynamics of heat, fuel, and ventilation to promote a slow, steady fire which may generate little open flame

and insufficient radiant heat to encourage fire growth. In some circumstances the fat rendered from a burning body can act in the same manner as the fuel in an oil lamp or candle. If the body is positioned so that oils rendered from it can drip or drain onto an ignition source, it will continue to fuel the flames. This effect is enhanced if there are combustible fuels—carpet padding, bedding, upholstery stuffing—that can absorb the oils and act as a wick (DeHaan 1991, 305).

Dr. Dougal Drysdale of Edinborough University agrees: "The idea that the body can burn like a candle isn't so far fetched [*sic*] at all. In a way, a body is like a candle—inside out. With a candle the wick is on the inside, and the fat on the outside. As the wick burns the candle becomes molten and the liquid is drawn onto the wick and burns. With a body, which consists of a large amount of fat, the fat melts and is drawn onto the clothing which acts as a wick, and then continues to burn" (Drysdale 1989). Experiments show that liquefied human fat burns at a temperature of about 250 degrees centigrade; however, a cloth wick placed in such fat will burn even when the temperature falls as low as 24 degrees centigrade (Dee 1965). In an 1854 English case, a woman's body had been partially destroyed in the span of two hours; it was explained that "beneath the body there was a hempen mat, so combustible, owing to the melted human fat with which it was impregnated, that when ignited it burnt like a link" (i.e., a pitch torch). (Stevenson 1883)

Even a lean body contains a significant amount of fat, which is present even in the bone marrow (Snyder 1967). Indeed, "once the body starts to burn, there is enough fat and inflammable substances to permit varying amounts of destruction to take place. Sometimes this destruction by burning will proceed to a degree which results in almost complete combustion of the body," as police officials reported in the Mary Reeser case (Blizin 1951). Moreover, in general, "women burn hotter and quicker than men, because proportionally, women carry more fat." (Bennett n.d.)

Arnold tries to compare favorably the partial destruction of bodies that occurs in his SHC cases (in which limbs, large segments of bone and other matter may remain, and that which does is rarely quantified or described scientifically) with the more complete destruction typical of crematories. But this is an apples-versus-oranges comparison at best. As Drysdale (1989) explains: "In a crematorium you need high temperatures—around 1,300 degrees C, or even higher—to reduce the body to ash in a relatively short period of time. But it's a misconception to think you need those temperatures within a living room to reduce a body to ash in this way. You can produce local, high temperatures, by means of the wick effect and a combination of smouldering and flaming to reduce even bones to ash. At relatively low temperatures of 500 degrees C—and if given enough time—the bone will transform into something approaching a powder in composition."

It is interesting that the major proponents of spontaneous human combustion—Michael Harrison (*Fire From Heaven*, 1977), Jenny Randles and Peter Hough (*Spontaneous Human Combustion*, 1992), and Larry E. Arnold (*Ablaze!* 1995)—are all popular writers who are credulous as to other paranormal claims. They stand in contrast to the physicists and chemists, the forensic specialists, and other scientists who question—on the evidence—the reality of spontaneous human combustion.

References

Arnold, Larry. 1995. *Ablaze! The Mysterious Fires of Spontaneous Human Combustion.* New York: M. Evans.

Bennett, Valerie (crematorium superintendent). n.d. Quoted in Randles and Hough 1992, 50.

Blizin, Jerry. 1951. The Reeser case. *St. Petersburg (Florida)Times*, Aug. 9.

Dee, D.J. 1965. A case of "spontaneous combustion." *Medicine, Science and the Law* 5: 37–38.

DeHaan, John D. 1991. *Kirk's Fire Investigation*, 3rd ed. Englewood Cliffs, N.J.: Prentice-Hall.

Drysdale, Dougal. 1989. Quoted in Randles and Hough 1992, 43.

Gaddis, Vincent. 1967. *Mysterious Fires and Lights.* New York: David McKay.

Liebig, Justus von. 1851. *Familiar Letters on Chemistry*, letter 22. London: Taylor, Walton & Maberly.

Nickell, Joe, and John F. Fischer. 1984. Spontaneous human combustion, *The Fire and Arson Investigator* 34 (March): 4–11; no. 4 (June): 3–8. This was published in abridged form in Joe Nickell with John F. Fischer, *Secrets of the Supernatural* (Buffalo, N.Y.: Prometheus, 1988), 149–57, 161–71.

Nickell, Joe, with John F. Fischer. 1992. *Mysterious Realms.* Amherst, N.Y.: Prometheus, 165–75.

Randles, Jenny, and Peter Hough. 1992. *Spontaneous Human Combustion.* London: Robert Hale.

Snyder, Lemoyne. 1967. *Homicide Investigation*, 2nd ed. Springfield, Ill.: C.C. Thomas, 233, 242.

Stevenson, Thomas. 1883. *The Principles and Practice of Medical Jurisprudence*, 3rd ed. Philadelphia: Lea, 718–27.

Chapter 5

Believe It or ——— ?

One of my old cases—solved twenty years ago—was never published. However, I recently rediscovered a souvenir of the investigation—a strange curio—at the bottom of a stored trunk. It has an interesting link to the "Believe It or Not" empire founded by Robert L. Ripley.

Ripley (1893–1949) began his career by combining a love of athletics and drawing to produce a series of sports cartoons. One day in 1918, facing a deadline and lacking any other idea, he transformed some notes on unusual sports events into a cartoon panel headed "Champs and Chumps." His editor at the *New York Globe* liked all but the title, and soon "Believe It or Not" was launched. The changed title permitted a much broader selection of oddities, and the cartoon went from a weekly to a daily feature. In 1929, it began to be distributed by King Features Syndicate.

Ripley's income skyrocketed, boosted by "Believe It or Not" books, radio programs, movies, "freak shows," and other venues and ventures. Seeking out the weird, the grotesque, and the amazing, he traveled worldwide, earning the sobriquet the "Modern Marco Polo." According to a biographer, Ripley was his own greatest oddity:

> He lived it up, this strange, mixed-up man. He would own the most expensive foreign cars obtainable, but never summon up enough courage to drive. He would pioneer in transatlantic radio broadcasting, but he would never dial a telephone, because in his curious mind there lurked the suspicion that he might be electrocuted in the process. He consumed enormous quantities of liquor and may have set a record for amorous dalliance, but he considered smoking and card playing

evil and would have nothing to do with them. He was, to those who knew him best, the very personification of shyness, but no contemporary matched him in flamboyance or in seeking notoriety. (Considine 1961, 16)

Although Ripley insisted that every "Believe It or Not" claim was true, his biographer observes: "The truth was that Ripley literally believed everything. He made flat statements such as 'Neils Paulsen, of Uppsala, Sweden, died in 1907 at the age of 160 and left two sons—one nine years old and the other 103 years of age.' His sources were usually reprints of old newspapers for items such as the long-lived Swede—rarely medical records, birth certificates, or such" (Considine 1961, 56). In addition to claims based on flimsy evidence, some of Ripley's assertions were largely provocative. An example appeared beneath a portrait of William F. Cody: "Buffalo Bill Never Shot a Buffalo in His Life." Ripley's substantiation was that Cody actually slew *bison*. If readers felt they had been "had," Ripley was all the more pleased (Considine 1961, 51, 54).

Ripley began to amass a collection of curios from his travels, including shrunken heads, strange effigies, and other oddities, including (his reputed favorite) a "genuine" Fiji mermaid. In 1933, he displayed such items along with live performers at his "Odditorium" at the Chicago World's Fair. Its success led to shows at various fairs and expositions, and in time Ripley's Believe It or Not Museums—twenty-seven so far—have spread around the world (Kemlo 1997).

My case began in the early 1970s at the Ripley museum in Niagara Falls, Canada. I used to visit it on my day off when I was Resident Magician at the nearby Houdini Magical Hall of Fame. (Admission at most Falls attractions was reciprocally free to employees.) I have always enjoyed the "Believe It or Not!" museums' displays, although I sometimes choose the "or Not" part of the equation. Such was my response to a particular item in the museum. It was a conical piece of wood accompanied by a display sign describing "A cypress growth found in the swamps of Florida with the word R I P L E Y written by nature." Obviously nature produces infinite random shapes that—given our tendency to make order out of chaos—we may perceive as recognizable forms, as by seeing pictures in clouds or envisioning images in ink blots. But the RIPLEY pattern seemed too good to be true. Each time I saw the object, I shook my head in disbelief and thought about how it might be scientifically examined or otherwise investigated.

After I left the Falls, I forgot about the mystery object until a few years later, in 1979, when I was traveling in Florida. On U.S. 27 near Palmdale, Florida, I came across the Cypress Knee Museum, with its accompanying factory and sales room and a three-quarter-mile catwalk that meandered through a cypress swamp. There I learned much about the curious growths known as cypress knees. The cypress is the only tree that has "knees," which form on the roots and rise, without limbs or leaves, above the water level of swamps. Their function is the subject of some conjecture, but being porous, they may aerate the roots during high water ("Tree-Root" 1937; Gaskins 1978, 18–19).

In the museum were many cypress knees "shaped by nature," their gnarled forms prompting their descriptive names like "Mother and Child," "Brown Bear," and the like. But one was strikingly evocative of the Ripley knee, bearing a name and address! Alarm bells were going off in my head. When I asked proprietor Tom Gaskins about this, telling him of my interest, he led me to a shed where he revealed *five more* "RIPLEY" knees! Therein lay an interesting tale.

Tom Gaskins pioneered in using cypress knees for decorative purposes, beginning in 1934 and advertising them in *House & Garden* in November of the following year. In 1937, he was awarded U.S. Patent 2,069,580, for "Articles of Manufacture Made from Cypress Knees." Basically, the knees are harvested from the swamp with an ax, peeled, and—without affecting the natural shape—modified by hollowing, drilling, etc., to produce "ornamental" items. These include flower holders, bird houses, lamp stands, ashtrays, candle holders, and other household articles.

Within a year of cutting his first knee, having observed a stump that had begun to heal and soon noticing the effects of scarring, he was struck by the idea "that it might be damage that caused knees to grow in strange shapes." He began to conduct experiments in "controlled knee growth" and produced test scarring in 1938. He stated he had learned that lettering, for example, could be cut into the knee and that subsequent growth would heal the wounds, producing raised wood where the cuts were made (Gaskins 1979).

In 1939, Gaskins spoke with a Ripley representative at the Odditorium at the New York World's Fair about the possibility of employing his technique "to produce a knee—purely for novelty effect—bearing the word "RIPLEY." He did later produce such a knee and sent it to the man who, as he recalled, subsequently asked for five more. He made the necessary

39

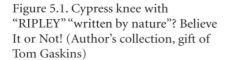

40

Figure 5.1. Cypress knee with "RIPLEY" "written by nature"? Believe It or Not! (Author's collection, gift of Tom Gaskins)

carvings but forgot about them. It was not until 1978 that he finally sent a photograph of a group of the completed five knees to the Ripley International Ltd. office in Toronto but was told that they did not require any more at the time (Gaskins 1979).

There was ample room for confusion and misunderstanding in all of this, and Tom Gaskins did not believe that anyone at Ripley ever intended to misrepresent how the "RIPLEY" knee was actually formed. During my investigation, a Ripley official reported to me that "This exhibit has been in the possession of Ripley's Believe It or Not! for many, many years, and we have no further details concerning it" (Copperthwaite 1979a). It remained for me to apprise Ripley's of the facts by means of an affidavit from Tom Gaskins, and subsequently to be advised that the display wording had been amended satisfactorily (Copperthwaite 1979b). (The RIPLEY knee is no longer on display at the Niagara Falls Museum.)

When I reported Ripley's prompt, appropriate action to Gaskins, I mentioned "luck" regarding my meeting him and learning the true Ripley story. He replied, "I have contemplated luck quite a great deal and use the word as it is commonly used now and then but with my tongue in my cheek. On account of, if you had not had [the] eyes you had and if a thousand other little parts had not been carefully put together, then this entertaining story would not ever have come out" (Gaskins 1979). Hmmm. As "Rip" would say, "Believe It or Not!"

References

Considine, Bob. 1961. *Ripley: The Modern Marco Polo.* New York: Doubleday.

Copperthwaite, Rita. 1979a. Letter to author from Ripley International, Oct. 19.

———. 1979b. Letter to author, Nov. 26.

Gaskins, Tom. 1978. *Florida Facts and Fallacies.* Palmdale, Fla.: Privately printed.

———. 1979 Personal communication (including letters and supplementary materials); affidavit of Nov. 13.

Kemlo, Karen. 1997. Educational booklet, n.p.: Ripley Entertainment.

Tree-root craftwork forms unique business. 1937. *Popular Science Monthly.* April, 66.

Chapter 6

Legend of the "Miraculous Stairway"

The CBS television movie, "The Staircase" (April 12, 1998), told how "a dying nun's wish to complete her order's chapel is fulfilled by a mysterious stranger" (Bobbin 1998). Starring Barbara Hershey as the terminally ill mother superior and William Peterson as the enigmatic carpenter, the movie is an embellishment of the legend of the "miraculous stairway" at the Sisters of Loretto Chapel in Santa Fe. The wooden, spiral stair is thought to be unique, and some claim its very existence is inexplicable.

The Loretto legend begins with the founding of a school for females in Santa Fe in 1852. A combined day and boarding school, the Loretto Academy was founded by the local Sisters of Loretto at the behest of Bishop John Lamy. In 1873, work was begun on a chapel. Unfortunately, some earthly—even earthy— events reportedly marred the work: the wife of Bishop Lamy's nephew caught the architect's eye, and he was killed for his interest—shot by the nephew who was distraught over his destroyed marriage.

At this time, work on the chapel was nearing completion, and although the choir loft was finished, the architect's plans provided no means of access. It was felt that installing an "ordinary stair" would be objectionable on aesthetic grounds as well as by limiting seating (Bullock 1978, 6, 8). "Carpenters and builders were called in," according to one source, "only to shake their heads in despair." Then, "When all else had failed, the Sisters determined to pray a novena to the Master Carpenter himself, St. Joseph" (the father of Jesus) (Bullock 1978, 8).

"On the ninth day," reportedly, their prayers were answered. A humble workman appeared outside, leading a burro laden with carpentry tools. He announced he could provide a suitable means of access to the loft, requiring only permission and a couple of water tubs. Soon, he was at work:

> Sisters, going in to the Chapel to pray, saw the tubs with wood soaking in them, but the Man always withdrew while they said their prayers, returning to his work when the Chapel was free. Some there are who say the circular stair which stands there today was built very quickly. Others say no, it took quite a little time. But the stair did grow, rising solidly in a double helix without support of any kind and without nail or screw. The floor space used was minimal and the stair adds to, rather than detracts from, the beauty of the Chapel.

As the tale continues:

> The Sisters were overjoyed and planned a fine dinner to honor the Carpenter. Only he could not be found. No one seemed to know him, where he lived, nothing. Lumberyards were checked, but they had no bill for the Sisters of Loretto. They had not sold him the wood. Knowledgeable men went in and inspected the stair and none knew what kind of wood had been used, certainly nothing indigenous to this area. Advertisements for the Carpenter were run in the *New Mexican* and brought no response.
>
> "Surely," said the devout, "it was St. Joseph himself who built the stair." (Bullock 1978, 8, 10)

No doubt the legend has improved over the intervening century, like good wine. As we shall see, there is more to the story. But Barbara Hershey concedes, "Those who want to believe it's a miracle can, and those who want to believe this man was just an ingenious carpenter can" (Bobbin 1998). Evidence for the latter is considerable, but first we must digress a bit to understand spiral stairs.

Spiral and other winding staircases reached a high point in development in sixteenth-century England and France, with several "remarkable" examples ("Stair" 1960; "Interior" 1960). To appreciate the problems such stairs present, we must recognize that builders use *turns* in staircases to save space or to adapt to a particular floor plan. The simplest is the *landing turn*, which is formed of straight flights joined at the requisite angle by a platform. A variation is the *split landing*, which is divided on a diagonal into two steps. Instead of a landing, the turn may be accomplished by a series of steps having tapered treads. Such staircases are called *winders* and include certain ornamental types, like that which takes the shape of a partial circle (known as circular stair) or an ellipse. An extreme form of winding staircase is a *continuous* winder in the form of a helix (a line that rises as it twists, like a screw thread). This is the popularly termed "spiral staircase" like the example at Loretto Chapel (Locke 1992, 135–36; Dietz 1991, 340–42). Helixes—in contrast to, say, pyramids—are not inherently strong weight-supporting structures. They require some kind of strengthening or support. Therefore, in addition to being secured at top and bottom, the spiral staircase is usually also braced by attachment along its height to a central pole or an adjacent wall (Dietz 1991, 342; "Stair" 1960).

Unfortunately, spiral and other winding staircases are not only problematical as to design but are also fundamentally unsafe. Explains one authority, "For safety, any departure from a straight staircase requires careful attention to detail in design and construction." Especially, "Because people tend to travel the shortest path around a corner, where a winder's treads are narrowest, the traveler must decide at each step where each foot falls. This may be an intellectual and physical exercise best practiced elsewhere. In short, winders are pretty but inherently unsafe" (Locke 1992, 135, 136). Other experts agree. According to Albert G.H. Dietz, Professor Emeritus of Building Engineering at MIT, winders "should be avoided if at all possible. No adequate foothold is afforded at the angle [due to the tapering] and there is an almost vertical drop of several feet if a number of risers converge on the same point. The construction is dangerous and may easily lead to bad accidents" (Dietz 1991, 341). As a consequence, winders are frequently prohibited by building codes. That is especially true of the spiral stair, which "contains all the bad features of the winder multiplied several times" (Dietz 1991, 342).

Such problems seem to have beset the staircase at Loretto, suggesting that, at most, the "miracle" was a partial one. Safety appears to have been a concern at the outset, since there was originally no railing. At the time the staircase was completed, one thirteen-year-old sister who was among the first to ascend to the loft told how she and her friends were so frightened—absent a railing—that they came down on hands and knees (Albach 1965). Nevertheless, despite the very real hazard, it was not until 1887—ten years after the staircase was completed—that an artisan named Phillip August Hesch added the railing (Loretto n.d.). No one claims it was a miracle, yet it is described as "itself a work of art" (Albach 1965). (See figure 6.1.)

Figure 6.1. The spiral stairway at Loretto Chapel in Santa Fe, New Mexico, is an alleged miracle of construction.

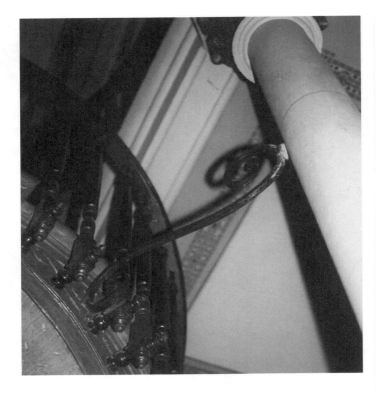

Figure 6.2. Iron support bracket (unmentioned in published accounts) reveals the "miracle" is a partial one. (Photos by Joe Nickell)

There were other problems over time relating to the double helix form. The helix, after all, is the shape of the common wire spring. There-fore, it is not surprising that people who trod the stairs reported "a small amount of vertical movement" or "a certain amount of springiness" (Albach 1965) and again "a very slight vibration as one ascends and de-scends rather as though the stair were a living, breathing thing" (Bullock 1978, 14).

Some people have thought the free-standing structure should have collapsed long ago, we are told, and builders and architects supposedly "never fail to marvel how it manages to stay in place," considering that it is "without a center support" (Albach 1965). In fact, though, as one wood technologist observes, "the staircase does have a central support." He observes that of the two wood stringers (or spiral structural members) the inner one is of such small radius that it "functions as an almost solid pole" (Easley 1997). There is also another support—one that goes unmentioned, but which I observed when I visited the now privately owned chapel in 1993. This is an iron brace or bracket that stabilizes the staircase by rigidly connecting the outer stringer to one of the columns that support the loft. (See figure 6.2.)

There is reason to suspect that the staircase may be more unstable and potentially unsafe than some realize. It has been closed to public travel since at least the mid-1970s (when the reason was given as lack of other egress from the loft in case of fire). When I visited in 1993, my understanding was that it was suffering from the constant traffic. Barbara Hershey implied the same when she stated, "It still functions, though people aren't allowed to go up it very often" (Bobbin 1998). It would thus appear that the Loretto staircase is subject to the laws of physics like any other.

The other mysteries that are emphasized in relation to the stair are the identity of the carpenter and the type of wood used. That the latter has not been identified precisely means little. The piece given to a forester for possible identification was exceedingly small (only about $3/4$ -inch square by $1/8$ -inch thick) whereas much larger (six-inch) pieces are preferred by the U.S. Forest Service's Center for Wood Anatomy (which has made many famous identifications, including artifacts taken from King Tut's tomb and the ladder involved in the Lindbergh kidnaping) (Knight 1997). The wood *has* reportedly been identified as to family, *Pinaceae*, and genus, *Picea*—i.e., spruce (Easley 1997), a type of "light, strong, elastic wood" often used in construction ("Spruce" 1960). But there are no fewer than thirty-nine species—ten in North America—so that comparison of the Loretto sample with only two varieties (Easley 1997) can scarcely be definitive.

As to the identity of an obviously itinerant workman, it seems merely mystery mongering to suggest that there is anything strange—least of all evidence of the supernatural—in the failure to record his name. As it happens, however, the identity of the enigmatic craftsman has finally been revealed. Credit for the discovery goes to an "intrepid and highly respected amateur historian" named Mary Jean Cook. She learned of a "hermit rancher," François-Jean "Frenchy" Rochas, who lived in "godforsaken" Dog Canyon, nine miles from Alamogordo. Learning that he had left behind a collection of "sophisticated carpentry tools," Cook searched for his death notice, which she found in the January 6, 1896, issue of *The Santa Fe New Mexican*. It described Rochas's murdered body being found at his isolated rock cabin and described him as "favorably known in Santa Fe as an expert worker in wood." He had built, the brief obituary noted, "the handsome staircase in the Loretto Chapel and at St. Vincent sanitarium."

Cook suspects the legend of St. Joseph began with the sisters at the Loretto Academy, "probably in response to questions from their students." However, she observes that "it wasn't until the late 1930s—when the story appeared in *Ripley's . . . Believe It or Not!*—that the story became an icon of popular culture. Although some rued the debunking of the pious legend, Archbishop Michael Sheehan promised, "It will always be referred to as a miraculous staircase. It was an extraordinary piece to have been done in its time" (Stieber 2000).

References

Albach, Carl R. 1965. Miracle or wonder of construction? reprint from *Consulting Engineer*, Dec., n.p.

Bobbin, Jay. 1998 . The staircase. Review in *TV Topics, Buffalo News,* April 12, 1, 24–25.

Bullock, Alice. 1978. *Loretto and the Miraculous Staircase.* Santa Fe, N.M.: Sunstone.

Dietz, Albert G.H. 1991. *Dwelling House Construction*, 5th ed. Cambridge, Mass.: MIT Press.

Easley, Forrest N. 1997. "A Stairway From Heaven?" Privately printed.

"Interior Decoration." 1960. *Encyclopaedia Britannica.*

Knight, Christopher. 1997. Just what kind of wood . . ? *Wall Street Journal*, Oct. 22.

Locke, Jim. 1992. *The Well-Built House*, revised ed. New York: Houghton Mifflin.

Loretto Chapel. n.d. Text of display card, photographed by author, 1993.

"Spruce." 1960. *Encyclopaedia Britannica.*

"Stair." 1960. *Encyclopaedia Britannica.*

Stieber, Tamar. 2000. Loretto staircase mystery unravels. *New Mexico* magazine. Jan., 62–66.

Chapter 7

Flying Saucer "Dogfight"

Did an extraterrestrial craft actually fire on a police helicopter? If not, what was the nature of a UFO that two officers reported attacked them over Louisville, Kentucky, in 1993? Is this the case that proves the reality of alien invaders?

Flying Saucers

The modern wave of UFOs began on June 24, 1947, when businessman Kenneth Arnold was flying his private airplane over the Cascade Mountains in Washington State. Arnold saw what he described as a chain of nine disc-like objects, each flying with a motion like "a saucer skipped across water." Whether Arnold saw a line of aircraft or mirages caused by temperature inversion or something else, the flying saucer phenomenon had taken flight. Once again reality followed fiction. Popular science-fiction magazines like *Amazing Stories* had been publishing wild tales of extraterrestrial visitations, complete with imaginative covers illustrating strange, circular spaceships.

UFO reports continue to be common. Most fall into two categories, the first being termed "daylight discs"—metallic, saucer-shaped objects. When properly investigated, these often turn out to be weather, research, and other balloons; aircraft; meteors; kites, blimps, and hang gliders; wind-borne objects of various kinds; and other phenomena. Photographs of such discs often turn out to be lens flares (the result of interreflection between lens surfaces), lenticular (lens-shaped) clouds, and other causes, including, of course, deliberate hoaxing. Many faked UFO photos have been produced simply by tossing a model spaceship in the air or suspending it on a thread. One fake photo, offered by a Venezuelan airline pilot, was made by placing a metal button on an aerial photograph and then rephotographing the view (Nickell 1994, 1995).

The second type of UFO sighting consists of nighttime UFOs—so-called "nocturnal lights"—which represent the most frequently reported UFO events. They are also the "least strange" ones, according to the late Dr. J. Allen Hynek, astronomer and former consultant to the U.S. Air Force's UFO research program, Project Blue Book (1952–1969). According to him, "An experienced investigator readily recognizes most of these for what they are: bright meteors, aircraft landing lights, balloons, planets, violently twinkling stars, searchlights, advertising lights on planes, refueling missions, etc. When one realizes the unfamiliarity of the general public with lights in the night sky of this variety, it is obvious why so many such UFO reports arise" (Hynek 1972, 41–42). (Note that balloons appear in both categories. They were extensively used in the past and were frequently reported as strange craft. A balloon can achieve high altitudes and, if caught in jet-stream winds, can reach speeds of more than two hundred miles an hour. Or it can stop and seem to hover, or move erratically, or execute sharp turns, depending on the winds. It can even appear to change its shape and color. Depending on how sunlight strikes the plastic covering, the balloon can appear to be white, metallic, red, glowing, and so on. In fact, so often have balloons of one type or another been reported as UFOs that, when lost, these chameleons of the sky have often been traced by following the reports of saucer sightings [Nickell 1989, 21].)

Most UFO researchers—proponents and skeptics alike—agree that the majority of UFO reports can be explained. The controversy is over a small residue—say two percent—of unsolved cases. Proponents often act as if these cases offer proof of extraterrestrial visitation, but to suggest so is to be guilty of the logical fallacy called *argumentum ad ignorantiam* (that is, "arguing from ignorance"). Skeptics observe that what is unexplained is not necessarily *unexplainable*, and they suspect that if the truth were known, such cases would fall not into the category of alien craft but into the realm of mundane explanations. But what about the attack on a patrolling police helicopter?

Close Encounter

"UFO Fires on Louisville, Ky. Police Chopper" was the headline on the *Weekly World News's* May 4, 1993, cover story, complete with fanciful illustration. But if the tabloid account seemed overly sensational in describing the "harrowing two-minute dogfight"—before vanishing into the night—it was only following the lead of the respected *Louisville Courier-Journal*. The *Courier* had used similar wording in relating the February 26 incident (which had not been immediately made public), headlining its front-page story of March 4—"UFO Puts on Show: Jefferson [County] Police Officers Describe Close Encounter."

Unfortunately, the *Weekly World News* did not cite the *Courier's* follow-up report explaining the phenomenon. Yet the tabloid's tale contained numerous clues that might have tipped off an astute reader. The first sighting was of what looked like "a fire" off to the patrol craft's left; the "pear-shaped" UFO was seen in the police spotlight "drifting back and forth like a balloon on a string"; after circling the helicopter several times, the object darted away before zooming back to shoot the "fireballs" (which fortunately "fizzled out before they hit"); and then—as the helicopter pilot pushed his speed to over one hundred miles per hour—the UFO "shot past the chopper, instantly climbing hundreds of feet," only to momentarily descend again before flying into the distance and disappearing. That the "flowing" object was only "about the size of a basketball" and that it had "hovered" before initially approaching the helicopter were additional clues from the original *Courier* account that the tabloid omitted.

The *Courier's* follow-up story of March 6 was headed "A Trial Balloon?" It pictured Scott Heacock and his wife, Conchys, demonstrating how they had launched a hot-air balloon Scott had made from a plastic dry-cleaning bag, strips of balsa wood, and a dozen birthday candles—a device familiar to anyone who has read Philip J. Klass's *UFOs Explained* (Vintage, 1976, 28–34, plates 2a and 2b). No sooner had the balloon cleared the trees, said Heacock, than the county police helicopter encountered it and began circling, shining its spotlight on the glowing toy.

The encounter was a comedy of errors and misperceptions. Likened to a cat chasing its tail, the helicopter was actually pushing the light-

Figure 7.1. Scott Heacock (left) puts the finishing touches on a model hot-air balloon like the one he had launched in Louisville, Kentucky, on February 26, 1993. Looking on is psychologist Robert A. Baker. (Photo by Joe Nickell)

weight device around with its prop wash. In fact, as indicated by the officers' own account, the UFO zoomed away in response to the helicopter's sudden propulsion—behavior consistent with a lightweight object. As to the "fireballs," they may have been melting, flaming globs of plastic, or candles that became dislodged and fell, or some other effect. (Heacock says he used the novelty "relighting" type of birthday candles as a safeguard against the wind snuffing them out. Such candles may sputter, then abruptly reflame.)

Although one of the officers insisted the object he saw that night traveled at speeds too fast for a balloon, he seems not to have considered the effects of the helicopter's prop-wash propulsion. Contacted by psychologist and skeptical investigator Robert A. Baker (with whom I investigated the case), the other officer declined to comment further, except to state his feeling that the whole affair had been "blown out of proportion" by the media. Be that as it may, a television reporter asked Scott Heacock how certain he was that his balloon was the reported UFO. Since he had witnessed the encounter and kept the balloon in sight until it was caught in the police spotlight, he replied, "I'd bet my life on it." To another reporter, his Mexican wife explained, "I'm the only alien around here."

References

Hynek, J. Allen. 1972. *The UFO Experience.* New York: Ballantine.

Nickell, Joe. 1989. *The Magic Detectives.* Buffalo, N.Y.: Prometheus.

———. 1994. *Camera Clues: A Handbook for Photographic Investigation.* Lexington: Univ. Press of Kentucky, 15.

———. 1995. *Entities: Angels, Spirits, Demons, and Other Alien Beings.* Amherst, N.Y.: Prometheus, 190–92.

⚛ Chapter 8

A Study in Clairvoyance

On March 16, 1992, I appeared on *The Jerry Springer Show* with what were billed as "today's outrageous psychics." They included an "aura" photographer, a pet prognosticator, and the self-proclaimed "world's greatest psychic," who was introduced as "Mr. B of ESP." Mr. B, Springer promised, would "use his extraordinary powers" to peer clairvoyantly inside a locked refrigerator. A uniformed security guard, baton in hand, stood dramatically beside the chained-and-padlocked appliance. After engaging in a bit of banter with Springer and boasting further of his psychic prowess, Mr. B approached the refrigerator. He asked "everybody to concentrate on the power of my eyes," adding with braggadocio that provoked smirks and giggles from some members of the audience, "If you can see these eyes, they penetrate through you, and I will now do the same thing with the refrigerator, and then I will come back and read you people like a book. . . . This I promise you."

As he began, he said, "It's kind of weird, ladies and gentlemen, because I'm not getting a clear vision, but what I'm getting here is—I'm looking at—looks like some apples are in here." Also he said there was what "looks like a cantaloupe." (There was some more banter as Springer, who had begun writing a bold list of Mr. B's pronouncements, admitted he was unsure how to spell the last word and wrote "c-a-n-t-e-l-o-p-e.") Mr. B continued, stating that he could see what "looks like jewelry, so I'm looking at some carrots," he said; "I would relate that to jewelry" (apparently making a pun on carats). He went on to say that he saw a carton of low-fat milk and jars of spaghetti sauce. Then he stated, "Basically, the last thing I'm going to say—which is totally incredible—is, I'm looking at a skull which looks to be almost like a human head." Springer responded by announcing (to applause), "If you're right, we've got another show!" And Mr. B made a punning quip that "[I]t's also a good way to get ahead in this world," adding, "Anyway, I do see something that looks like a human head." When Springer suggested, "Maybe it's a head of lettuce," Mr. B replied, "It could be. And this is basically—at this moment this is all I'm able to pick out."

55

Springer then unfastened the padlock, removed the chain, and opened the refrigerator. Reaching in and holding up each item in turn, to applause, he brought out "the milk, low fat, two percent," next an apple, a honeydew melon (not a cantaloupe but "pretty close," Springer noted), then a bunch of carrots. Impressively, he next extracted a grotesque novelty head! During the hubbub that followed, he also discovered a jar of sauce. Displaying the head, Springer gushed to Mr. B, "I swear to God, unless the staff is lying to me, you really didn't know what was in here!" He added, "This guy's special." After a commercial break he stated, "I have to tell you, I'm blown away. I'm very, very impressed!"

After Mr. B had done readings for the audience and after the other psychics had given dubious performances, I was brought on. My anger showed: unknown to the audience, backstage I had had an exchange with a producer; I had expressed my suspicions about the refrigerator test, and his response was what I interpreted as a guilty look. After Springer introduced me, I made a skeptical statement about the lack of evidence for psychic ability and disparaged the readings that had been given. (A later analysis showed that Mr. B. had indeed achieved a very poor score.)

I then suggested there was something odious about the "fridge" demonstration, to which Springer replied, "I have to tell you . . . I do not believe the staff would lie to me, but they swore to me that he did not know what was going to be put in there. That's the only thing I can vouch for; I can't vouch for anything else . . . but that I know, he did not know what was in that refrigerator." Remaining unconvinced, I said, "That's why I brought my own test," explaining that in twenty years of investigation I had yet to discover anyone who could "reveal a simple three-letter word" under test conditions. Suiting action to words, I produced a set of three envelopes (each containing a three-letter word) and a check for one thousand dollars, which I offered as a reward for a successful demonstration.

The psychics were immediately defensive, claiming among other things that the TV studio did not represent test conditions. Springer seemed to shift from annoyance with me to delight at the sparks of conflict that had begun to fly. He pointed out to Mr. B that "You could tell us what was in the refrigerator, okay? With the studio lights and the live audience you could tell us what was in the refrigerator." I added that, if it would help, I would draw a picture of a refrigerator on the front of the envelope! Mr. B did not appear to find that amusing but finally did attempt to divine the three target words. But although he afterward rearranged letters and then words to produce a semblance of accuracy, in fact he failed completely, and during a break I tore up the check.

After the show, I continued to be rankled over the suspicious demonstration, although I did appear on a later *Springer* show (Dec. 16, 1992) about guardian angels. Over subsequent years, the show degenerated even further in quality as it soared in ratings. Episodes about cross-dressers and unfaithful lovers typically lapsed into on-camera brawls (*Springer* 1999). In 1998, as the fisticuffs and hair-pulling fights proliferated, there were accusations that the fights were staged (*Good Morning Sunday* 1998). Indeed, former guests told *Inside Edition* (May 1, 1998) that Jerry Springer producers encouraged antagonism and promised combatants one hundred dollars per blow. Springer was dubbed "the ringmaster of TV's best-watched circus" (Gray 1998). When ratings slipped from the top slot to a tie with *Oprah, Broadcasting & Cable* magazine cited sources at the show who maintained the fights were even "turned up a notch" during the sweeps' period ("Brawls continue" 1998). Springer denied the charges. He responded to critics by saying he did not know what all the fuss was about, that his was only "a silly show" (*Good Morning Sunday* 1998). Certainly Jerry Springer has been no stranger to controversy. A one-time Cincinnati councilman, he left office after an FBI raid on a nightclub turned up a $25 check he had tendered for a "tryst with a prostitute" (*Inside Edition* 1998). (Undaunted, Springer went on to become mayor, then ran a failed campaign for governor before becoming a TV anchor in the 1980s.)

In light of evidence that the *Jerry Springer* shows may have involved staged elements, I decided to reexamine the refrigerator-divination segment. First of all, recall that it was Springer himself who raised the prospect of fakery by using the phrase "unless the staff is lying to me." Obviously, the possibility had crossed his mind. Moreover, it would have been quite easy to rig Mr. B's demonstration. All that would have been required would have been a few words relayed to the "psychic" before the show. Since producers invariably speak to guests prior to their appearing before the audience and cameras, this would have been easily accomplished.

In addition, as already indicated, a critical analysis of Mr. B's audience readings and his failure in the envelope test indicate an utter lack of extrasensory ability. That alone raises questions about his fridge demonstration. So does his demeanor. He trivialized what was supposed to be a significant accomplishment by making silly puns about "carrots"/"carats" and "a head"/"ahead," giving the distinct impression that he was doing nothing more than trying to entertain.

The most telling evidence, I think, comes from a careful analysis of what Mr. B claimed to "see" in the refrigerator, compared with what was actually inside it. If Mr. B did as Springer advertised (to "psychically look inside") or as he himself claimed (to use the "power of my eyes," eyes that "penetrate through" targets, etc.), he would be demonstrating a form of extrasensory perception (ESP) known as clairvoyance (from the French for "clear seeing"). More specifically he would presumably be exhibiting a form known as "X-ray clairvoyance," defined as "the ability to see through opaque objects such as envelopes, containers, and walls to perceive what lies within or beyond" (Guiley 1991)—hence the appropriateness of my envelope test. If Mr. B indeed used X-ray clairvoyance, the resulting match of predicted items and actual objects in the refrigerator should be *visually* significant. On the other hand, if some other mechanism were employed (for example, information secretly imparted by a producer), the match might be only *cognitive*, consistent with a verbal communication. That the latter is the case is shown repeatedly. For example, Mr. B's first pronouncement is that "I'm looking at—looks like some apples are in here," whereas there is but a single apple, a visual non sequitur. Little can be made of the cantaloupe or the carrots, although the punning reference to "carats" works only verbally or cognitively—not visually.

The description of the next item, the milk, is telling. Whereas Mr. B described a "carton" and gratuitously mentioned it "looks like it's a little bit dented," the actual article was visually quite unlike that description. It was instead a white plastic milk jug, with a handle. Mr. B's statement that it "looks like some kind of skim milk or some kind of milk that's not very high in calories" indicates confusion, that he may not have been quite sure of what was meant by "two percent," the type of milk provided. Then there were "jars of some kind of spaghetti sauce or—I don't know, it's hard to explain." In fact, there was what Springer called "the sauce," a *single* container, that looked like a jar of salsa. Once again, the match was a confused, cognitive one, not visually similar. Finally there was the "skull which looks to be almost like a human head." This was not a skull at all, but a comically grotesque head with one bulging eye. Mr. B's description indicates he did not know exactly what the object was, hence his agreement with Springer when the host suggested it might be "a head of lettuce." Of course it *looked* nothing like that.

In addition to the visual inaccuracy of Mr. B's alleged viewings, there is the fact that he missed some items completely: a large bottle of Canada Dry ginger ale (which stood beside the milk) and a bunch of bananas. If Mr. B was peering (psychically) into the refrigerator, he should have seen and named those items, but if he had been given a quick verbal list, it might have been incomplete or Mr. B might have incompletely remembered it. Assuming the hypothesis that Mr. B was tipped off as to the refrigerator's contents, we can almost reconstruct the wording of the list that would have been provided: "apple," "melon," "carrots," "two-percent milk," "sauce," and "severed head."

Of course, this is only one interpretation of the evidence. Mr. B might claim, for instance, that he was receiving information from spirits, who translated what they saw inside the fridge into verbal statements. Or there might be some other rationalization for the visual inaccuracy. For example, Mr. B's guesses might have been only that. While such luck would seem phenomenal, all of the items in the refrigerator were rather common ones except for the head, and Mr. B might have thought of it for the same reason that a *Springer* producer probably did: news reports about serial killer Jeffrey Dahmer told how he had kept the severed head of one of his victims in his refrigerator (Ubelaker and Scammell 1992). In any event, the question is begged, why does the evidence not support what the "world's greatest psychic" claimed to do? It would seem that the least likely interpretation of the results is that ESP was involved.

References

Brawls continue on Jerry Springer show. 1998 *Good News*, Sept.

Croteau, Maureen, and Wayne Worcester. 1993. *The Essential Researcher.* New York: HarperCollins, 106, 108.

Good Morning Sunday. 1998. ABC television, April 26.

Gray, Ellen. 1998. Here are television's least fascinating people of 1998, Buffalo
    News, Dec. 28.
Guiley, Rosemary Ellen. 1991. *Harper's Encyclopedia of Mystical & Paranormal
    Experience.* New York: HarperCollins, 111–13.
Springer offers little defense for show. 1999. *Buffalo News,* Jan. 3.
Ubelaker, Dr. Douglas, and Henry Scammell. 1992. *Bones: A Forensic Detective's
    Casebook.* New York: HarperCollins, 265.

Chapter 9

The Kennedy Curse

The tragic death of John F. Kennedy Jr. on July 16, 1999, sparked renewed claims of a "Kennedy curse"—only the latest in a series of alleged popular hexes such as the Hope Diamond jinx and the curse of King Tut's mummy. During live CBS coverage of the search for Kennedy's missing airplane, anchorman Dan Rather referred to "the alleged Kennedy curse," while after the bodies of Kennedy and his wife and sister-in-law were recovered, *U.S. News & World Report* (July 26, 1999) ran a front-cover story unequivocally titled "The Kennedy Curse." A *Buffalo (New York) News* headline spoke more factually of a "litany of Kennedy tragedies" (Anthony 1999), a list that varies from source to source but generally includes the following misfortunes in the family of Joseph and Rose Fitzgerald Kennedy:

1941: Daughter, Rosemary, is institutionalized due to retardation and the effects of an unsuccessful lobotomy.

1944: Son, Joseph Jr., dies in airplane explosion in World War II.

1948: Daughter, Kathleen, dies in plane crash in France.

1963 (August 9): Grandchild, Patrick, (son of President John F. and Jacqueline Kennedy) dies after premature birth.

1963 (November 22): Son, President John F., is assassinated.

1964: Son, Edward, is injured in plane crash that kills an aide.

1968: Son, Robert F., is assassinated while campaigning for Democratic presidential nomination.

1969: Son, Edward, narrowly escapes death when car plunges off bridge on Chappaquiddick Island, killing passenger.

1973: Grandson, Joe (son of Robert and Ethel), overturns a Jeep, paralyzing a passenger.

1973: Grandson, Edward M. Kennedy Jr., has leg amputated due to cancer.

1984: Grandson, David (son of Robert and Ethel), dies of drug overdose.

1991: Grandson, William Kennedy Smith (son of Jean Ann Kennedy), is charged with rape but acquitted in trial.

1994: Daughter-in-law, Jacqueline, dies of cancer.

1997: Grandson, Michael (son of Robert and Ethel), is killed in "ski football" accident.

And this is only a partial list. Senator Edward Kennedy's son Patrick sought treatment for drug addiction in 1985, and Michael Kennedy, before his fatal accident, was disgraced due to an alleged affair with a fourteen-year-old baby sitter (Davis 1984; Thomas 1998; Anthony 1999; Salkin 1999; Kelly and Walsh 1999).

Certainly the list is as long as it is filled with tragedy. But is it evidence of a curse? What exactly is meant by the term?

Curses: Foiled Again

Actually a "curse"—also known as a "hex" or "jinx"—is an alleged paranormal assault that can supposedly result in physical or mental injury or illness—even death. Known to New Age mystics as a "psychic attack" (Guiley 1991), it is an ancient concept said to have either human direction (as from a sorcerer) or a supernatural one (such as by angry gods, demonic spirits, or the like). As an example of the first, in the Old Testament when Noah became displeased by his son Ham, he placed a curse on him (Genesis 9:21–27), and as a supernatural example, Jehovah dealt with an intransigent pharaoh by visiting upon him ten plagues (Exodus 7–12).

Various occurrences could spark belief in the existence of psychic attacks. For example, although the plagues on pharaoh are not mentioned in any source other than the Bible (Asimov 1968), and some see the account as pure allegory (Graham 1979), such phenomena can occur naturally. (Proliferations of locusts and frogs, for instance, are not unknown, and the water turning to "blood" could be equated with a "red Nile" wherein flood waters are colored by lake deposits [Keller 1995; Acuistapace 1991].)

A phenomenon that can actually simulate a psychic attack is the "hag syndrome." Typically the "victim" awakens to feel a weight pressing on the chest and to see bizarre imagery (e.g. an "old hag," incubus, vampire, or the like). Known from ancient times, and estimated to occur presently in some fifteen percent of the world's adult population (Guiley 1991), the syndrome is popularly termed a "waking dream" and occurs in the twilight between being asleep and awake (Nickell 1995). Because such an experience may seem quite real to the "victim," it could appear to prove to that person that he or she was actually accursed.

Apart from such dramatic "evidence," however, belief in curses is simply a superstition—that is, "a belief that some action not logically related to a course of events influences its outcome" or "any belief, practice, or rite unreasoningly upheld by faith in magic, chance or dogma" (*American Heritage* 1981). As with other superstitions (such as the fear of Friday the Thirteenth), once the idea of a curse is planted, it can take root in the imagination so that any harmful occurrence is counted as evidence for the jinx, while beneficial events are ignored. In this way, superstitious or magical thinking tends to start with an answer and work backward to the evidence, in contrast to scientific or rational thinking that allows evidence to lead to an answer.[5]

Tut et al.

This process of focusing only on negative evidence clearly perpetuates many popular "curses," including alleged "Jinxed Seas" like the so-called "Devil's Triangle" of the Atlantic, where ships and planes supposedly vanish without a trace. In fact, however, as Lawrence David Kusche demonstrated in his investigative classic *The Bermuda Triangle Mystery Solved* (1975), the disappearances are actually tragedies involving a combination of bad weather, heavy sea and air traffic, equipment failure, human error, and journalistic exaggeration and misattribution. (Many incidents attributed to the zone in fact occurred elsewhere.)

Another such example is the site near Niagara Falls known as "Devil's Hole" that is allegedly "cursed with an aura of sheer bad luck." Indeed, asserts one writer, "Those ghost hunters who wish to explore Devil's Hole must do so at tremendous personal risk. Only those blessed with extremely good luck or who feel that they have nothing left to lose should even attempt to study this site. The forces at work in this area are so

Figure 9.1. Cursed cave? *Skeptical Inquirer* managing editor Ben Radford tempts gloomy Devil's Hole near Niagara Falls.

strong and unpredictable that even experienced ghost hunters with extraordinary climbing, survival, and caving skills are likely to fall victim to the cave's intense aura" (Blackman 1998). Actually, *Skeptical Inquirer* managing editor Ben Radford and I challenged Devil's Hole on May 20, 1999 (see figure 9.1) and lived to tell about it. (In fact, park official Barry Virgilio told us that despite heavy pedestrian traffic, there was not a high incidence of injury in the area and that accidents were typically due to risky behavior.)

Other examples of "curses" involving a selective focus include those attributed to King Tut's tomb and the infamous Hope Diamond. After the discovery of Tutankhamen's lost burial chamber in 1922, expedition financial Lord Carnarvon died of blood poisoning from an infected insect bite, and in 1926 his former nurse died in childbirth. The archaeologist who discovered the tomb, Howard Carter, lost two assistants to what newspapers began to call "King Tut's Curse." They reported that there was an inscription over the tomb's entrance that read, "Death shall come to he who touches the tomb." Over the years, some archaeologists and tourists became ill or even died after they visited the site. Some have suggested that a mysterious bacteria or fungus in the tomb causes people to become ill.

In fact, there was no curse inscription on or in the tomb. In 1980, the site's former security officer admitted the story of the curse had been circulated in order to frighten away would-be grave robbers. As to the misfortunes, there was no pattern to them, the "victims" dying of a variety of causes. Some may have been ill anyway, and the added effects of travel, climate, and other stressful factors may have contributed to any illness-related deaths. In fact, balancing the list of misfortunes is the fact that ten years after the pharaoh's tomb was opened, all but one of the five who first entered it were still living. Carter himself lived on until 1939, dying at the age of sixty-six. Lord Carnarvon's daughter and others associated with the tomb, including the photographer and Egypt's Chief Inspector of Antiquities, lived normal life spans. And Dr. Douglas Derry—the man who actually dissected the mummy of Tutankhamen—lived to be over eighty years old (Nickell 1989).

But has the Hope Diamond—a.k.a. the "Diamond of Doom"—indeed "left a trail of death, debt and disaster among its owners" ("Diamond" 1976)? The seventeenth-century French trader, Jean Baptist Tavernier, who first acquired and sold the magnificent blue gem to Louis XIV for a King's ransom, later suffered financial ruin. Louis XVI, who cut the diamond into the shape of a heart, gave it to his queen, Marie Antoinette, before both were taken to the guillotine by French revolutionaries. Stolen by thieves, the gem—or rather a portion of it, cut to its present oval shape—surfaced in London, where it was bought in 1830 by a rich banker named Henry Thomas Hope. The faceted stone then passed through a succession of owners who reportedly suffered such misfortunes as bankruptcy, suicide, even murder. In the obituary for one alleged victim who died in 1947, a United Press story declared, "The Hope diamond has a long reputation as a 'jinxed' stone whose ownership carried with it a cloud of tragedy" (MacDougall 1983).

Figure 9.2. Jinxed jewel? Once allegedly doom-laden, the Hope Diamond now reposes serenely in the Smithsonian. (Photos by Joe Nickell)

As with "King Tut's curse," however, evidence for the Hope Diamond "jinx" depends on a selective process. According to Curtis D. MacDougall in his *Superstition and the Press* (1983), "Study of the complete history of the fabulous jewel reveals that at least half of those who owned or used it seemingly were not affected by any curse. How unusual is it for about half the members of any family to experience bad luck?" Moreover, he says, since acquiring the stone in 1958, "[T]he Smithsonian Institution has not suffered from fire, theft or death as a result of its famous possession. Because of the prominence of many of the diamond's owners the press has kept alive the myth of a curse, translating every untoward occurrence to fit the pattern." (See figure 9.2.)

Interestingly, once the selective process changes focus, as happened with the quartz effigy known as the "Crystal Skull," so do the imagined consequences. Once said to have the power to cause death (Mitchell-

Hedges 1954), a claim utterly lacking support (Nickell 1988), the erstwhile "Skull of Doom" has become a talisman to New Agers, who now "channel" hopeful messages from it and credit it with wonderful psychic "energies," even placing their own crystals next to it to supposedly "charge" them (Bryant and Galde 1991).

In Camelot

A similar process of selection and hype helps promote "the Kennedy curse." In 1984, *Newsweek* continued a long journalistic tradition of describing the family as a "star-crossed dynasty" (Beck et al. 1984) and later headlined a report on Michael Kennedy's accidental death "The Camelot Curse" (Thomas 1998). In reporting on the John F. Kennedy Jr. tragedy, one wire service story proclaimed that "The legendary Kennedy family curse had struck again" (quoted in *Times Record* 1999).

Actually, the Kennedys themselves have not been blameless in the matter. For example, in his television to the people of Massachusetts in the wake of the Chappaquiddick tragedy, Ted Kennedy (1969) admitted that among his "irrational" thoughts of the period had been the question of "whether some awful curse did actually hang over all the Kennedys." And Michael Kennedy had said of RFK's assassination, "It was as if fate had turned against us. There was now a pattern that could not be ignored" (Kelly and Walsh 1999).

Despite the hype, there has also been much appropriate skepticism. A German daily editorialized: "A plane crash is a dreadful, horrible banality. But when a member of the Kennedy dynasty crashes a plane, the accident becomes a sign of inescapable destiny . . . and the global infotainment industry has its raw material—the curse of the Kennedys" (quoted in "Curse or Hubris" 1999). Commendably, the Wichita Falls, Texas, *Times Record News* had this to say:

> The notion that a family is cursed harkens back to the Dark Ages or the early days in this country when women were burned at the stake because they were believed to be witches and men were drawn and quartered because they were believed to be inhabited by evil spirits. Yet, even if educated reporters and editors don't actually believe in the fact that a family or an individual can be cursed, we see that idea promoted to a public that borders on scientific illiteracy already and, as

proven by the popularity of all sorts of magical, mystical cures for ailments, the popularity of horoscopes and psychic readings, that is pretty darn gullible.

The editorial went on to indicate various factors that were actually responsible for the alleged curse and concluded that for the notion to be entertained, "there needs to be proof that's more reputable than the zero proof offered right now. Extraordinary claims require extraordinary proof" ("Irresponsible" 1999).

The *Times Record News* editorial writers joined other skeptics in pointing out the real factors that can lead to the perception of a curse. Tacitly acknowledging selectivity, *U.S. News* conceded that the Kennedy family was "blessed and cursed all at once" (Kelly and Walsh 1999). And former JFK special counsel Ted Sorensen (1999), wrote: "The Kennedys are not accursed but blessed. True, they have endured, with remarkable religious faith, more than their proportionate 'share' of pain (though that is never allotted by the law of averages anyway). But they have also been endowed with good genes, good brains, good looks, good health and good fortune, with both instincts and opportunities for serving their country and helping those less fortunate."

In addition to the selective process, there is the sheer size of the Kennedy family. With nine children producing twenty-nine grandchildren, there have been increased opportunities for tragedy. Observes Temple University mathematics professor John Allen Paulos (1999), "If we look at large families we can sometimes find more death, disease and tragedy than is generally expected."

Still another factor is the common tendency to connect the unconnected. Much like the impulse that prompts us to see pictures in clouds or other random forms, there is the impetus to find dubious relationships between events—a sort of connect-the-dots tendency that the *Times Record News* (1999) observed "seems to be one characteristic of human nature." Asks the editorial, "When traffic accidents cluster around one intersection, would we blame our luck on the curse of the car gods or would we recognize that congestion or some other factor might play the major role in the number of accidents occurring there?"

The *News* joined others in pointing out the evident Kennedy "propensity for risk-taking" (Paulos 1999). Although Sorensen (1999) insists that the family is characterized by an adventurous rather than foolhardy spirit, the line between the two often blurs. Michael Kennedy died as a result of the risky family pastime of "ski football"—a game the Aspen, Colorado, ski patrol had warned against (Thomas 1998, 23). And a friend of JFK Jr. stated that the son of the thirty-fifth president "loved to dance on the edge" (Barlow 1999), a tendency that may have been involved in his chancing a nighttime flight. Apart from mere adventurousness, simply seeking political office obviously brings increased risk of assassination—a factor that belies the notion of a curse in the deaths of JFK and RFK.

And speaking of assassination, there is another factor that aids the perception of a curse: visibility. Paulos (1999) notes that "When a celebrity's private life and death become public, news gets disseminated so rapidly and so thoroughly that we're blinded to everyone else's lives"—as happened with JFK's assassination. Also, the Kennedy family's involvement in various aspects of American society—an involvement that increases the family members' visibility—can help foster "the perception of more misfortunes" (Paulos 1999).

Especially when taken together, these factors may help promote superstitious belief in a Kennedy curse, although it is never stated who or what has cursed them or why. But as presidential historian Doris Kearns Goodwin (1999) said of the cumulative tragedies, the family's willingness to carry on demonstrated "a love of life that's just the opposite of giving in to a curse." And conservative columnist William Saffire concluded (1999), "There is no curse that hangs over anybody. It's against our idea of free will, whether you buy the Hope diamond or enter King Tut's tomb."

References

Acquistapace, Fred. 1991. *Miracles That Never Were: Natural Explanations of the Bible's Supernatural Stories.* Santa Rose, Calif.: Eye-Opener, 39–79.

The American Heritage Desk Dictionary. 1981. Boston: Houghton Mifflin, s.v. "superstition."

Anthony, Ted. 1999. Litany of Kennedy tragedies seen as product of risk-taking lifestyles, *Buffalo News*, July 18.

Asimov, Isaac. 1968. *Asimov's Guide to the Bible*, vol. 1. New York: Avon.

Barlow, John Perry. 1999. Appearance on *Larry King Live*, July 19.

Beck, Melinda, et al. 1984. A Kennedy shadow legacy? *Newsweek*, July 2, 25.

Blackman, W. Haden. 1988. *The Field Guide to North American Hauntings.* New York: Three Rivers, 92–94.

Bryant, Alice, and Phyllis Galde. 1991. *The Message of the Crystal Skull.* St. Paul, Minn.: Llewellyn, 49–63, 203–07.

Curse or hubris—Europe's press mourns JFK Jr. 1999. London: Reuters, July 19.

Davis, John H. 1984. *The Kennedys: Dynasty and Disaster.* New York: McGraw-Hill.

Diamond of doom. 1976. In Perrott Phillips, ed., *Out of This World*, vol. 1. n.p.: Phoebus, 47–50.

Goodwin, Doris Kearns. 1999. Appearance on *Tim Russert*, CNBC, July 24.

Graham, Lloyd M. 1979. *Deceptions and Myths of the Bible.* New York: Bell, 157–63.

Guiley, Rosemary Ellen. 1991. *Harper's Encyclopedia of Mystical & Paranormal Experience.* New York: HarperCollins, 472–74.

Irresponsible: The media should rethink the "Kennedy family curse." 1999. Wichita Falls, Texas, *Times Record News*, July 20.

Keller, Werner. 1995. *The Bible as History*, 2nd revised ed. New York: Barnes & Noble, 124.

Kelly, Brian, and Kenneth T. Walsh. 1999. The curse. *U.S. News & World Report*, July 26, 17–21.

Kennedy, Ted. 1969. Live TV broadcast, July 25, text given in James E.T. Lange and Katherine DeWitt, Jr. 1992. *Chappaquiddick: The Real Story.* New York: St. Martin's, 171–75.

Kusche, Lawrence David. 1975. *The Bermuda Triangle Mystery Solved.* Reprinted Buffalo, N.Y.: Prometheus, 1986.

MacDougall, Curtis D. 1983. *Superstition and the Press.* Buffalo: Prometheus, 206–09.

Mitchell-Hedges, F.A. 1954. *Danger My Ally.* London: Elek, 243.

Nickell, Joe. 1995. *Entities: Angels, Spirits, Demons, and Other Alien Beings.* Amherst, N.Y.: Prometheus, 41, 117.

———. 1989. *The Magic Detectives.* Buffalo, N.Y.: Prometheus, 55–56.

———. 1988. *Secrets of the Supernatural*, with John F. Fischer. Buffalo, N.Y.: Prometheus, 29–46.

Paulos, John Allen. 1999. Curse of the Kennedys? http://abcnews.go.com/sections/science/WhosCounting/paulos990720.html, July 20.

Rather, Dan. 1999 CBS live broadcast, July 17.

Saffire, William. 1999. Appearance on *Tim Russert*, CNBC, July 24.

Salkin, Allen. 1999. Clan history is written in tears. *New York Post*, July 18, 12–13.

Sorensen, Theodore C. 1999. The Kennedy curse, and other myths. *New York Times,* July 23.

Thomas, Evan. 1998. The Camelot curse. *Newsweek*, Jan. 12, 23–29.

Chapter 10

Riddle of the Circles

For years a mysterious phenomenon has been plaguing southern English crop fields. Typically producing swirled, circular depressions in cereal crops, it has left in its wake beleaguered farmers and an astonished populace—not to mention befuddled scientists and would-be "investigators"—all struggling to keep apace with the proliferating occurrences and the equally proliferating claims made about them.

The Mystery and the Controversy

The circles range in diameter from as small as three meters (nearly ten feet) to some twenty-five meters (approximately eighty-two feet) or more. In addition to the simple circles that were first reported, there have appeared circles in formations; circles with rings, spurs, and other appurtenances; and yet more complex forms, including "pictographs" and even a crop triangle! While the common depression or "lay" pattern is spiral (either clockwise or counterclockwise), there are radial and even more complex lays (Delgado and Andrews 1989; Meaden 1989; "Field" 1990). In most cases, the circles' matted pinwheel patterns readily distinguished them from fairy rings (rings of lush growth in lawns and meadows, caused by parasitic fungi) (Delgado and Andrews 1989). The possibility that they were due to the sweeping movements of snared or tethered animals, or rutting deer, seemed precluded by the absence of any tracks or trails of bent or broken stems. And the postulation of helicopters flying upside-down was countered by the observation that such antics would produce not swirled circles, but crashed helicopters ("England" 1989; Grossman 1990).

A "scientific" explanation was soon attempted by George Terence Meaden, a onetime professor of physics who later took up meteorology as an avocation. In his book *The Circles Effect and Its Mysteries,* he claims, "Ultimately, it is going to be the theoretical atmospheric physicist who will successfully minister the full and correct answers." Meaden's notion is that the "circles effect" is produced by what he terms the "plasma vortex phenomenon." He defines this as "a spinning mass of air which has accumulated a significant fraction of electrically charged matter." When the electrically charged, spinning mass strikes a crop field, Meaden contends, it produces a neat crop circle (1989, 3, 10–11). Variant forms, he asserts, are also allowed by his postulated vortices. However, as even one of Meaden's staunchest defenders concedes, "Natural descending vortices . . . are as yet unrecognized by meteorologists" (Fuller 1988). Meaden himself acknowledges that "some from among my professional colleagues who have expressed surprise at the discovery of the circles effect and questioned why it has not previously attracted the attention of scientists, prefer to deny its existence and reject the entire affair as a skillful hoax" (Meaden 1989, 15).

In contrast to Meaden's approach is that of Pat Delgado and Colin Andrews (1989), two engineers who have extensively studied and recorded the crop-circle phenomenon. The pages of their *Circular Evidence* are filled with digressions and irrelevancies—all calculated to foster mystery. Overall, Delgado and Andrews hint most strongly at the UFO hypothesis—perhaps not surprisingly, since both have been consultants to *Flying Saucer Review* (Grossman 1990). Although they profess "guarded views" about whether circles and rings have an extraterrestrial source, they frequently give the opposite impression. For example, they go out of their way to observe that a 1976 circle "appeared about seven weeks before a Mrs. [Joyce] Bowles had seen a UFO [and a silver-suited humanoid] just down the road." Again, after visiting one circle Andrews met two teenagers, one of whom had earlier seen "an orange glowing object" nearby. Other mysterious lights and objects are frequently alluded to in connection with crop circles(Delgado and Andrews 1989, 17, 63, 98).

Almost predictably, a hybrid of the main theories has appeared in "eyewitness" form. Late one evening in early August 1989, or so they claimed, two young men witnessed a circle being formed near Margate, Kent. One of them, a nineteen-year-old, described "a spiraling vortex of flashing light" (a nod to Meaden et al.), which, however, "looked like an upturned satellite TV dish with lots of flashing lights" (a gesture to flying saucer theorists). The youth kept a straight face while posing with the circle for a news photo ("A Witness" 1989–1990).

As the crop-circle phenomenon entered the decade of the nineties—bringing with it the emergence of ever more complex forms that earned the sobriquet "pictograms"—the main circular theorists rushed into print their various "Son of Crop Circles" sequels. For example, Paul Fuller and Jenny Randles (who are Meaden's disciples, although, ironically, they are ufologists) followed their *Controversy of the Circles* with *Crop Circles: A Mystery Solved*. Several periodicals devoted to the phenomenon also sprang up, such as *The Cereologist*, *The Crop Watcher*, and *The Circular*, which was published by the Centre for Crop Circle Studies (Chorost 1991). If critics of the main theories were not capitalizing on an expanding market of interest in crop circles, they were nevertheless busily poring over the data and pointing out that the prevailing circle theories were, well, full of holes.

Data Analyses

Forensic analyst John F. Fischer and I launched an investigation into the crop-circle mystery. It soon seemed apparent that the crop-circle phenomenon had a number of potentially revealing characteristics. Cereologists—whether of the "scientific" or "paranormal" stripe—tend either to deny these characteristics or to posit alternative explanations for them, for the implications are serious. While any single attribute may be insufficient to identify a phenomenon, since other phenomena may share that feature, sufficient multiple qualities may allow one to rule in or out certain hypotheses so as to make an identification.

The identification alluded to is hoaxing. The characteristics that point to it include an escalation in frequency, the geographic distribution, an increase in complexity over time, and what we call the "shyness effect," as well as a number of lesser features.

An Escalation in Frequency

This aspect of the phenomenon has been well reported. Although there have been reports of circles and rings in earlier years and in various countries—e.g., circles of reefs in Australia in 1966 and a burned circle of grass in Connecticut in 1970—only a few had the flattened swirl feature, and not many of those were well documented at the time (Delgado and

Andrews 1989, 179–89; Story 1980, 370–71). In any case, by the mid 1970s, what are now regarded as "classic" crop circles had begun to appear. In 1976, swirled circles in tall grass were shown near a Swiss village by a man who claimed he was regularly visited by extraterrestrials (Kinder 1987), and Delgado and Andrews (1989) claim an instance in England that same year. When Delgado saw his first circles in 1981, his response was "to share the experience with other people, so I contacted several national papers, along with the BBC and ITN." Then, he says, "Local papers jumped on the bandwagon as soon as they could get the story into print" (Delgado and Andrews 1989, 11–17).

Delgado's use of the word "bandwagon" seems appropriate, since the term refers to an increasingly popular trend or fad. It was in an attempt to quantify and assess such perceptions that we decided to create a data bank of information on the circles. We used the data in Delgado and Andrews's *Circular Evidence*, which reviewers praised for its "level of detail" (Shoemaker 1990). Of course, we considered that the incidences of the phenomenon in their book did not represent a complete list, but we intended to look at other sources of data as a cross-check on the sample.

With these caveats in mind, a copy of *Circular Evidence* was provided to computer expert Dennis Pearce, an advisory engineer with Lexmark International. Plotting the number of circles per year, he determined, showed a definite (i.e., significantly greater than exponential) increase in the number of crop circles annually from 1981–1987 (Pearce 1991). This was well supported by data from Meaden's (1989–1990) article in *Fortean Times*, "A Note on Observed Frequencies of Occurrence of Circles in British Cornfields." Figures for the four years from 1980 to 1983 were, respectively, 3, 3, 5, and 22; Meaden (1989–1990) does not give exact figures for the next few years but notes they were "rising"; then, during the years from 1987 to 1989, the totals went from 73 to 113 to "over 250" annually. For 1990, the figure had again jumped remarkably—to 700 circles in Britain, at least according to Randles (1991a). Small wonder that even moderate voices in the controversy insisted the phenomenon was increasing.

Dennis Pearce also examined statistics on crop-circle articles that appeared in the London *Times* from 1986 to 1990, and he specifically commented on "the rapid rise in both locations and number of circles in the years following the London *Times* reports," which, he said, "is to me evidence of human intervention."

Geographic Distribution

A second observed feature of the patterned crops phenomenon is its predilection for a limited geographic area. As we have seen, prior to the mid-1970s, crop circles appeared sporadically at scattered locations in various countries, but since then they have flourished in southern England—in Hampshire, Wiltshire, and nearby counties. It was there that the circles effect captured the world's attention.

In plotting the occurrences of formations among English counties, Pearce confessed that he was "surprised at how localized the phenomenon is." Although there are known exceptions, such as an occurrence in adjacent Wiltshire in 1980, all the pre-1986 cases published by Delgado and Andrews in *Circular Evidence* were in Hampshire, with the vast majority remaining there during the period surveyed (Pearce 1991). Other sources provide additional evidence for this geographic preference. In 1989, *Time* magazine concluded: "While there have been reports of circles from as far away as the Soviet Union, Japan, and New Zealand, by far the greatest number have appeared in Hampshire and Wiltshire" (Donnelly 1989). The Associated Press, citing a total of 270 circles for the summer of 1989, reported that "two-thirds appeared in a square-mile zone near Avebury in Wiltshire's rural terrain, including 28 in one field" ("England" 1989).

Looking beyond the Wessex area, just as the popular media's increasing reportage of the cornfield phenomenon appears to have produced an increase in circle totals—as even Jenny Randles concedes—it also correlates well with the spread of the phenomenon elsewhere. In view of just the data in *Circular Evidence*, Dennis Pearce observed that the number of reported geographical locations in England each year grew at a faster than exponential rate. "I would suspect," he said, "that a natural phenomenon would be either consistently localized or consistently spread about, but not spreading rapidly over time." Also, whereas the circles' pre-English distribution was exceedingly sparse, after newspaper and television reports on the phenomenon began to increase in the latter eighties, circles began to crop up in significant numbers around the world. For example, in September 1990 two circles appeared in a Missouri sorghum field and were immediately followed by reports in three other fields—one in Missouri and two in Kansas (McGuire and Adler 1990). About this time they also had begun to appear in significant numbers in Japan and Canada.

Increase in Complexity

A third characteristic of the patterned-crops phenomenon is the tendency of the configurations to become increasingly elaborate over time. Looking first at the data in *Circular Evidence* alone, we see a definite trend. Delgado and Andrews (1989) themselves state, "Before the late 1970s it looked as though single circles were all we had to consider; but, as has always been the pattern, and as we have learnt over the years, something, maybe some intelligent level, keeps one or more jumps ahead" (122). Again they say, "As soon as we think we have solved one peculiarity, the next circle displays an inexplicable variation, as if to say, 'What do you make of it now?'" (12).

While there were some moderately complex forms in earlier periods, the overall evolution of forms within the Wessex area still seems well established, and worldwide the emergence of the pictograms in 1990 clearly represented a new phase. According to Meaden, "Admittedly, 1990 does look to be exceptional, but just because the reasons for this wait to be clarified, it would be fatuous to decree [that] an alien intelligence is at hand" (Meaden, in Noyes 1989, 85).

The pictograms are wildly elaborate forms with a distinctly pictorial appearance. There have been circles with key shapes and clawlike patterns; complex designs, consisting of circles and rings linked by straight bars and having various appendages and other stylized features; and still other configurations, including free-form "tadpole" shapes and even a crop *triangle* ("Field" 1990; Noyes 1990). Small wonder that Delgado and Andrews, as well as others, suspect that the force making the designs is being "intelligently manipulated" ("Mystery" 1990).

At least the pictograms enabled Jenny Randles to wake up to the unmistakable evidence that hoaxes were not only occurring but were running rampant. She has admitted (1991a), "I do not believe that wind vortices created the pictograms, though serious research into that possibility continues. . . . I can think of very good reasons why the pictograms might well be expected, based on our sure knowledge that crop-circle hoaxing was greatly increased from just a few known cases before 1989 to a far higher figure deduced from my own personal site investigations in 1990. I would put the hoaxes to comprise something over 50 percent of the total." However, Randles still believes that beyond the hoaxes is a genuine, wind-vortex-caused phenomenon, whereas there seems no need to postulate such. If the "experts" like Meaden, Delgado, and Andrews cannot tell the genuine crop circles from hoaxed ones in fifty percent of the cases, one wonders just what the other 50 percent consist of.

The Shyness Factor

A fourth characteristic of the patterned-crop phenomenon is its avoidance of being observed in action. There is considerable evidence of this fact. First, there is its nocturnal aspect. Delgado and Andrews (1989, 156), who appear to have done the most extensive documentation of the phenomenon, state, "Many . . . confirmations of nighttime creations come from farmers and people living near circle sites. 'It wasn't there last night, but I noticed it first thing this morning,' has become almost a stock statement. The evidence is overwhelming that circle creations only occur at night." Randles and Fuller (1990, 53) agree that "most seem to form during the night or in daylight hours around dawn."

Not only does the circle-forming mechanism seem to prefer the dark, but it appears to specifically resist being seen, as shown by Colin Andrews's Operation White Crow. This was an eight-night vigil maintained by about sixty cereologists at Cheesefoot Head (a prime circles location) beginning June 12, 1989. Not only did the phenomenon fail to manifest itself in the field under surveillance, but—although there had already been almost a hundred formations that summer, with yet another 170 or so to occur—not a single circle was reported for the eight-day period anywhere in England! Then a large circle and ring (the very set that, being swirled in the same direction, seemed to play a joke on Meaden by upsetting his hypothesis) was discovered about five hundred yards away on the very next day! (Noyes 1990, 28; Michell 1989–1990, 47–58)

The following year, the cereologists attempted to profit from their mistakes. This time they conducted a "top secret" operation termed Operation Blackbird, which lasted three weeks beginning on July 23, 1990. They took $2 million worth of technical equipment-including infrared night-viewing camera equipment-to an isolated site where they maintained a nighttime vigil. Reuters quoted the irrepressible Colin Andrews as explaining what happened in the early morning hours: "We had many lights, following that a whole complex arrangement of lights doing all sorts of funny things. It's a complex situation. . . . But there is undoubtedly something here for science" (L. Johnson 1991). Pressed by reporters, Andrews denied that his group could have been fooled by a hoax.

However, when they and reporters converged on the site, they discovered a hastily flattened set of six circles, with a wooden cross and a Ouija board placed at the center of each.

The Hoax Hypothesis

Taken together, the characteristics we have described—the escalation in frequency, the geographic distribution, the increase in complexity, the "shyness effect," and other features—are entirely consistent with the work of hoaxers. That there *are* hoaxed crop circles no one can deny; the question is of the extent of the hoaxing—that is, whether, if all the hoaxes were eliminated, there would still be a residue of genuine circles that would require postulating some hitherto unproved phenomenon, such as wind vortices or extraterrestrial visitations.

In several technical papers, W.C. Levengood (1994) purports to show that "Plants from crop formations display anatomical alterations which cannot be accounted for by assuming the formations are hoaxes." Unfortunately, there are serious objections to Levengood's approach. First of all, while he uses various control plants for his experiments, nowhere in the papers I reviewed is there any mention of the work being conducted in double-blind manner so as to minimize the effects of experimenter bias. There is, in fact, no satisfactory evidence that a single "genuine" (i.e., vortex-produced) crop circle exists, so Levengood's reasoning is circular: although there are no guaranteed genuine formations on which to conduct research, the research supposedly proves the genuineness of the formations. But if Levengood's work were really valid, he would be expected to find that some among the putatively "genuine" formations chosen for research were actually hoaxed ones—especially since even some of Meaden's most ardent defenders admit there are more hoaxed circles than "genuine" ones.

Although Levengood finds a correlation between "structural and cellular alterations" in plants and their location within crop-circle-type formations (as opposed to those of control plants outside such formations), he should know the maxim that "Correlation is not causation." That Levengood's work does not go beyond mere correlation in many instances is evident from his frequent concessions: for example, "Taken as an isolated criterion," he says, "node size data cannot be relied upon as a definite verification of a 'genuine' crop formation." Again he admits,

"From these observed variations, it is quite evident that [cell wall] pit size alone cannot be used as a validation tool." Until his work is independently replicated by qualified scientists doing "double-blind" studies and otherwise following stringent scientific protocols, there seems no need to take seriously the many dubious claims that Levengood makes, including his similar ones involving plants at alleged "cattle mutilation" sites (Nickell 1996).

If the cereologists cannot offer much in the way of positive evidence, they nevertheless make several negative claims, notably that hoaxers cannot produce circles with the qualities of the "genuine" ones. But what are these qualities? When I debated Delgado on a Denver radio program, it was difficult to get a straight answer from him on this issue. Delgado's main argument was the alleged lack of broken-stemmed plants in the "genuine" formations, a point he and Andrews make repeatedly in *Circular Evidence*. For example, they say of one circle that "the root end of each stem is bent over and pressed down hard with no damage to the plants, which is why they continued to grow and ripen horizontally" (138). In response, his various equivocations were pointed out; e.g., in one instance "most" of the plants were undamaged (or rather unbroken; some had "serration" marks on them!) (51). His contradictions were also noted. For instance, Andrews states of one crop ring, "Between the two radial splays was a line of buckled plants. Each one was broken at the knuckle along its stem length." Did he regard the formation as a hoax? No. He only said, as mysteriously as possible, "These collapsed plants appeared to have suffered whiplash damage, possibly caused by opposing forces meeting" (63–64). In other words, if the plants are unbroken, that is a mystery; if broken, that is another mystery.

It is entirely possible that the circles with broken plants are merely the less skillfully hoaxed ones. Also, the moistening effect of dew on plants bent at night might mitigate against breakage, while agronomists I talked with pointed out that from mid-May to early August the English wheat was green and could easily be bent over without breaking—indeed, could only be broken with difficulty (Blitzer 1990; Daugherty 1990). Another supposed impossibility is for hoaxers to produce circles without leaving tracks—there allegedly being none in the case of "genuine" circles. But a study of numerous crop-circle photographs in the various publications reveals that virtually every circle would have been accessible by the tractor "tramlines" that mark the fields in closely spaced, parallel rows. In any case, one can carefully pick one's way through a field without leaving apparent tracks.

In several cases, hoaxers have come forth and confessed; although, often the reaction of cereologists is to doubt them. Then, in September 1991, two "jovial con men in their sixties" claimed they had been responsible for many of the giant wheat-field patterns made over the years. In support of their claim, they fooled Delgado, who declared a pattern they had produced for the tabloid *Today* to be authentic; he said it was of a type no hoaxer could have made. The men said their equipment consisted of "two wooden boards, a piece of string and a bizarre sighting device attached to a baseball cap" (Schmidt 1991). They demonstrated the technique for television crews, e.g., on ABC-TV's *Good Morning America,* September 10, 1991, and their proclaimed hoax was publicized worldwide.

The burden remains with the cereologists to justify postulating anything other than such hoaxes for the mystery circles. In the meantime, an insightful reviewer has characterized the circles effect as "a form of graffiti on the blank wall of southern England" (J. Johnson 1991). Although the phenomenon has clearly exhibited aspects of social contagion like other fads and crazes—the goldfish-swallowing contest of 1939 comes to mind (Sane 1967, 789–92)—the graffiti analogy is especially apt. Just as graffiti is a largely clandestine activity produced by a variety of scribblers and sketchers possessed of tendencies to indulge in mischief, urge religious fervor, provide social commentary, show off elaborate artistic skills, or the like, so the crop-circle phenomenon has seemingly tapped the varied motives of equally varied circle makers—from bored or mischievous farmhands to UFO buffs and New Age mystics, to self-styled crop artists, and possibly to others. The phenomenon is indeed mysterious, but the mystery may be only the ever-present one of human behavior.

Additional information on crop circles comes from what I can literally call my field research. On Sunday, June 18, 1994, I went on an expedition into the vast wheat crops, conducted especially for me by veteran crop-circle investigators Chris Nash and John Eastmond (both of Southampton University), with an assist from the United Kingdom's *Skeptical Inquirer* representative, Michael J. Hutchinson (who did not, however, accompany us on the trip). With Chris at the wheel, the three of us motored into the picturesque Wiltshire countryside. We passed through charming thatched-roof villages—including that of Avebury, set amid a

Figure 10.1. British skeptic Chris Nash examines the swirled-grain pattern in this slightly elevated view of a Wiltshire pictogram.

great prehistoric circle of standing stones—and came upon a hillside adorned with a giant white horse (one of several ancient effigies formed by exposing the underlying chalk). By nightfall, we had discovered a handful of circles and pictograms. Two that were reasonably accessible are shown in the accompanying photos. The first was composed of a line of circles—a dozen by my count, or, as Chris waggishly clarified, mocking the exaggerating tone of crop-circle enthusiasts, "exactly a dozen." (Rather than follow the tractor "tramlines" into the figure, we took a shortcut, carefully picking our way through the wheat.) It is of course easier to see the overall pattern on a slope from a distance rather than from within the pictogram. The skeptics did not have with them their pole-mounted camera, but John bravely climbed atop my shoulders for a better view and a snapshot from my camera. (See figure 10.1.) Examining the swirl pattern, Chris thought the figure a rather ordinary example of a relatively simple pictogram.

The second one we examined was more unusual, with a crescent-and-circle design, but it appeared somewhat older, since the wheat was recovering from having been matted. Amusingly, the farmer had placed crude signs at the gate, requesting that visitors please use the footpath so as not to damage the crop and announcing huffily: "The Circle—It's a Hoax." Located just opposite the ancient man-made mound, Silbury Hill

Figure 10.2. John Eastmond (left) and author examine the "hoax" pictogram located opposite the famous manmade mound, Silbury Hill, seen in the background.

(figure 10.2), the pictogram was nevertheless pronounced genuine by a group of local dowsers who had preceded us to the site. One of them twitched his magical wands for the camera and explained that the swirled patterns were produced by spirits of the earth. He observed that the figure was on a "ley line" (a supposed path of mystical energy) that ran from nearby West Kennet Long Barrow through Silbury Hill to another ancient site.

Subsequently, we made our way to the top of the hill to the nearby ancient barrow, where we encountered a group of young Christian evangelists. As we explored the barrow's tunnel-like passage with its flanking burial niches, overhead the young people sang and rhythmically clapped their hands to "bless" the site and counter any evil forces. Off in the distance was another hill slope adorned with a large pictogram. After dark we rested over refreshments at an old stone tavern, where cereologists had once congregated in droves. It was now hosting, among others, a group of jockeys and three skeptics—at least one of whom was tired but delighted with the afternoon's rich and colorful experiences.

References

BBC program, "County File," 1988. Oct.

Blitzer, Morris J. 1990. Interview by Joe Nickell, Aug. 28.

Chorost, Michael. 1991. Circles of note: a continuing bibliography. *MUFON UFO Journal*, 276: 14–17, April.

Daugherty, Charles T. 1990. Interview by Joe Nickell, Aug. 28.

Delgado, Pat, and Colin Andrews. 1989. *Circular Evidence*. Grand Rapids, Mich.: Phanes.

Donnelly, Sally B. 1989. Going forever around on circles. *Time*, Sept. 11, 12.

England perplexed by crop-field rings. 1989. *Denver Post*, Oct. 29.

Field of dreams. 1990. *Omni*. Dec., 62–67.

Fuller, Paul. 1988. Mystery circles: Myth in the making. *International UFO Reporter*, May/June, 4–8.

Grossman, Wendy. 1990. Crop circles create rounds of confusion. *Skeptical Inquirer* 14: 117–18.

Johnson, Jerold R. 1991. Pretty pictures. *MUFON UFO Journal*, 275: 18, March.

Johnson, Larry F. 1991. Crop circles. *Georgia Skeptic*, 4(3), n.p.

Kinder, Gary. 1987. *Light Years*. New York: Atlantic Monthly.

Levengood, W.C. 1994. Anatomical anomalies in crop formation plants. *Physiologia Plantarum* 92: 356–63.

McGuire, Donna, and Eric Adler. 1990. More puzzling circles found in fields. *Kansas City (Missouri) Star*, Sept. 21.

Meaden, George Terence. 1989. *The Circles Effect and Its Mystery*. Bradford-on-Avon, Wiltshire: Artetech.

———. 1989–1990. A note on observed frequencies of occurrence of circles in British cornfields. *Fortean Times*, 53: 52–53, winter.

Michell, John. 1989–1990. Quarrels & calamities of the cereologists. *Fortean Times*, 53: 42–48, winter.

Mystery circles in British cornfields throw a curve to puzzled scientist. 1990. *Newark Star-Ledger*, Jan. 10.

Nickell, Joe. 1996. Levengood's crop-circle plant research. *Skeptical Briefs* 6.2 (June): 1–2.

Noyes, Ralph. 1989. Circular arguments. *MUFON UFO Journal*, 258: 16–18, Oct.

———, ed. 1990. *The Crop Circle Enigma*. Bath, England: Gateway.

Pearce, Dennis. 1991. Report to Joe Nickell. July 21.

Pickering, Keith. 1990. Unpublished monograph, Dec. 3.

Randles, Jenny. 1991a. Nature's crop circles nature's UFOs. *International UFO Reporter*, May/June, 14–16, 24.

———. 1991b. Measuring the circles. *Strange Magazine*, 7: 24–27, April.

Randles, Jenny, and Paul Fuller. 1990. *Crop Circles: A Mystery Solved.* London: Robert Hale.

Sann, Paul. 1967. *Fads, Follies and Delusions of the American People.* New York: Bonanza.

Schmidt, William E. 1991. Two "jovial con men" take credit (?) for crop circles. *New York Times*, Sept. 10.

Shoemaker, Michael T. 1990. Measuring the circles. *Strange Magazine*, 6: 32–35, 56–57.

Story, Ronald D. 1980. *The Encyclopedia of UFOs.* Garden City, N.Y.: Doubleday.

A witness from Whitness. 1989–1990. *Fortean Times* 53: 37, winter.

Chapter 11

Cult of the "UFO Missionaries"

Marshall Herff Applewhite (1931–1997) and Bonnie Lu Trousdale Nettles (ca. 1927–1985) were styled "UFO missionaries extraordinary" in a 1976 book by that name compiled by ufologist Hayden Hewes and paranormal pulp writer Brad Steiger (Hewes and Steiger 1976). The story of Applewhite and Nettles is a bizarre tale of fantasy that led eventually to psychosis and to the annihilation of an entire cult.

Fantasy Proneness

In their pioneering study of the fantasy-prone personality, Sheryl C. Wilson and Theodore X. Barber (1983) stated that, as suggested by their research data, "individuals manifesting the fantasy-prone syndrome may have been overrepresented among famous mediums, psychics, and religious visionaries of the past" (371). Wilson and Barber found that they could use biographies of mystics—like Helena P. Blavatsky (1831–1891), the founder of Theosophy—to determine whether or not such a person had the requisite fantasy characteristics. Discovering in the affirmative in the case of Madame Blavatsky, Wilson and Barber reported: "When we look further back in history, we find that famous psychics and mediums of the past also had the characteristics we have found in fantasy-prone subjects" (371). Sixteenth-century occultist Jerome Cardan, visionaries Joan of Arc and St. Bernadette of Lourdes, and others, like Christian Science founder Mary Baker Eddy (who talked with spirits), exhibited the traits of fantasy proneness. Also, "almost all [of their research subjects] who had many realistic out-of-the-body experiences and all who had the prototypic 'near-death experience,'" were fantasy prone (371–72).

I found numerous fantasy-prone characteristics among a group of persons who believed they had been abducted by aliens (Nickell 1996). Subsequently, I have been applying Wilson and Barber's suggestion about famous mystics to a number of contemporary and historical individuals, ranging from psychic sleuth Dorothy Allison and the prophetess Jeane Dixon, to faith healer Kathrynn Kuhlman, hierophant Aleister Crowley, and "sleeping prophet" Edgar Cayce. In each case, after I determine from biographies or autobiographies that the person was fantasy prone, I then write a short life history of him or her, being sure to include in the sketch sufficient evidence of the fantasy traits. I have considered fourteen potential characteristics from Wilson and Barber for these "fantasy-assessment biographies" (as I call them):

   (a) being an excellent hypnotic subject,
   (b) having imaginary playmates as a child,
   (c) fantasizing frequently as a child,
   (d) adopting a fantasy identity,
   (e) experiencing imagined sensations as real,
   (f) having vivid sensory perceptions,
   (g) reliving past experiences,
   (h) claiming psychic powers,
   (i) having out-of-body or floating experiences,
   (j) receiving poems, messages, etc., from spirits, higher intelligences, and the like,
   (k) being involved in "healing,"
   (l) encountering apparitions,
   (m) experiencing hypnagogic hallucinations (waking dreams), and
   (n) seeing classical hypnagogic imagery (such as spirits or monsters from outer space).

I have considered the possession of six or more of these characteristics to indicate fantasy proneness.

The following is an example of a fantasy-assessment biography. Actually it is a combined biography of the two "UFO missionaries" who founded Heaven's Gate, the cult whose adherents shocked the world with their mass suicide in Rancho Santa Fe, California, in 1997.

Marshall Applewhite was the son of a domineering Presbyterian minister of the same name. Little is known of his childhood, but he was born in Spur, Texas, in 1931. He was, his sister said, "very outgoing and caring" as a child (Winant 1997). In 1948, he graduated from Corpus

Christi High School, then attended Austin College and, briefly, Union Theological Seminary in Richmond, Virginia, where he studied sacred music. In addition, he served in the U.S. Army Signal Corps. He received a master's degree in music from the University of Colorado and was choir director at a Presbyterian school in Kingsville, Texas. Subsequently, he held the same post at several other churches (Hewes and Steiger 1976, 24–27). At some point, Applewhite married and became the father of two children.

From 1966 to 1970 he taught at the University of St. Thomas, a Roman Catholic school in Houston, and frequently sang with the Houston Grand Opera. In 1970, however, he was granted a "terminal leave of absence." According to a St. Thomas spokesperson, "He was an extremely talented musician who had health problems of an emotional nature" (Hewes and Steiger 1976, 24). The following year he reportedly checked into a Houston hospital, asking to be "cured" of homosexual desires. By this time he was divorced and had been living with a male companion. He was also "suddenly hearing voices," and he had a vision in which he was given knowledge about the world (Fisher and Pressley 1997; Hewitt et al. 1997). According to *Newsweek*, "He told his sister he had suffered a 'near-death experience' after a heart attack, but he may actually have suffered from a drug overdose, according to Ray Hill, a radio-show host in Texas who knew Applewhite at the time. 'He was kind of a Timothy Leary type,' said Hill" (Thomas et al. 1997, 31).

During this period, Applewhite met a nurse named Bonnie Lu Trousdale Nettles. They shared an interest in astrology and believed they had been acquainted in earlier lives. Nettles, who was four years his senior and married with four children, shared an asexual relationship with Applewhite, who at some point underwent castration. Early in their association they claimed to be channeling an apparition, the spirit of a nineteenth-century monk named Brother Francis, whom Nettles had been communicating with even prior to meeting Applewhite. They would later claim that anyone who followed them would have a spirit or guardian angel to direct them in perfecting their meditation (Sachs 1980, 153; Hewes and Steiger 1976, 37). According to one biographical source, "Herff experienced unnerving astral voyages at night, and he and Bonnie were in daily contact with unseen forces and entities. . . . Both Herff and Bonnie told of vivid dreams in which beings from UFOs urged them to abandon their earthly lives" (Balch 1982, 37).

The Two

The couple set out on a tour of the United States, during which time they formulated their flying saucer religion. They saw their mission revealed in chapter eleven of the Book of Revelation, which told how two messengers from the heavens would prophesy "a thousand two-hundred-and-three-score days, clothed in sack cloth." The two would then be killed, but they would return to life in three and a half days, ascending into heaven in a cloud that Applewhite and Nettles believed was actually a UFO. Calling themselves "The Two," they began to recruit followers at special meetings. Converts were expected to renounce family ties and give away all their worldly possessions in anticipation of the UFO voyage. This was predicted to occur in six months; when it did not, many disillusioned followers deserted the cult, while Applewhite and Nettles responded by extending the deadline for the expected events.

When The Two were briefly arrested on auto theft charges in 1974, Applewhite, who was sentenced to four months in jail, reportedly told the prosecutor that "a force from beyond the earth" made him keep the car (Hewitt et al. 1997, 40). Interviewed in 1974 by Hewes, both "Herff" and "Bonnie" claimed to be aliens from "another level" (Hewes and Steiger 1976, 68). "The Two" also referred to themselves as "Bo and Peep," due to their role as extraterrestrial shepherds. At times during the interview, Applewhite "would go into a trance-like state" (70). This was apparently explained in a later interview with Brad Steiger when they claimed that their "Fathers in the next kingdom" communicated with them "mentally" (84). As special messengers of God, they taught that the body could actually be "healed" from death and taken to "the next level" (89).

Their imaginings were apparently quite real to them. One interviewer came away convinced that "what they're talking about and what they're preaching about they believe in one-hundred percent" (quoted in Hewes and Steiger 1976, 77). Step by step, of course, they were creating their own reality. After Nettles died in 1985, Applewhite continued to lead the cult. Then came Comet Hale-Bopp and an amateur astronomer's photo of a "UFO" apparently trailing behind. Although this was actually a distant star, Applewhite and his followers apparently saw it as their long-awaited ride into the heavens. Dressed in their identical, asexual manner with short haircuts, the eighteen men and twenty-one women packed small bags of their belongings and committed suicide in shifts, eating drug-laced applesauce or pudding and lying on their bunk beds to await the prophesied encounter.

There is, I think, sufficient evidence to warrant the conclusion that both Applewhite and Nettles were fantasy-prone individuals, each exhibiting several characteristics from the above list (he: a, d, e, h, i, j, l, and m; and she: d, e, h, j, k, l, and m). Eventually, however, Applewhite completely lost contact with reality and became psychotic. A psychiatry professor who studied videotapes of his final statements concluded he was delusional, paranoid, and sexually repressed (Fisher and Pressley 1997). Thus did fantasies of the paranormal lead to gruesome reality.

References

Balch, Robert W. 1982. Bo and Peep: A case study of origins of messianic leadership. In *Millennialism and Charisma*, edited by Roy Wallis. Belfast, Northern Ireland: The Queen's University, 13–72.

Bearak, Barry. 1997. Odyssey to suicide. *New York Times*, April 28, cover story.

Fisher, Marc, and Sue Ann Pressley. 1997. Cult leader evolved from being married, gay to anti-sex prophet. *Washington Post*, reprinted in *Buffalo News*, March 29.

Hewes, Hayden, and Brad Steiger, comps. and eds. 1976. *UFO Missionaries Extraordinary*. New York: Pocket.

Hewitt, Bill, et al. 1997. Who they were. *People*, April 14, 40–56.

Internet, radio may have inspired belief that UFO trailed comet. 1997. Associated Press, *Buffalo News*, March 28.

Nickell, Joe. 1996. A study of fantasy proneness in the thirteen cases of alleged encounters in John Mack's *Abduction*. *Skeptical Inquirer* 20(3): 18–20, 54.

Sachs, Margaret. 1980. *The UFO Encyclopedia*. New York: Perigree, 152–53.

Thomas, Evan, et al. 1997. The next level. *Newsweek*, April 7, 28–35.

Wilson, Sheryl C., and Theodore X. Barber. The fantasy-prone personality. In *Imagery: Current Theory, Research and Application*, edited by Anees A. Sheikh. New York: John Wiley & Sons, 1983.

Winant, Louise. 1997. Interview on ABC's *Good Morning America*, March 28.

Chapter 12

The Electronic Poltergeist

In the late 1990s, a strange entity calling himself Sommy harassed an Emeryville, Ontario, family for months, supposedly using "high-tech" means to stalk Debbie and Dwayne Tamai and make their lives miserable. As reported on *Dateline NBC*, the harassment began with the telephone—at first clicks, like someone was on the other extension; then the Tamais' calls would be disconnected whenever they attempted to phone out. Things got worse when the couple went on a vacation, leaving their fifteen-year-old son Billy in the care of a house sitter and friend, Cheryl McCaulis. Now the power went off and on intermittently, although the power company could find nothing amiss. Then the password (pin number) on the voice mail was changed, although Bell Canada officials declared that impossible.

As the disturbances increased, Cheryl began keeping a log, even recording some of the noises made by Sommy. He made obscene and threatening calls, claiming he was watching the house. On other occasions he would just cut in on the line and make burping or grunting noises. By week's end he had cut the telephone lines. When the Tamais returned from vacation, they had trouble believing their friend. Soon, however, Debbie had herself talked to Sommy. "It was freaky," she said. "The first time I heard him, I'll never forget him. My hair stood on ends, my arms— I was goose bumps, it was just the—the meanest voice." Asked why he was doing this, Sommy replied, "I just want a friend."

He reportedly learned to control the TV set, and he used the Tamais' telephone number to call others and harass them. He changed the ringing device on the Tamais' phone so that it sounded strange. Worse, he even devised a way to eavesdrop on the family, telling them things, they insisted, that he could only learn by monitoring their every word—from information on Debbie's birthday to the Tamais' bank card pin number.

According to *Dateline*, "So far no one, not the police, not the utility companies, not private surveillance teams, or even a former member of the Canadian Mounties, has been able to find this not-so-friendly ghost. Though not for the lack of trying. The Tamais believe Sommy got into their house while it was under construction ... and planted devices they've ripped out walls trying to find. Or they think he could have tapped into a line down the street with so many wires above ground in this still unfinished subdivision. In fact, experts tell us with all the digital and computer technology these days, it is theoretically possible." *Dateline* teamed up with the Discovery Channel to hire a private security firm, to take— as reporter Chris Hansen put it—"our own shot at ghostbusting." But after more than six hours, the team was forced to announce they had discovered nothing.

Unfortunately, *Dateline* failed to enlist the real ghostbusters. Some of us at CSICOP headquarters, and no doubt elsewhere, formed a hypothesis as soon as we saw the program. We realized that many of the phenomena described, such as the eavesdropping, could have been accomplished more easily by someone in the house, negating such an elaborate hypothesis as that involving highly sophisticated electronic wizardry. We also knew that such mischief is typically due to a disturbed youngster in the household. For example, the mystery behind several fires that plagued an Alabama house was solved by the confession of the family's nine-year-old son. He had had a simple motive: he wanted his family to return to the city from which they had recently moved. In another case— in a Louisville, Kentucky, home—boxes, bottle caps, and other objects were hurled about. Eventually an eleven-year-old girl admitted she was responsible for the trouble. Her mother was away, in a hospital, and the girl had felt neglected and needed attention. But she said, "I didn't throw all those things. People just imagined some of them" (Nickell 1995, 82– 92). To catch a culprit, investigators have used a variety of techniques, ranging from use of dye powder (which stains the hands of a person touching a treated object) to hidden cameras. (One revealing film sequence, featured on Arthur C. Clarke's *Mysterious World* series, portrayed a little girl, caught flagrante delicto, smashing an object.)

Following the Friday night broadcast, however, before CSICOP could reply to urgings from our readers on the Internet, there came new developments. On Saturday, when the Tamais planned to take their son to the Ontario Provincial Police (OPP) station in order to defend him from rumors claiming he was guilty of the harassment, he instead confessed. An OPP spokesperson reported the next day that nothing would be gained by prosecuting the youth for what was "an internal family matter." The Tamais explained, "It started off as a joke with his friends and just got so out of hand that he didn't know how to stop it and was afraid to come forward and tell us in fear of us disowning him." They went on to "apologize" to the world for any pain or harm that was caused, and added that they would seek professional counseling for the boy ("Teen-Age" 1997).

References

Dateline NBC. 1997. April 18.

Nickell, Joe. 1995. *Entities: Angels, Spirits, Demons, and Other Alien Beings.* Amherst, N.Y.: Prometheus.

Teen-age son confesses to harassing his family,1997. *Buffalo News*, April 21.

Chapter 13

The Silver Lake Serpent

On the night of July 13, 1855, in Wyoming County, New York, two boys and five men were fishing from a boat on Silver Lake near the village of Perry. After several minutes of watching a floating log, one man exclaimed, "Boys, that thing is moving!" Indeed, according to the *Wyoming Times*, after bobbing in and out of sight, suddenly, "the SERPENT, for now there was no mistaking its character, darted from the water about four feet from the stern of the boat, close by the rudder-paddle, the head and forward part of the monster rising above the surface of the water. . . . All in the boat had a fair view of the creature, and concur in representing it as a most horrid and repulsive looking monster." One estimated its above-water circumference as about that of a flour barrel.

The group reached the shore safely but were "frightened most out of their senses." Two of the men—all of whom were "persons of character"—signed an affidavit before a justice of the peace attesting to the incident. Several days later, one of the men was again on the lake—this time with his family—and all of them spied the monster, described as having a head as large as a calf's and a fin, apparently, upon its back ("Silver Lake Serpent" 1855).

Soon, others were reporting sightings of the monster, and excitement spread far and wide. As reported in an 1880 pamphlet, *The Silver Lake Serpent*, "People came on foot, by carriage, on horseback, and in fact, by any means of locomotion in their power, to see if even a glimpse of the monster could be obtained, and the hotels [in the village of Perry] found they had 'struck a bonanza'" (3). In response to a reward of a dollar per foot for the monster's skin, the *Wyoming Times* wondered, "Where's

Barnum? What will he give for the Serpent, dead or alive?" (6) Several expeditions were launched—ranging from a whaleman with a harpoon, to a vigilance society of men armed with guns, to a company having a capital stock of one thousand dollars and bent on capturing the creature (*Silver Lake Serpent* 1880, 3–21).

This was all to no avail, and the excitement eventually died down. Then, reports a modern account: "Several years later [1857] a fire broke out in the Walker Hotel. Firemen rushed to the scene to put out the blaze. When they worked their way into the attic they came upon a strange sight. In the midst of the flames they saw a great green serpent made of canvas and coiled wire" (*Legend* 1984, 11). Another source says, "The truth was then revealed by Mr. Walker himself" who "built that monster serpent with his friends to pick up the business at the Walker House Hotel" ("True" 1974).

Mr. Walker was Artemus B. Walker (1813–1889), and the scheme attributed to him and "a few of his intimate and trustworthy friends" is described in a local history by Frank D. Roberts in 1915:

> The serpent was to be constructed of a body about 60 feet long, covered with a waterproof canvas supported on the inside by coiled wire. A trench was to be dug and gas pipe laid from the basement of a shanty situated on the west side of the lake, to the lake shore. A large pair of bellows such as were used in a blacksmith shop, secreted in the basement of the shanty connected to that end of the pipe, and a small light rubber hose from the lake end to the serpent. The body was to be painted a deep green color, with bright yellow spots added to give it a more hideous appearance. Eyes and mouth were to be colored a bright red. The plan of manipulating the serpent was simple. It was to be taken out and sunk in the lake, and then when everything was ready, the bellows were to be operated and air forced into the serpent, which naturally would cause it to rise to the surface. Weights were to be attached to different portions of the body to insure its sinking as the air was allowed to escape. Three ropes were to be attached to the forward portion of the body, one extending to the shore where the ice house now stands; one across the lake, and the other to the marsh at the north end; the serpent to be propelled in any direction by the aid of these ropes (Roberts 1915, 200–01).

Roberts adds that "Many nights were spent" in the construction of the creature, after which it was transported to the lake one night and

94

Figure 13.1. Balloon's-eye view of Silver Lake, Wyoming County, New York, site of 1855 lake monster sightings. (Photo by Joe Nickell)

sunk at a depth of some twenty feet. Then came Friday evening, July 13, 1855, and—you know the rest of the tale. Today, Perry's city limits signs sport a sea monster, and the town annually hosts a lighthearted Silver Lake Serpent Festival—most recently featuring hot-air balloons. (One of these was an inflated sea serpent in which I flew over the scenic lake and countryside. See figure 13.1.)

The hoax story is a colorful yarn, but is it true? It has certainly been reported as factual, even by writers inclined to promote mysterious monsters—providing a touch of skepticism that seemed to enhance those writers' credibility. For example John Keel's *Strange Creatures from Time and Space* (1970, 260–61) claims the case proves "that a sea serpent hoax is possible and was possible even in the year 1855. It's too bad there were no psychologists and sociologists in 1855 who could have visited Silver Lake and made a thorough study of the 'monster mania' that developed there." Keel (260) also claims that "witnesses generally gave a very accurate description of what they had seen." He is echoed by Roy P. Mackal, whose *Searching for Hidden Animals* (1980, 209) specifically states that the Silver Lake creature was "described as . . . shiny, dark green with yellow spots, and having flaming red eyes and a mouth and huge fins." Other sources follow suit, including the *History of Northwestern New York*, which states that watchers "beheld a long green body, covered with yellow spots . . . and a large mouth, the interior of which was bright red" (Douglass 1947, 562). Alas, these writers are merely assuming people saw what Roberts's description of the fake serpent indicates they *should* have seen. In fact, not one of the original eyewitness reports mentions the yellow spots or the red mouth. Keel concedes the omission of the spots but rationalizes that the eyewitnesses might have simply "missed" them, or, he says, "perhaps, the newspaper editors felt that 'yellow polka-dots' were a bit much and deliberately deleted that detail from the published accounts" (Keel 1970, 260). But several of the reports were sworn affidavits, apparently given in their entirety ("Silver Lake Serpent" 1855; *Silver Lake Serpent* 1880). A 1955 account of the sightings repeated the yellow-spots canard and claimed "general agreement" from eyewitnesses that the denizen also sported "red eyes and a savage-looking mouth equipped with sharp fangs and a long pointed tongue" (Douglass 1955, 118).

Among the problems with the hoax story is that—while a wonderfully skeptical tale—it exists in a suspicious number of often-contradictory variants. For example, whereas Roberts's previously cited account of the hoax's discovery refers to a wire-and-canvas monster being found by firemen in the hotel attic, other sources give a very different explanation. Noting that the Walker House burned to the ground on December 19, 1857, they state that "in the debris left by the fire were found the remains of the Silver Lake Monster" (Mackal 1980, 209), specifically the remains were "the frame of the serpent" ("Silver Lake Serpent Revived" n.d.) or maybe just "remnants of wire and green canvas" (Fielding 1998).

An account in the *New York Folklore* newsletter notes that "there is some discrepancy" as to when and how the hoax was discovered. While "some say" it was the fire that uncovered evidence of the monster, "others report the hoax was revealed in 1860 when one of the men involved in the hoax simply got mad at A.B. Walker, the instigator of the hoax, and for one reason or another blurted out the truth in a moment of anger" (Kimiecik 1988).

At least one source asserts that "The creators of this stupendous hoax soon afterward confessed" (Peace 1976), and monster hunter Mackal (1980, 209) names the "confessed" perpetrators as Walker and *Wyoming Times* editor Truman S. Gillett. However, an analytical account attributes the newspaper's alleged involvement to "rumor" (Kimiecik 1988, 10), and a longtime local researcher, Clark Rice, insists that Walker was only *suspected* and that "No one ever admitted to helping him" (Fielding 1998).

Due to the many variations—what folklorists term *variants*—the story is appropriately described as a "legend," "tale," or even "the leading bit of folklore of Perry and Silver Lake" (*Perry* 1976, 145). States Rice: "It was a subject that was bantered around when you were growing up, and everyone had a different version" (Vogel 1995). Invariably the books and articles that give a source for the tale cite Frank D. Roberts's previously quoted account. Writing in 1915—sixty years after the alleged hoax— Roberts gives no specific source or documentation, instead relying on a fuzzy, passive-voice grammatical construction to say, "to the late A.B. Walker *is credited* the plan of creating the Silver Lake sea serpent" (emphasis added) having supposedly been assisted by "a few of his intimate and trustworthy friends"—who, alas, remain unnamed. He adds, "*It is said that* the serpent was made in the old Chapin tannery" (emphasis added), further indication that Roberts is reporting rumor (Roberts 1915, 200, 202).

The elaborateness of the literally monstrous 1855 mechanism raises further suspicion about the tale. Never mind the alleged laying of the "gas pipe," when gas lines did not come to Perry until 1909 nor piped water until 1896 (*Perry* 1976, 119, 124), raising questions about the availability of the pipe. And never mind the "small light rubber hose" that reportedly extended from shore to serpent, when the availability of that seems equally doubtful in a mid-nineteenth-century village. One account, seemingly cognizant of this problem, asserts that "Materials were ordered in Boston" (Douglass 1955, 120). There *is* a large old bellows, attributed to the hoax, that reposes in the Pioneer Museum at Perry (see figure 13.2), but its display card states only that it is "*believed* to have been used to inflate the Silver Lake sea serpent" (emphasis added). And a dredged-up millstone that some supposed had been ballast for the monster was discovered off the shore *opposite* the one from which the monster was re-

Figure 13.2. Author with bellows (probably a blacksmith's) allegedly used to inflate a fake rubber serpent as part of an elaborate hoax.

portedly operated. A knowledgeable source reports that some local boys once rolled the stone downhill and along a dock to its underwater site (Rice 1998). The questionable attribution of such artifacts to the hoaxed-serpent legend demonstrates the burgeoning nature of the tale.

Materials aside, the complexity of the alleged contraption as described by Roberts provokes skepticism. Although such a monster would not seem to preclude the laws of physics (Pickett 1998), the propulsion method Roberts describes raises serious questions. The three ropes that were reportedly attached to the serpent and extended to three lakeside sites would have greatly complicated the operation, not to mention multiplying the danger of detection. A far simpler and more credible method of creating a lake monster would have been that which artist Harry Willson Watrous (1857–1940) reportedly employed. In 1934, he confessed that the Lake George, New York, "hippogriff" that had frightened vacationers three decades before had been merely a log operated from shore by a rope and pulley (MacDougall 1958, 114).

In contrast, the Silver Lake contrivance would seem to have been a rather remarkable engineering feat—especially for a hotelier and some village friends. One suspects they would have sewed a lot of canvas and made many experiments before achieving a workable monster, yet Roberts (1915, 202) claims theirs worked on the first attempt. In fact, over the years attempts to replicate the elaborate monster have failed. "They have kept on trying to make one that submerged and came up," stated Clark Rice (Fielding 1998). One news source, calling it an "unresolved issue" as to "how the canvas and wire serpent swam at all," reports on an attempt by the Perry Jaycees to duplicate the creature: "They were unsuccessful. Their Serpent was too heavy and unwieldy to 'swim.' The club wished to hold a money-raising festival around Silver Lake and needed a Sea Serpent to attract crowds, so they tried making it with other materials and finally settled on a papier-mache and fiberglass construction. It could float but moved woodenly through the water" (Peace 1976).

Despite the claim that Walker originated the serpent, the 1855 newspaper accounts make clear that there was an earlier Indian tradition about a Silver Lake serpent and that, furthermore, such a monster had been "repeatedly seen during the past thirty years" ("Silver Lake Serpent" 1855).[6] On July 19, 1855, just six days into the monster scare, the *Wyoming Times* published a letter about a similar experience of "some 21 or 22 years ago" (cited in *Silver Lake Serpent* 1880, 13).

Certainly, not all of the 1855 sightings can be explained by the monster contraption Roberts described. According to his account, it was installed near the northern end of the lake, where both the inlet and outlet are located—indeed, one of the three operating ropes allegedly being anchored at "the marsh at the north end" (Roberts 1915, 200). Yet on Thursday, August 16, farmer John Worden and others who were "on the west shore of the lake *between two and three miles above the outlet*" (emphasis added) reportedly sighted "the monster" about a quarter mile distant ("Silver Lake Serpent" 1855). Surely no one imagines the fake monster being controlled from more than two miles away! Neither can the monster apparatus explain sightings of a distinct *pair* of creatures at the same time ("Silver Lake Serpent" 1880, 19–20).

Seeking to assess the hoax tale and working backward from Roberts's 1915 narrative, we come to the 1880 *History of Wyoming County, N.Y.* It describes the serpent tale as "a very successful canard" that was circulated locally, and that "afterward, by the connivance of certain editors," was "spread through the entire country." It states that "An intrepid whaleman, armed with a harpoon . . . cruised daily in search of the monster. It afterward 'leaked out' that a certain fun loving Boniface [i.e., a hotel proprietor[7]] had hired him to do this, and it was whispered that an attempt was made to manufacture an india-rubber serpent in order to meet an evident demand for a humbug" (*History* 1880, 240–41). This seems to be the basis of the legend: a *rumor* (i.e., what was "leaked out" and "whispered") concerning an *effort* ("an attempt") being made—apparently unsuccessful—"to manufacture an india-rubber serpent," which does not quite tally with Roberts's canvas-and-wire creature. The term "Boniface" does seem to indicate that the rumors focused on A.B. Walker—one of two hoteliers in Perry in 1855 who profited from the crowds attracted to the lake. But the rumors may have originated as speculation merely *because* Walker benefited.

The earliest mention of the hoaxed serpent appears to be a report in the *Wyoming County Mirror* of December 12, 1860, claiming that a Perry resident had gotten angry at Walker "and divulged the secret" of his fake sea monster (Douglass 1955, 120).

As we have seen, there has always been speculation about the role of Truman Gillett, editor of the *Wyoming Times.* Gillett certainly hyped the sea-serpent story. He had begun the newspaper just two months before, filling a vacuum left by the demise of the short-lived *Wyoming Advertiser* (Roberts 1915, 238). The leviathan tale was a bonanza for the *Times.* Described as the "village paper," it "'made hay while the sun shone,' and issued extras, illustrated with cuts [woodcut pictures] of the Lake and the monster supposed to live within its depths, and the papers had a large sale" (*Silver Lake Serpent* 1880, 3). That Gillett fanned the flames of excitement cannot be denied, but that he sparked the events by helping to create a fake monster is at most unproved.

As to the "intrepid whaleman" who was allegedly "hired" to search out the monster as part of the fun, he too has undergone modification. The 1880 pamphlet states, "An old whaleman, by the name of Daniel Smith, was imported for the scare" (*Silver Lake Serpent* 1880, 3). Later sources state that "professional harpooners were brought in" (*Legend* 1984, 10). In fact, the original newspaper accounts specifically make clear that Daniel Smith was one of "four young men from an adjoining town." He was therefore a resident rather than an import. Described as a "sailor, who has been for four years upon the Pacific engaged in the capture of whales," Smith had "but recently returned" to the area. He and his friends had been fishing on the lake and seem merely to have been caught up in the serpent hunt. Far from trying to foment excitement, he responded to an article describing his and his friends' own sighting by stating "that he had not intended to make it public, but to continue his investigations until such time as he might be able to capture the monster" (*Silver Lake Serpent* 1880, 13, 15, 18).

Finally, local lore has it that A.B. Walker left town because his hoax was exposed. Says Keel (1970, 260): "Those were rough-and-ready days, you must remember, and tar-and-feathering were common practices. Mr. Walker did not even linger long enough to collect his fire insurance. He departed immediately for Canada." It is true that Walker moved away, but he may well have done so for business or other reasons—there is no proof that he fled. His absence may have simply invited gossip. The alleged exposure by an angry resident did not come to light until 1860, three years after Walker's departure. In any event, he returned in 1868, after a lapse of eleven years, to resurrect the Walker House hotel. By this time, raconteurs state, he had supposedly been forgiven his deception and residents "decided that he was a hero instead of a villain" (Keel 1970, 260). But if that is true, then why did not the 1880 county history proudly tell the story—especially since Walker was still alive at the time and could have corroborated the story and supplied the authentic facts?

In fact, the earliest version of the hoax tale appeared in the December 12, 1860, *Wyoming County Mirror*. "Everyone remembers," stated the brief article, "that during the Silver Lake snake excitement, at Perry, the hotel there reaped a rich harvest of visitors. A correspondent of the *Buffalo Commercial* says that when about two years and a half ago, the hotel was partially burned, a certain man discovered the serpent in the hotel." This "was made of India rubber," and supposedly "corresponded minutely" with a *Buffalo Republic* description of the serpent. The man who discovered the rubber fake "has just got mad at the landlord and divulged the secret." The newspaper story ended on a skeptical note: "We suppose this last game is just about as much of a 'sell' as the original snake."

In sum, the historical evidence diminishes as we work backward to the alleged hoax, whereas, conversely, details of the story increase the farther they are from the supposed event. Therefore it appears it was the story—rather than the serpent—that became inflated. If Walker and/or others did perpetrate a hoax, it is unlikely to have involved an elaborate contraption like Roberts described. There *were* hoaxes associated with the 1855 frenzy, but they were largely played out in the newspapers of the day, which treated the whole affair as great sport. For example, the Buffalo *Republic*, while expressing skepticism, published a lithographic illustration of the "captured snake!" A contemporaneous report says it "brought scores of visitors from a distance" (Douglass 1955, 119). In September, the *Chicago Times* reported that two visitors had seen the monstrous serpent harpooned and towed to shore. The newspaper jocosely reported that come nightfall the creature uprooted the tree to which it was tethered and returned to the lake. It was recaptured the next day, said the *Times*, whereupon it "awoke, threw its head 60 feet into the air; lurid eyes glared like balls of flame and its tongue, like flashes of forked lightning, 10–12 feet long, vibrated between its open jaws" (Douglass 1955, 119).

In the journalistic interplay of the day, accusations of hoaxing (or worse) were often made against rival newspapers, as happened with the Silver Lake brouhaha. At one point during the media uproar, the *Hornellsville Tribune* suggested that "if the origin of the Silver Lake Snake humbug is ever revealed, it will be discovered that some *one* or *two* in Perry village have been playing 'nigger in the fence' for the sole purpose and with the hopes of selfish benefit."[8] A clergyman, the Reverend J.S. Page, pastor of the Perry Presbyterian Church, wrote to the *Rochester Democrat*, lamenting: "The idea is abroad that it is merely a hoax to entice visitors to Silver Lake and Perry [and that] is entirely without foundation" (Douglass 1955, 119).

Such insinuations of hoaxing probably elicited an early statement by *Wyoming Times* editor Gillett. On August 8, 1855, he wrote: "We assert, without fear of contradiction, that there is not a log floating on the water of Silver Lake—that nothing has been placed there to create the serpent story" and that the paper had published what was related by truthful people ("Silver Lake Serpent" 1855).

Even if there was a hoax—either a fake serpent or a journalistic scheme—that does nothing to explain the earlier sightings. At this late date we can only round up the usual lake-monster suspects. As the perpetual saga at Scotland's Loch Ness demonstrates, "monsters" may be created by floating trees and driftwood, leaping fish, swimming otters and deer, wind slicks, and many other culprits—often seen under such illusory conditions as mirage effects and diminished visibility (Binns 1984). For example, some of the Silver Lake sightings, including the one that launched the 1855 frenzy, occurred at night— when visibility would have been relatively poor and imaginations heightened. On the 27th, two farmers working in a nearby field "saw something that *appeared like a log,* but three or four rods long" (emphasis added) (*Silver Lake Serpent* 1880, 11).

Eyewitnesses typically insisted the object was a living creature, sometimes with its head above the water. A possible candidate is the otter, which "when swimming seems a very large creature" (Scott 1815). While treading water, an otter can raise its head and neck well above the surface and otherwise simulate a monstrous serpent, especially if swimming with one or two others in a line (Binns 1984, 186–91). The large North American otter (*Lutra canadensis*) inhabits "virtually the whole of the New World" (Chamin 1985, 6). On one of my visits to Silver Lake, I was startled while walking along a nature trail to glimpse a creature swimming in a nearby stream; it quickly vanished and I was puzzled as to its identity until, later commenting to a resident about all the wildlife I had glimpsed (woodchuck, woodpecker, squirrels, etc.), I was asked if I had seen "one of the otters" that had recently been reintroduced there.

I subsequently talked with New York State wildlife experts about otters possibly being mistaken for mid-nineteenth-century "lake serpents." Bruce Penrod, Senior Wildlife Biologist with the Department of Environmental Conservation, stated it was "very probable" that otters were in the Silver Lake area in 1855. And if the sightings were not hoaxes, he said, he would clearly prefer otters—or even muskrats, beavers, or swimming deer—over sea monsters as plausible explanations for such sightings.

His view was echoed by Jon Kopp, Senior Wildlife Technician with the department. Kopp had an illuminating story to tell. In 1994, he was involved in banding ducks and was sequestered in a blind on Lake Alice in Clinton County. It was dark, when suddenly he saw a huge snakelike creature making a sinuous, undulating movement, heading in his direction! As it came quite close, he saw that the "serpent" was actually a group of six or seven otters swimming in single file, diving and resurfacing to create the serpentine effect. "After seeing this," Kopp said, "I can understand how people can see a 'sea serpent'" (Kopp 1998).

I thought of otters especially when I studied two previously mentioned accounts of 1855 that described a *pair* of "serpents" estimated at twenty to forty feet in length. Possibly the witnesses in each case saw two or more otters, which, together with their wakes, gave the appearance of much longer creatures. All of the witnesses were observing from considerable distances—in one case through a spy glass ("Silver Lake Serpent"

1880, 19–20)—distances that could easily be overestimated, thus exaggerating the apparent size of the creature. Because otters are "great travelers," with nomadic tendencies (Kopp 1998), it is possible that a group of them came into Silver Lake in the summer of 1855 and later moved on, thus initiating and then ending that particular rash of sightings.

The least likely explanation for the Silver Lake reports is that some exotic creature inhabited its waters. Noting that as a result of the "extravagant stories" Silver Lake "became more thoroughly advertised than it could have been by any other process," the *History of Wyoming County* (1880) concluded: "It is doubted, however, whether any snake larger than those which, under certain circumstances, infest people's boots, was ever seen." Whatever people did see, the situation was hyped in turn by the local newspaper and the antics of would-be monster hunters. People's expectations were thus heightened, and that in turn led to misperceptions. Psychological contagion (the spreading of beliefs and/or behavior to others as by suggestion) yielded the "monster mania" that soon ran its course. It is well known that people expecting to see something could be misled by anything having a slight resemblance to it. Gould (1976) called this tendency "expectant attention" and it is the basis of many paranormal claims—apparently including sightings of the Silver Lake Serpent, a case of the tale wagging the monster.

References

Binns, Ronald. 1984. *The Loch Ness Mystery Solved.* Buffalo, N.Y.: Prometheus.

Chamin, Paul. 1985. *The Natural History of Otters.* New York: Facts on File.

Douglass, Harry S. 1947. "Wyoming County," in John Theodore Horton et al., *History of Northwestern New York.* New York: Lemis Historical Publishing.

———.1955. The legend of the serpent: 1855–1955. *Historical Wyoming* 8.4 (July): 115–21.

Fielding, Todd. 1998. It came from Silver Lake. *The Daily News* (Batavia, N.Y.), July 25.

Gould, Rupert T. 1976. *The Loch Ness Monster and Others.* Secaucus, N.J.: Citadel Press, 112–13.

History of Wyoming County, N.Y. 1880. New York: F.W. Beers & Co.

Keel, John A. 1970. *Strange Creatures from Time and Space.* Greenwich, Conn.: Fawcett, 254–59.

Kimiecik, Kathy. 1988. The strange case of the Silver Lake sea serpent. *New York Folklore* 9.2 (summer): 10–11.

Kopp, Jon. 1998. Interview by author, Sept. 18.

The Legend of the Silver Lake Sea Serpent. 1984. Silver Lake, N.Y.: Serpent Comics and Print Shop.

MacDougall, Curtis D. 1958. *Hoaxes.* New York: Dover.

Mackal, Roy P. 1980. *Searching for Hidden Animals.* Garden City, N.Y.: Doubleday, 209–10.

Peace, Carolyn. 1976. The Silver Lake sea serpent. *Buffalo Courier-Express*, May 16.

Penrod, Bruce. 1998. Interview by author, Sept. 14.

Perry, New York, As It Was and Is. 1976. Perry, N.Y.: Perry Bicentennial Committee.

Pickett, Thomas J. 1998. Personal communication, Sept. 18.

Rice, Clark. 1998. Interview by author, Aug. 1.

Roberts, Frank D. 1915. *History of the Town of Perry, New York.* n.p. [Perry, N.Y.]: C.G. Clarke & Son, 184–203.

Scott, Sir Walter. 1815. Letter quoted in Binns 1984, 186–87.

The Silver Lake serpent. 1855. *Wyoming Times*, Sept. 26 (citing earlier issues of July 18–Sept. 19).

The Silver Lake Serpent: A Full Account of the Monster as Seen in the Year 1855. 1880. Castile, N.Y.: Gaines and Terry.

Silver Lake serpent revived for Jaycee festival, undated clipping ca. 1960s, vertical file, Perry Public Library.

"The True and Unembellished Tale of the Great Serpent of Silver Lake," 1974. Song, published in *Legend* 1984, 1.

Vogel, Charity. 1995. Perry recalls fishy tale of sea serpent. *Buffalo News*, July 22.

Chapter 14

Miraculous Rose Petals

It has long been common, especially within the Catholic tradition, to discover faces of holy personages in random patterns and to suggest that these are miraculous. In my book *Looking for a Miracle* (Nickell 1993), and in a recent article in *Free Inquiry* magazine (Nickell 1997), I recounted several of these, including the famous image of Jesus discovered in the skillet burns on a New Mexico tortilla in 1978. Usually, these simulacra are the result of the inkblot or picture-in-the-clouds effect: the mind's tendency to create order out of chaos. On occasion, however, they are faked.

On Good Friday 1995, when I appeared on a special live episode of *Oprah* to discuss miracles, I met a daughter of Mrs. Maria Rubio, the woman who had discovered the tortilla Jesus. Afterward, as we were waiting in a limousine for a ride to the airport, I also talked with a self-styled visionary who had been on the show. She showed me a "miraculous" rose petal that bore a likeness of Jesus, one of several such items that supposedly came from the Philippines. Examining the petal with my Bausch & Lomb illuminated Coddington magnifier (a penlighted loupe), I was suspicious and asked to borrow the object for further study. (See figure 14.1.)

I subsequently examined the rose petal by viewing it with transmitted light, using a fluorescent light box and a stereomicroscope (figure 14.2). I noted that everywhere there were markings there was damage to the rose petal, resembling hatch marks made with a blunt tool (figure 14.3). In contrast, ordinary rose petals had no such markings. (See figure 14.4, top right).

Figure 14.1. Rose petal with "miraculous" portrait of Jesus.

Figure 14.2 (below). Author conducting examination of rose petal in CSICOP laboratory.

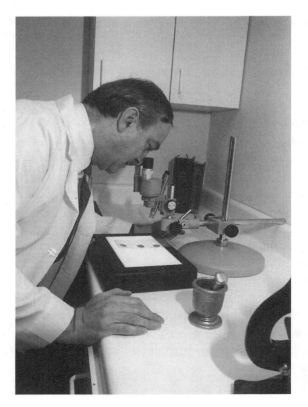

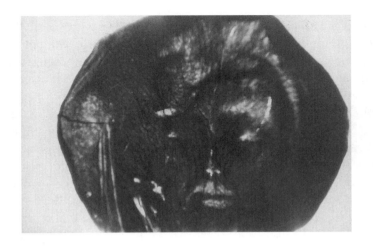

Figure 14.3. Facial markings constitute damage, resembling stylus marks.

Figure 14.4. An ordinary rose petal (top right) lacks markings, but a stylus (upper left) can be used to produce faces such as the three shown at bottom.

However, I found that faces could easily be drawn with a blunt stylus (figure 14.4, top left). I obtained dried rose petals, rejuvenating them with boiling water, then smoothing out the wrinkles on the surface of a light box and drawing the requisite pictures. They have characteristics similar to the "miraculous" one (figure 14.4, bottom).

Other imaged rose petals were shown on the Fox television network's special, "Signs From God" (July 28, 1999). The program hyped numerous miracle claims, while more prosaic explanations were glossed over or, worse, unmentioned. When an art conservator and a botanist each demonstrated that the images on the petals had been faked—they even duplicated the effects by pressing petals with small medallions—journalist Michael Willessee became flustered. He suggested that fakery was unlikely because the "miracle" petals were not being sold, ignoring the possibility of what skeptics term "pious fraud"—deception used in an end-justifies-the-means manner to promote religious belief.

As these examples show, paranormal claims are not solved by assumptions (e.g. that rose petals have mottled patterns that could yield a facial image) but rather by investigation on a case-by-case basis.

References

Nickell, Joe. 1993. *Looking for a Miracle: Weeping Icons, Relics, Stigmata, Visions and Healing Cures.* Amherst, N.Y.: Prometheus.

———. 1997. In the eye of the beholder. *Free Inquiry* 17 (2): 5.

Chapter 15

Paranormal Lincoln

His guiding of the United States through its greatest crisis and his subsequent martyrdom have caused the shadow of the tall, sixteenth president to loom still larger. Called "the most mythic of all American presidents" (Cohen 1989, 7), Abraham Lincoln has long been credited with supernatural powers. These include an early mirror-vision, prophetic dreams, and spiritualistic phenomena. His ghost, some say, even haunts the White House.[9]

In the Looking Glass

Many people have portrayed Lincoln as a man given to belief in omens, particularly with respect to his assassination. An incident often cited in this regard occurred at his home in Springfield, Illinois. Lincoln related it to a few friends and associates, including Noah Brooks in 1864. Brooks shared it with the readers of *Harper's New Monthly Magazine* the following July—three months after Lincoln's death—recounting the president's story "as nearly as possible in his own words":

> It was just after my election in 1860, when the news had been coming in thick and fast all day, and there had been a great "Hurrah, boys!" so that I was well tired out, and went home to rest, throwing myself down on a lounge in my chamber. Opposite where I lay was a bureau, with a swinging-glass upon it—[and here he got up and placed furniture to illustrate the position]—and, looking in that glass, I saw myself reflected, nearly at full length; but my face, I noticed, had *two* separate and distinct images, the tip of the nose of one being about three inches from the tip of the other. I was a little bothered, perhaps startled, and

got up and looked in the glass, but the illusion vanished. On lying down again I saw it a second time—plainer, if possible, than before; and then I noticed that one of the faces was a little paler, say five shades, than the other. I got up and the thing melted away, and I went off and, in the excitement of the hour, forgot all about it—nearly, but not quite, for the thing would once in a while come up, and give me a little pang, as though something uncomfortable had happened. When I went home I told my wife about it, and a few days after I tried the experiment again, when [with a laugh], sure enough, the thing came again; but I never succeeded in bringing the ghost back after that, though I once tried very industriously to show it to my wife, who was worried about it some-what. She thought it was "a sign" that I was to be elected to a second term of office, and that the paleness of one of the faces was an omen that I should see life through the last term (Brooks 1865, 224–25).

The same story was told by Ward Hill Lamon in his book *Recollections of Abraham Lincoln*. Lamon was a friend of Lincoln's, a fearless man who accompanied him to Washington for his protection, being given the special title, Marshal of the District of Columbia. In discussing the matter of the double image in the mirror, Lamon stated: "Mr. Lincoln more than once told me that he could not explain this phenomenon" and "that he had tried to reproduce the double reflection at the Executive Mansion, but without success." In Lamon's account it was not Mrs. Lincoln but the president himself who thought the "ghostly" image foretold "that death would overtake him" before the end of his second term (Lamon 1995, 111–12).

In recent years, paranormalists have gotten hold of Lincoln's anecdote and offered their own interpretations. Hans Holzer states that "What the President saw was a brief 'out of the body experience,' or astral projection," meaning "that the bonds between conscious mind and the unconscious are temporarily loosened and that the inner or true self has quickly slipped out" (Holzer 1995, 65). However, such an explanation fails to fit the evidence. Lincoln did not describe an out-of-body experience—a feeling of being outside one's physical self—but according to Brooks (1865, 225), "The President, with his usual good sense, saw nothing in all this but an optical illusion."

The nature of this optical illusion can be deduced from the circumstances. The double image was of Lincoln's face only, could be seen in a particular mirror but not others, and vanished and reappeared with respect to a certain vantage point. Taken together, these details are cor-

Figure 15.1. Double image of author (and photographer Rob McElroy) reproduces a curious effect experienced by Abraham Lincoln in 1860 and thought by Mrs. Lincoln to be an omen.

roborative evidence that the mirror was to blame. An ordinary mirror can produce a slight double-image effect due to light reflecting off the *front* of the glass as well as off the silvering on the back. With modern mirrors this is usually not noticeable, and the shift in the image is slight in any event. But in the case of old mirrors, whose glass plates "were generally imperfect" (Cescinsky 1931), a distinct double image might be produced, like that shown in figure 15.1. (Unfortunately, the actual mirror-topped bureau Lincoln described is no longer to be found at the Lincoln Home National Historic Site, much of the furniture having been dispersed in earlier years [Suits 1998].)

Although Lincoln thought the effect essentially an optical illusion, nevertheless, said Noah Brooks (1865, 225), "the flavor of superstition which hangs about every man's composition made him wish that he had never seen it. But," Brooks added, "there are people who will now believe that this odd coincidence was 'a warning.'"

Dreams of Death

The mirror incident sets the stage for claims of even more emphatically premonitory experiences. These were dreams Lincoln reportedly had that foretold dramatic events—one of which he related to his cabinet on April 14, 1865. The previous night, he had dreamed he was in some mysterious boat, he said, "sailing toward a dark and indefinite shore." In another version, it was of "a ship sailing rapidly" (Lewis 1973, 290). When Lincoln was assassinated only hours later, the dream was seen as weirdly prophetic. The story grew in the retellings that spread, says Lloyd Lewis in *Myths After Lincoln* (1973, 291) "around the world."

In fact, Lincoln had not thought the dream presaged his death. He had actually mentioned it in reply to General Grant, his guest that Good Friday afternoon, who had expressed worries about General Sherman's fate in North Carolina. Lincoln felt that Sherman would be victorious because, he said, the dream had often come to him prior to significant events in the war. According to Lewis (1973, 290), "For a President of the United States, in a time like the Civil War, to dream that he was sailing rapidly to an unseen shore was certainly not remarkable. Most of his waking hours, across four years, were spent in wondering where the Ship of State was going."

Not long before his assassination, Lincoln supposedly described an even more ominous dream to Mrs. Lincoln, then again to Ward Hill Lamon (1895, 115–16), who reconstructed Lincoln's words as follows:

> About ten days ago, I retired very late. I had been up waiting for important dispatches from the front. I could not have been long in bed when I fell into a slumber, for I was weary. I soon began to dream. There seemed to be a death-like stillness about me. Then I heard subdued sobs, as if a number of people were weeping. I thought I left my bed and wandered downstairs. There the silence was broken by the same pitiful sobbing, but the mourners were invisible. I went from room to room; no living person was in sight, but the same mournful sounds of distress met me as I passed along. It was light in all the rooms; every object was familiar to me; but where were all the people who were grieving as if their hearts would break? I was puzzled and alarmed. What could be the meaning of all this? Determined to find the cause of a state of things so mysterious and so shocking, I kept on until I arrived at the East Room, which I entered. There I met with a sickening sur-

prise. Before me was a catafalque, on which rested a corpse wrapped in funeral vestments. Around it were stationed soldiers who were acting as guards; and there was a throng of people, some gazing mournfully upon the corpse, whose face was covered, others weeping pitifully. "Who is dead in the White House?" I demanded of one of the soldiers. "The President," was his answer; "he was killed by an assassin!" Then came a loud burst of grief from the crowd, which awoke me from my dream. I slept no more that night; and although it was only a dream, I have been strangely annoyed by it ever since.

Lamon's account may be true, although he has been criticized for having "fed the fire of superstition that people were kindling about the name of Lincoln" (Lewis 1973, 294). In fact, however, Lamon had added a sequel to the story that is invariably ignored: "Once the President alluded to this terrible dream with some show of playful humor. 'Hill,' said he, 'your apprehension of harm to me from some hidden enemy is downright foolishness. For a long time you have been trying to keep somebody—the Lord knows who—from killing me. Don't you see how it will turn out? In this dream it was not me, but some other fellow, that was killed. It seems that this ghostly assassin tried his hand on some one else'"(Lamon 1895, 116–17).

In any event, that Lincoln should have dreamed of assassination—even his own—can scarcely be termed remarkable. Prior to his first inauguration in 1861, Pinkerton detectives had smuggled Lincoln into Washington at night to avoid a change of trains in Baltimore, where an assassination plot had been uncovered (Neely 1982, 16–17). Lincoln had subsequently "received [an] untold number of death threats" (St. George 1990, 66), and on one occasion had a hole shot through his top hat by a would-be assassin (Neely 1982, 282).

Among the Spirits

Lamon (1895, 120) insisted that Lincoln "was no dabbler in divination—astrology, horoscopy, prophecy, ghostly lore, or witcheries of any sort." Yet soon after his death, spiritualists sought to use Lincoln to give respectability to their practices by citing the occasions he had permitted séances in the White House, as well as to claim contact with his own departed spirit. The extent of Lincoln's involvement with spiritualism has been much debated. Daniel Cohen (1989, 7) says the president "seems to have had some genuine interest in ghosts and spirits while he was still alive," and spiritualists later tried to claim him "as one of their own" (Holzer 1995, 63).

Actually, it was *Mrs.* Lincoln who was involved with spiritualists. She turned to them in her bereavement over the death of Willie, the Lincolns' beloved eleven-year-old son who died of "bilious fever" in 1862. One such spiritualist medium was Henrietta "Nettie" Colburn (1841–1892). Mary Todd Lincoln met her at a "circle" or séance at the Georgetown home of Cranstoun Laurie, chief clerk of the Post Office in Washington. On one occasion, a séance with Nettie was being held in the White House's Red Parlor when the president stumbled upon them and watched with curiosity. Another time, he accompanied Mary to a séance at the Lauries' home. At least one biographer has suggested that Lincoln's marginal involvement may have stemmed from a desire "to protect his gullible wife" (Temple 1995, 199).

That was exactly what Lincoln did with regard to a trickster named Charles J. Colchester. Styling himself "Lord Colchester," he conducted séances wherein "spirit rappings" were produced. A concerned Lincoln asked Dr. Joseph Henry (1797–1878), the secretary of the Smithsonian Institution, for his advice about Colchester, whereupon Dr. Henry invited the medium to give a demonstration at his office. The scientist determined that the sounds came from Colchester, and he suspected trickery. Later, Noah Brooks caught the medium cheating and warned Colchester not to return to the executive mansion (Temple 1995, 200). Lincoln himself was not interested in séances, but according to Lloyd Lewis's *Myths After Lincoln* (1973, 301), "In these dark hocus-pocuses Mrs. Lincoln found comfort, and Lincoln let them go on for a time, careless of whether the intellectuals of the capital thought him addle-pated or no."

Spectral Visits

It is ironic that Lincoln did not believe in spiritualism, when his ghost is now reportedly so active. Although his Springfield home is decidedly *un*haunted, according to curator Linda Suits (1998), who says neither she nor anyone she knows has had a ghostly encounter there, other places compete for attention. There have been numerous reported sightings of Lincoln's ghost at his tomb in Springfield as well as at Fort Monroe in Virginia and, in Washington, at both the White House and Ford's Theater (where Lincoln was assassinated) (Cohen 1989, 11; Winer and Osborn 1979, 125; Jones 1996, 15). Understandably, perhaps, it is the White House that seems to receive the most attention—especially the "Lincoln Bedroom" (which, in Lincoln's time, was actually his office). The notion that his ghost frequents the stately rooms and corridors doubtless began with Mrs. Lincoln's post-assassination séances, and it was probably given impetus by a figurative remark made by President Theodore Roosevelt (who served from 1901–1909): "I think of Lincoln, shambling, homely, with his strong, sad, deeply-furrowed face, all the time. I see him in the different rooms and in the halls" (St. George 1990, 84). Such feelings are still common and may trigger sightings among imaginative people and those predisposed to see ghosts. The first person to report actually seeing Lincoln's ghost was Grace Coolidge (First Lady from 1923 to 1929), who saw his tall figure looking out an Oval Office window (Scott and Norman, 1991, 74; Cohen 1989, 10). During her tenure, guests were lodged in the "Lincoln bedroom" and "Every newcomer was informed of the legend that when the great light over the front door was dimmed for the night the ghost of Abraham Lincoln was supposed to pace silently to and fro on the North Porch" (Ross 1962, 109).

Since that time, there have been many alleged sightings of Lincoln's ghost by "White House staff, official visitors and members of presidential families," even, it is said, by "hard-boiled Secret Service men" who "have acknowledged observing the shadowy form of the martyred president gliding at night through the quiet hallways of the White House" (Jones 1996, 9). Among the Lincoln sightings was one by Queen Wilhelmina of the Netherlands (who had a prior interest in spiritualism). She was a guest of President Franklin D. Roosevelt when she heard a knock during the night at her bedroom door. Opening it, the drowsy queen saw the figure of Abraham Lincoln looking down at her, causing her to swoon (Ronan 1974, 40; Cohen 1989, 10). Religious leader Norman Vincent Peale claimed that a prominent actor (whom he would not name) had been a White House guest when he awoke to Lincoln's voice pleading for help. The actor sat up to see "the lanky form of Lincoln prostrate on the floor in prayer, arms outstretched with fingers digging into the carpet" (Winer and Osborn 1979, 135). And President Reagan's daughter Maureen said she had occasionally seen Lincoln's ghost—"an aura, sometimes red, sometimes orange"—during the night. So had her husband Dennis Revell (Caroli 1992, 39).

These examples are typical of many ghost sightings that are due to common "waking dreams," an experience that occurs when someone is just going to sleep or waking up and perceives ghosts, lights, or other strange imagery (Nickell 1995, 41, 46). Other apparitions are most likely to be seen when one is tired, daydreaming, performing routine chores, or is otherwise in a reverie or dissociative state (see e.g., Mackenzie 1982). This may help explain such sightings as one by Eleanor Roosevelt's secretary, who passed by the Lincoln Bedroom one day and was frightened to see the ghostly president sitting on the bed and pulling on his boots (Alexander 1998, 43; Jones 1996, 8).

Once the notion of a ghost is affixed to a place, almost anything—an unexplained noise, mechanical malfunction, misplaced object, or the like—can be added to the lore. For example, "When FDR's little Scottish terrier, Falla, would begin barking for no particular reason, some would say that the dog could see the ghost but no one else could" (Cohen 1989, 10). A similar situation was reported by the Reagans. On one of my appearances on *The Michael Reagan Show,* Mike told me an anecdote about his father and their dog Rex. According to President Reagan, when passing the Lincoln bedroom, Rex would often bark but would refuse to enter the room (Reagan 1998; see also Caroli 1992, 39, and Alexander 1998, 45). Mike related the story as more of a novelty than as proof of a supernatural occurrence. (President Reagan's daughter, Patti Davis, once asked her father if he had ever seen Lincoln's ghost. "No," my father answered— a bit sadly, I thought. "I haven't seen him yet. But I do believe he's here" [Davis 1995].) Neither the Bushes nor, as far as they could tell, their dog Millie ever saw the ghost of Lincoln, or indeed any of the other historical specters who are occasionally reported (Alexander 1998, 45).

Not all of the reports of Lincoln's ghost, however, have featured apparitions. In earlier times, there were frequent reports of sounds that were variously interpreted, by some as heavy footfalls (Cohen 1989, 10; Jones 1996, 8), by others as knockings at the door, with Lincoln's ghost typically being thought responsible. Not only Queen Wilhelmina but also "Presidents from Theodore Roosevelt to Herbert Hoover and Harry Truman all said they heard mysterious rappings, often at their bedroom doors" (Scott and Norman 1991, 74). However, ghost hunter Hans Holzer (1995, 70) concedes: "President Truman, a skeptic, decided that the noises had to be due to 'natural' causes, such as the dangerous settling of the floors. He ordered the White House completely rebuilt, and perhaps this was a good thing: It would surely have collapsed soon after, according to the architect, General Edgerton."

For all his greatness, Abraham Lincoln was of course human. Among his foibles were a tendency to melancholy, a sense of fatalism, and a touch of superstition from his frontier upbringing. However, as this investigation demonstrates, neither his life nor his death offers proof of paranormal or supernatural occurrences—not his very human apprehensions of mortality, not his wife's sad seduction into spiritualism, and not the evidence, even if expressed as anecdotes of ghostly apparitions, that his great legacy lives on.

References

Alexander, John. 1998. *Ghosts: Washington Revisited.* Atglen, Pa.: Schiffer.

Brooks, Noah. 1865. "Personal Recollections of Abraham Lincoln," *Harper's New Monthly Magazine.* July, 222–26.

Caroli, Betty Boyd. 1992. *Inside the White House.* New York: Canopy.

Cescinsky, Herbert. 1931. *The Gentle Art of Faking Furniture.* Reprinted New York: Dover, 1967, 135.

Cohen, Daniel. 1989. *The Encyclopedia of Ghosts.* New York: Dorset.

Davis, Patti. 1995. *Angels Don't Die.* New York: HarperCollins, 65.

Holzer, Hans. 1995. *Ghosts, Hauntings and Possessions: The Best of Hans Holzer,* ed. by Raymond Buckland. St. Paul, Minn.: Llewellyn.

Jones, Merlin. 1996. *Haunted Places.* Boca Raton, Fla.: Globe Communications.

Lamon, Ward Hill. 1895. *Recollections of Abraham Lincoln 1847–1865.* Chicago: A.C. McClurg.

Lewis, Lloyd. 1973. *Myths After Lincoln.* Gloucester, Mass.: Peter Smith.

Mackenzie, Andrew. 1982. *Hauntings and Apparitions.* London: Heinemann.

Neely, Mark E., Jr. 1982. *The Abraham Lincoln Encyclopedia.* New York: Da Capo.

Nickell, Joe. 1995. *Entities: Angels, Spirits, Demons, and Other Alien Beings.* Amherst, N.Y.: Prometheus.

Reagan, Michael. 1998. *The Michael Reagan Show,* Oct. 30.

Ronan, Margaret. 1974. *Strange Unsolved Mysteries.* New York: Scholastic.

Ross, Ishbel. 1962. *Grace Coolidge and Her Era.* New York: Dodd, Mead.

Scott, Beth, and Michael Norman. 1991. *Haunted Heartland.* New York: Dorset.

St. George, Judith. 1990. *The White House: Cornerstone of a Nation.* New York: G.P. Putnam's.

Suits, Linda Norbut (curator, Lincoln Home, Springfield). 1998. Interview by author.

Temple, Wayne C. 1995. *Abraham Lincoln: From Skeptic to Prophet.* Mahomet, Ill.: Mayhaven.

Winer, Richard, and Nancy Osborn. 1979. *Haunted Houses.* New York: Bantam.

⚛ Chapter 16

The Roswell Legend

More than a half century ago, in the summer of 1947, the modern UFO craze began. Fed by fantasy, faddishness, and even outright fakery, the mythology has become so well nourished that it has begun to spawn bizarre religious cults like Heaven's Gate. In 1997, the Roswell controversy reached out to involve U.S. Senator Strom Thurmond and a former aide, Philip J. Corso, in a dispute over a memoir by Corso for which Thurmond wrote the foreword. The book claims that the U.S. government used alien technology to win the Cold War ("Thurmond" 1997). This controversy only intensified the planned fiftieth-anniversary hoopla July 1–6 at Roswell, New Mexico, the site of ufology's Holy Grail. From near Roswell, according to a burgeoning legend, in late June or early July of 1947, a crashed alien spacecraft and its humanoid occupants were retrieved and hidden away at a secret government installation.

The "Roswell Incident," as it is popularly known, was propelled into history on July 8, 1947, by an unauthorized press release from a young but eager public information officer at the Roswell Army Air Base. He reported that a "flying disc" had been retrieved from an area ranch where it had crashed (Korff 1997, Berlitz and Moore 1980). This came in the immediate wake of the first modern UFO sighting, the famous string of "flying saucers" witnessed by private pilot Kenneth Arnold on June 24. Just such sightings had long been anticipated by pulp science-fiction magazines, like *Amazing Stories*, and by the earlier writings of a crank named Charles Fort. Called "the world's first ufologist," Fort reported on unidentified objects in the sky that he believed indicated visits from space aliens, reports taken from old newspaper and magazine accounts. Soon after the press release about the Roswell sighting made headlines around the world, the young officer was reprimanded and new information was announced: the unidentified flying object had really been a weather balloon, said officials, and photographs of the "wreckage"—some flexible, silvery-looking material—were distributed to the press.

In 1949 came the first of the crashed-saucer hoaxes—a science-fiction movie, *The Flying Saucer*, produced by Mikel Conrad, which contained scenes of a purportedly captured spacecraft; an actor hired by Conrad actually posed as an FBI agent and swore the claim was true. The following year, writer Frank Scully reported in his book *Behind the Flying Saucers* that the United States government had in its possession no fewer than three alien spaceships, together with the bodies of their humanoid occupants. Scully was fed the story by two confidence men who had hoped to sell a petroleum-locating device allegedly based on alien technology (Clark 1993).

Other crash-retrieval stories followed, as did photographs of space aliens living and dead: one gruesome photo merely portrayed the charred body of the pilot of a small plane, his aviator's glasses still visible in the picture. In 1974, Robert Spencer Carr began to promote one of the crashes from the Scully book and to claim firsthand knowledge of where the pickled aliens were stored. According to the late claimant's son, Carr was a spinner of yarns who made up the entire story (Carr 1997). In 1977, a pseudonymous "Fritz Werner" claimed to have "assisted in the investigation of a crashed unknown object" in Arizona. This included, he said, his actually seeing the body of one four-foot-tall humanoid occupant that had been placed in a tent. Unfortunately, there were suspicious parallels between the Werner and the Scully stories and other evidence of hoaxing, including various inconsistencies in Werner's tale.

In 1987, the author of a book on Roswell released the notorious "MJ-12 documents," which seemed to prove that a saucer had indeed crashed near Roswell and that its humanoid occupants really were recovered. The documents purported to show that there was a secret "Operation Majestic Twelve" authorized by President Truman to handle clandestinely the crash/retrieval at Roswell. A "briefing document" for President-elect Eisenhower was also included. However, MJ-12 was another Roswellian hoax, the documents merely crude pasteup forgeries that utilized signatures cut from photocopies of actual letters and documents. The forger even slipped one document into the National Archives so that it could be "discovered" there. (The Archives quickly cast doubt on its authenticity.)

Forensic analyst John F. Fischer and I contributed to the evidence, conducting a lengthy, independent investigation of the documents that had me traveling to the Truman Library in Independence, Missouri, and the National Archives in Washington, D.C. Our report was published in *International UFO Reporter* (Nickell and Fischer 1990; see also Nickell 1996).

In 1990, Gerald Anderson responded to an *Unsolved Mysteries* telecast about the alleged 1947 UFO crash (placing it between Roswell and Corona, New Mexico). He claimed that he and other family members, including his uncle Ted, were rock hunting in the desert when they came upon a crashed saucer with injured aliens among the still-burning wreckage. Anderson released a diary his uncle had kept that recorded the event. Alas, examination by a forensic chemist showed that the ink used to write the entries did not exist in 1947 but had first been manufactured in 1974. (Anderson claimed that the tested pages were copies, but he never made the alleged original available.)

The boldest of the Roswell hoaxes came in 1995 when an "alien autopsy" film surfaced, showing the purported dissection of a retrieved humanoid corpse (see "Extraterrestrial Autopsy?" chapter in this book). More recently, there was the Roswell "UFO fragment" of 1996. . . . And so the hoaxes continue. Many ufologists have heralded the Roswell incident as providing the primary evidence for the UFO invasion of planet Earth. Supporting evidence, of course, purportedly comes from myriad UFO reports (most of which eventually become IFOs: *Identified* Flying Objects) and "alien abductions" (experiences that skeptics have shown are fantasy-based).

Ironically, the government's claim that a weather balloon instead of a "flying disc" landed at Roswell was itself a deception although not necessarily intentional. It was not of course the grandiose cover-up of extraterrestrial visitation that conspiracy theorists now imagine. The best current evidence indicates that the crashed device was in reality a secret United States government spy balloon—part of Project Mogul, an attempt to monitor sonic emissions from anticipated Soviet nuclear tests. As a consequence of these sordid events, the Roswell incident has left a half-century legacy of bizarre cult mythology, anti–government conspiracy theories, and unrelenting sky watching by self-styled ufologists who seem to fancy themselves on the brink of a momentous discovery. What crashed at Roswell was the truth, plain and simple.

References

Berlitz, Charles, and William L. Moore. 1980. *The Roswell Incident.* New York: Grosset and Dunlap.

Carr, Timothy Spencer. 1997. Son of originator of "Alien Autopsy" story casts doubt on father's credibility. *Skeptical Inquirer* 21.4 (July/Aug. 1997): 31–32.

Clark, Jerome. 1993. UFO hoaxes, in *Encyclopedia of Hoaxes*, ed. by Gordon Stein. Detroit: Gale Research, 267–78.

Korff, Kal K. 1997. What *really* happened at Roswell? *Skeptical Inquirer* 21.4 (July/Aug.): 24–30.

Nickell, Joe. 1996. *Detecting Forgery: Forensic Investigation of Documents.* Lexington: Univ. Press of Kentucky.

Nickell, Joe, and John F. Fischer. 1990. The crashed-saucer forgeries.*International UFO Reporter*, March/April, 4–12.

Thurmond disputes book . . . 1997. *New York Times*, June 5.

Chapter 17

Investigating
Police Psychics

The subject is nothing if not controversial. On one television show an experienced detective insists that no psychic has ever helped his department solve a crime, while another broadcast features an equally experienced investigator who maintains that psychics are an occasionally valuable resource, citing examples from his own solved cases. Who is right? Is it a matter of science versus mysticism as some assert? Or is it an issue of having an open mind as opposed to a closed one, as others claim? Let's look at the evidence.

Psychic Claims

In ancient times, those who sought missing persons or who attempted to uncover crimes could consult oracles or employ various other forms of divination, including astrology. After dowsing became popular in the sixteenth century, certain practitioners used divining rods to track down alleged culprits. Throughout the nineteenth century, certain "sensitive" persons received information regarding crimes in their dreams, while during the heyday of spiritualism, some mediums claimed to solve crimes through information provided by spirits of the dead.

Today virtually all of the old, supposedly discredited techniques are in vogue. Psychics like the late Dorothy Allison, regarded as America's most famous psychic sleuth, employ astrology at times, while Sylvia Browne receives information from her "spirit guides." Dutch psychic Marinus Dykshoorn and others have plied their dowsing rods and pendulums in the supposed service of crime detection. Noreen Renier employs still another old divination technique called psychometry, by which she purportedly gets psychic impressions from objects connected with a particular person. Some psychics claim to use clairvoyance ("clear-seeing") whereby they supposedly "see" remote images and scenes as if they were viewed on a movie screen. Psychic Bill Ward even studies people's "auras" and reads the lines in their palms.

At least on the face of it, this disparity of approach—in which one technique seems to work about as well as another—does not seem to provide a credible basis for psychic sleuthing. Neither do specific tests. For example, the seventeenth-century French dowsing sleuth, Jacques Aymar, was extensively tested in Paris, with embarrassing results: he failed to detect the guilty and even accused those who were innocent, while inventing absurd excuses for his failures. In 1991, tests of British "police psychic" Nella Jones indicated that her ability to "psychometrize" possible murder weapons was nonexistent. Indeed, tests conducted by Los Angeles Police Department researchers, reported in the *Journal of Police Science and Administration*, showed that information generated by psychics was no better than chance would allow (Reiser et al. 1979).

Psychic "Sting"

Indeed, a cleverly conceived and strikingly effective psychic test was conducted in May 1995 by Philadelphia WCAU-TV's Herb Denenberg. A starting point for the investigation was Jody Himebaugh, whose eleven-year-old son Mark disappeared November 25, 1991. Although Himebaugh conceded that the likelihood of his son being found alive was very small, more than one hundred alleged psychics had contacted him with their visions. He said they typically saw a "dark car," "the number 5," or similar "clues" that were never any help.

Prompted in part by the Himebaugh case, Denenberg first consulted with me to devise a suitable strategy. Then he and other members of his "Newscenter 10" unit went undercover to test the alleged powers of "so-called psychics," some of whom, the investigative segment announced, "prey on the parents of missing children." As the focus of their test, Denenberg's team utilized a fifteen-year-old named Kate. Although film clips showed her playing softball in her front yard, various tarot card readers and "psychic advisors"—as well as certain 900–number clairvoyants—were told that the schoolgirl had been missing since January. In response, some psychics saw her experiencing "physical harm"; one collected a fee of $50 for seeing her "confined against her will"; another charged $180 to report that the girl had run away and was "probably pregnant"; and while one psychic envisioned her only two miles from home, another saw her far away in Florida. Not one among the several psychics ever divined the truth about the teenager—that she was not missing—or about the true purpose of Channel 10's investigation.

When confronted with the evidence that their psychic powers were inoperative, the alleged clairvoyants chose not to appear on camera. However, a spokesman for "Miss Ruby, Psychic Reader and Advisor," conceded she should have foreseen the sting operation, and she refunded the TV station's money. Denenberg's investigative report also featured Frank Friel, who has thirty years of experience in law enforcement. He stated that he had never had a psychic provide a valuable clue, and he criticized the alleged seers for their phony offerings, which he described as "catastrophic to the well-being" of the families concerned, and, indeed, "out-and-out fraud." Himebaugh said psychics took an "emotional toll" on families. He said he had twice ended up in the hospital suffering from anxiety attacks brought on by psychics' false hopes.

Sting II

On May 11, 2000, the television show *Inside Edition* featured a similar exposé. A producer and researcher had contacted me about alleged police psychics, and we discussed the evidence in between their reading of my *Psychic Sleuths* (Nickell 1994). This book presents the results of a special "task force" of experienced researchers and investigators I enlisted to help me investigate the claims of those who offer themselves as psychic crime solvers. I also made *Inside Edition* aware of Herb Denenberg's psychic sting.

Subsequently, the TV reporters obtained a childhood photo of a staffer and presented it to a professional "psychic" who claimed that the "missing child" was dead, while a hidden camera secretly recorded the session. Later, *Inside Edition* arranged to interview the alleged clairvoyant, whose powers once again failed to alert him to the setup. Even when the targeted individual was introduced to him, he initially refused to accept the truth. Finally, under pointed questioning he broke off the interview. The segment went on to expose Sylvia Browne's claim, on the *Montel Williams* TV show, to having solved a case that in fact continued to remain unsolved. The *Inside Edition* reporter admitted that—like other media—in the past, they had aired uncritical reports about psychic sleuthing because they knew such stories were popular. Their new program helped make up for past lapses.

Retrofitting

But what about testimonials from experienced homicide detectives who have actually used psychics? Most reported successes appear to be like the one that a New Jersey police captain attributed to Dorothy Allison. Her predictions "were difficult to verify when initially given," he said. "The accuracy usually could not be verified until the investigation had come to a conclusion" (quoted in Dennett 1994). Indeed, this after-the-fact matching—known as "retrofitting"—is the secret behind most alleged psychic successes. For example, the statement, "I see water and the number seven," would be a safe offering in almost any case. After all the facts are in, it will be unusual if there is not some stream, body of water, or other source that cannot somehow be associated with the case. As to the number seven, that can later be associated with a distance, a highway, the number of people in a search party, part of a license plate number, or any of countless other possible interpretations.

Other explanations for psychics' reputed successes include the following: (1) Some psychics exaggerate their successes, even claiming positive results in cases that were failures or that never even existed. (2) Psychics may use ordinary means of obtaining information that they then present as having been psychically obtained. For example, psychics have been accused of impersonating police and even of bribery of police officers in order to gain information. In one instance the psychic, unknown to a detective, had actually been briefed on the case by others. Shrewd psychics can brief themselves by studying newspaper files or area maps, and some make use of the fortune-teller's' technique of "cold reading" (a technique in which the psychic fishes for information while watching the listener's face for reactions that suggest correctness or error). (3) Another potential explanation for psychics' apparent successes is faulty recollection of what was actually said. The fallibility of memory is well known, and many stories of psychic success get better as they are told and retold. (4) Many psychics deal in vague generalities: for example, one psychic reported perceiving, "the names 'John' or 'Joseph' or something like that." (5) And there are social and psychological factors that may influence people to accept the accuracy of information. Obviously their own belief system will have an effect (Nickell 1994, 11–20). These factors—combined with the ever-present technique of retrofitting—can make a "psychic" of almost anyone. The result is like painting the bull's-eye around the arrow after it has been shot. Some credulous police officers even help the psychic in the reinterpretation necessary to convert a failure into an apparent "hit." For example, in one case when there was no nearby church as had been predicted, property owned by a church was counted as fitting the criterion.

The Bottom Line

Except in the extremely rare case in which a psychic was actually involved in the crime or had apparently received secret information (as from a tip), psychics rarely lead police to concealed bodies or unknown assailants. Of course they may use their own logical skills, or they may benefit from luck or perseverance, but there is no credible scientific evidence that psychic power ever solved a crime. Instead, crimes are invariably solved by police who search crime scenes, interview witnesses, and perform all of the myriad tasks necessary to locate a missing person or to convict a criminal. Common sense suggests that if psychics really had the powers they claim, then they would long ago have identified the "Unabomber" or have discovered the remains of missing Teamster boss Jimmy Hoffa. If they cannot accomplish such missions individually, how much more telling is their collective inability to do so.

Actually, the case against psychics is worse than just their inability to provide information that actually solves crimes. A far more serious problem exists with regard to the wasted resources of police departments who expend precious time and human activity in following up on a psychic's meaningless "clues." In one instance, the Nutley, New Jersey, police spent the whole of an afternoon digging up a drainage ditch that Dorothy Allison mistakenly thought contained the body of a missing boy. In another case, the fire department pumped the water from the flooded basement of an abandoned building in a fruitless search for a boy's remains, which eventually were discovered across town. Even worse, psychics have wrongfully accused persons of committing crimes, a memorable example being that of Peter Hurkos, "the man with the radar brain," who mistakenly identified an innocent man as the notorious Boston Strangler (Nickell 1994). These examples answer the question that is often asked by those who defend the use of psychics, "What harm can it do?" Another argument defenders use is that on occasion, a psychic's pronouncements prompted further search efforts, resulting in the discovery of the missing person's body, even though the psychic did not actually identify the location. But surely police should not have to rely on psychics to urge them to do more thorough work.

In brief, knowledgeable police officials resist the temptation to employ psychics. They know that psychic claims lack any scientific verification and that, in fact, psychics do not solve crimes. No longer should police solve crimes and let publicity-seeking occult pretenders take the credit.

127

References

Nickell, Joe. 1994. *Psychic Sleuths.* Buffalo, N.Y.: Prometheus.

Dennett, Michael. 1994. "America's Most Famous Psychic Sleuth: Dorothy Allison," in Nickell 1994, 42–59.

Reiser, Martin, et al. 1979. An Evaluation of the Use of Psychics in the Investigation of Major Crimes. Appendix A of Nickell 1994, 193–203.

Chapter 18

Ghostly Photos

A rash of new "ghost" photographs is plaguing the western world. I first became aware of the mysterious phenomenon when I received a call at my office at the Center for Inquiry. It was from a Lockport, New York, couple who were experiencing some spooky occurrences and were concerned about their young children. The most unusual phenomenon, they said, was found in some of their color snapshots. Although they had seen nothing at the time either of two photos was taken, each contained strange, unusually white shapes the couple could not explain. (See figures 18.1 and 18.2).

Similar pictures were taken by another couple. They had appeared with me on "The Danny Show" (where they presented UFO video sequences). Afterward, discovering I had written a book they praised, *Camera Clues: A Handbook for Photographic Investigation* (1994), they gave me some snapshots that puzzled them. Looking at them later, I recognized a few that had similarities to the earlier photos. A Post-It Note on one indicated it had been made in Mexico and was "similar to photo [in] *Fate* magazine." Naturally, the notation led me to the October 1995 issue of *Fate*, which featured a nationwide ghost photo contest. It was (to quote Yogi Berra) deja-vu all over again! Beginning with the Grand Prize Winner's photo, the mysterious strandlike forms infected all six winning photos. Citing my book *Camera Clues* at the end, the accompanying *Fate* article explained how some of the ghost effects in the photos the editors had received were due to such causes as film-processing errors, lens flares (caused by interreflection between lens surfaces), and outright hoaxes. What was left, they opined, "were a few pictures that may represent an

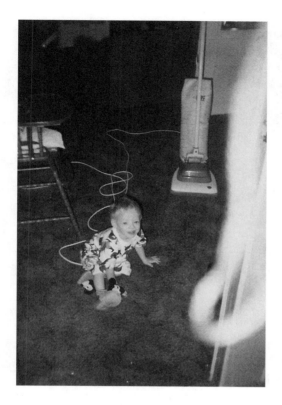

Figures 18.1 and 18.2. "Ghostly" forms in photos like these made by a New York state couple are becoming common.

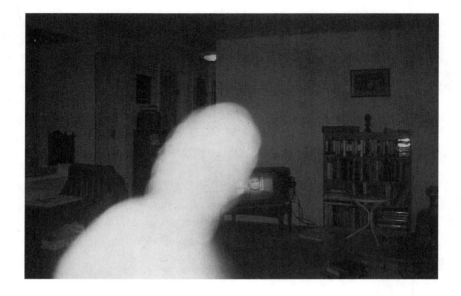

Figure 18.3. Experimental photograph by the author reproduces similar ghostly effects.

ectoplasmic energy or kinetic energy often associated with the presence of a ghost; however, experts tell us that kinetic energy can be related to a living being as well" ("*Fate* Ghost Contest" 1995).

Yet again, the mysterious, fluid form appears in a British photo in Jane Goldman's embarrassingly credulous *The X-Files Book of the Unexplained* (1995, reviewed in *Skeptical Inquirer*, May/June 1996). Goldman's caption suggests the white shape is a ghost; "Or is it fogged film?" Goldman asks in a rare moment of doubt. Actually it is neither. I learned the source of the ghostly phenomenon when the first young couple visited my office and, at my request, brought their camera and film for me to keep for a few days. Examination of the negatives revealed nothing remarkable, but by the next day I had the answer: the strand- or looplike form was caused by the new subcompact camera's hand strap getting in front of the lens. Since the viewfinder on this type of camera does not see what the camera sees (as it does in a single-lens reflex type camera), the obtruded view goes unnoticed. Although such camera straps are typically black and photograph black (or dark) in normal light, their sheen en-

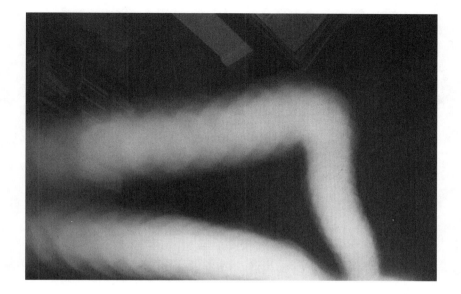

Figure 18.4. Another experimental photo is typical of many "ghost" snapshots.

ables them to reflect brightly the flash from the camera's self-contained flash unit.

Some of my experimental snapshots are shown in figures 18.3 and 18.4. The braiding of the strap can even be seen in some pictures. When the cord is quite close to the lens, the result is softer, more mistlike. It follows that analogous effects could occur if other articles were placed before the lens—either deliberately or inadvertently. For example, flash-reflected hair, jewelry, articles of clothing, a fingertip, or the like could produce distinctive effects that might not be easily recognized.

It is instructive to note that in each of the cases I have related, including the six examples in *Fate* magazine, no one saw anything out of the ordinary but simply discovered the anomolous shapes when the photos came back from the film processors. As I point out in *Camera Clues*, that situation is a good indication that the paranormal phenomenon in question—ghost, UFO, or other entity—is really only some sort of photographic glitch caused by camera, film, processing, or other element. In this case, a new type of camera was the culprit in a rash of allegedly supernatural pictures.

References

The *Fate* ghost contest. 1995. *Fate*, Oct., 42–45.

Goldman, Jane. 1995. *The X-Files Book of the Unexplained.* London: Simon & Schuster, 25.

Nickell, Joe. 1994. *Camera Clues: A Handbook for Photographic Investigation.* Lexington: Univ. Press of Kentucky.

Chapter 19

The Lake Utopia Monster

"Maritimers better lock up their ghosts," the Canadian Press writer advised residents of the Atlantic provinces. "Professional skeptic Joe Nickell is touring the region," announced the tongue-in-cheek warning in Canadian newspapers, "and not a lake monster, a beloved spectre or even the Oak Island treasure is safe from the penetrating glare of his cold, hard logic" (Morris 1999). The mock advisory was prompted by my June–July 1999 visit to "the Maritimes," initially by invitation of the Royal Canadian Mounted Police in Fredericton, New Brunswick. There I addressed forensic experts at the annual conference of the Canadian Identification Society and (incidentally) promoted my new book *Crime Science* (1999).

Rather than fly to Fredericton just for the event, however, I decided to drive and thus be able to investigate a number of regional enigmas. Naturally I prepared extensively, studying such works as *Mysterious Canada* by my friend John Robert Colombo (1988), formulating hypotheses and investigative strategies, contacting museum curators and others, and packing a large investigative kit customized for the trip, with camera equipment, tape recorder and notebooks, stereomicroscope (for examining a mystery inscription), among other items.

I passed through Maine (spending my first evening at the "haunted" Kennebunk Inn [see "Haunted Inns" chapter in this book]), then continued on to Canada, where I promptly conducted my first investigations. According to Micmac Indian legend, century-old tales, and modern eyewitness reports, Lake Utopia, in southern New Brunswick, is reportedly home to a fearsome monster. As with other lake leviathans, it is varyingly described, although only rarely glimpsed and more often per-

Figure 19.1. Guide Tony Wilson sets out with author on a jet-ski exploration of New Brunswick, Canada's, Lake Utopia in search of the fabled monster.

Figure 19.2. Although armed with a camera to shoot over his guide's shoulder, the author reported the monster a no-show.

ceived by a churning of the water and debris sent up from the depths. There are no known photographs of the alleged creature, but in the early settlement period were reported tracks, or rather a "slimy trail"—with claw marks—leading into the water (Martinez 1988; Colombo 1988). Today, it appears that most local people are skeptical of the monster's existence, although a few have reported seeing an unexplained wake (Murray 1999), or what they believed was a large animal (Gaudet 1999), or perhaps they know someone who has had such a sighting (K. Wilson 1999; T. Wilson 1999).

On June 27, I visited nearby St. George, N.B., where I collected local accounts of the fabled monster and hired a guide, Tony Wilson of All Wet Aquatics, to take me on a jet-ski trip (via the Magaguadavic River and a natural canal) into and around the 3,409-acre lake. Despite my efforts, however, the imagined creature did not have the courtesy to show itself, let alone pose for my camera. (See figures 19.1–19.2.)

As with similar claims, a major problem with the possibility of such a monster is the difficulty of a lake providing sufficient food—not merely for one leviathan, but for a breeding herd that would be necessary for the continuation of a species. Also, many mundane phenomena can simulate a monster. Local candidates include floating logs; wind slicks; salmon, sturgeon (Gaudet 1999), and schools of smaller fish; and Silver Eels (once so plentiful that they clogged the pulp mill's water wheels ["Brief History" n.d.]). Other potential culprits include such swimming wildlife as deer, muskrats, beavers, and otters ("St. George" 1999)—especially otters, who could have produced many of the effects reported (Nickell 1995, 1999).

In the preface to his *Mysterious Canada*, John Robert Colombo (1988, v) insisted quite properly that "We should know more about the mysteries that surround us." And he predicted: "Anyone who looks long and hard enough will no doubt find rational explanations for the mysteries in this book. There is no need to resort to a supernatural explanation to account for any one of them." And that is just what my series of investigations has shown, I think, that if we steer between the extremes of gullibility and dismissiveness—in other words, if our minds are neither too open nor too closed—we may learn more about our world and ourselves. We may even have some fun doing it.

References

Brief History of the Magaguadavic. n.d. [St. George, N.B.]: Magaguadavic Watershed Management Association, 13.

Colombo, John Robert. 1988. *Mysterious Canada: Strange Sights, Extraordinary Events, and Peculiar Places.* Toronto: Doubleday Canada.

Gaudet, Sam. 1999. Interview by Joe Nickell, June 27.

Martinez, Lionel. 1998. *Great Unsolved Mysteries of North America.* Secaucus, N.J.: Chartwell, 6–7, 12.

Morris, Chris. 1999. Skeptic shoots holes in Maritimes tales. *Globe and Mail* (Toronto), June 30.

Nickell, Joe. 1995. *Entities: Angels, Spirits, Demons, and Other Alien Beings.* Amherst, N.Y.: Prometheus, 241–43.

———. 1999. The Silver Lake serpent. *Skeptical Inquirer* 23.2 (March/April): 18–21.

"St. George, New Brunswick, the Granite Town." [1999]. Brochure published by Town of St. George.

Chapter 20

Memory of a Past Life

Perhaps not since the famous "Bridie Murphy" case of the 1950s—when American housewife Virginia Tighe supposedly discovered she was the reincarnation of an Irishwoman—has a single "past-life regression" case received such widespread attention as that of an English resident named Jenny Cockell. Since childhood, Mrs. Cockell relates, she has had constant dream-memories of another Irishwoman, eventually identified as Mary Sutton, who died more than two decades before Cockell was born, leaving behind eight young children. However, investigation shows not only that the reincarnation claims are unconvincing but also that there is quite a different hypothesis that best accounts for the proffered evidence.

Jenny Cockell was born in 1953 in rural England. Now a wife and mother, she lives and works as a registered chiropodist (i.e., podiatrist) in Northhamptonshire. Her unusual story has been told on such television programs as *Unsolved Mysteries* and in her own book, *Across Time and Death: A Mother's Search for Her Past Life Children* (Cockell 1993). Therein, as a self-described "withdrawn and nervous child," she relates how she frequently woke sobbing with her "memories of Mary's death" and her expressed "fear for the children I was leaving behind" (1). In addition to her childhood dreams, she would frequently echo Mary's domestic work during her play: making "bread" by mixing grass seeds in water, sweeping with a broom, and acting out other chores (14). "I was also constantly tidying and clearing out my room and toys," she writes, "something that I enjoyed almost more than playing with them" (5). At this time, she did not know Mary's last name and was unaware of countless other details about her origins and life. Somewhat artistically inclined, Jenny frequently sketched maps of Mary's Irish village, although there were admitted variations in the supposed landmarks (5). Among the reasons for Jenny's withdrawal was the unhappy atmosphere of her home, there being, as she described it, "an impossible tension" between her parents (14). "I usually played alone," she writes, "and the only company I regularly enjoyed was that of my two imaginary male friends" (15). Although she had a high IQ (which would later earn her membership in Mensa, the "genius" society), she reports that she was thought a slow learner due to her "dreamlike state of mind" that carried even into the classroom (15).

Although she describes her supposed memories as "dreams" and refers to her "private trance world" in which she was "oblivious to external activity," the memories were vivid and seemingly real. As is often the case, this was especially so under hypnosis. In 1988—by then married and the mother of two young children—Cockell was hypnotized for the first time. Under hypnosis, she seemingly became Mary. "I cried as she cried," she states; "I knew her pain as my own" (33). Tears rolled uncontrollably down her cheeks. Although under hypnosis she seemed to exist partly in the past and partly the present, she says, "Yet I was Mary, and the past had become very real. I could smell the grass on the slopes outside a large farmhouse, and I breathed in the fresh spring air" (36). Again, "As the questions were being asked and answered in this strange, mechanical way, I seemed to be free to wander through the places I saw— tangible, vivid places. I felt the wind in my hair; I could touch and smell the air as though I were there" (37).

Under hypnosis she also explored what she believed were her "psychic abilities." In addition to her past-life memories, she was already convinced she had the power of psychometry (object reading) and dream premonitions (13, 28). The hypnotic sessions also took her on an out-of-body experience as part of a dubious test of clairvoyance. (Also, in an earlier session, as "Mary," she had died, then went out of body to see the surroundings of her "now vacant body" [40, 55].) Not surprisingly, the hypnotic sessions also tapped other past-life experiences. "By chance I found myself," she reports, "in one of the memories that had been with me since childhood." One of several such memories, this involved a little French girl from the eighteenth century (40–41). Ultimately, however, the hypnosis helped little in her quest to identify Mary or Mary's family, leaving her "almost where I was before the hypnosis started" (69). She bemoaned "the lack of concrete details such as that forever elusive surname" (70).

She turned then to actual research, publishing an ad in a Mensa magazine, sending out numerous form letters, acquiring maps, and so on. Eventually she turned up a village (Malahide), a road (Swords Road), and finally a woman named Mary Sutton who roughly fit the target. The story ended with Mrs. Cockell making contact with some of Mary's surviving children. Although they were supposedly her own offspring, they were—ironically and somewhat bizarrely—old enough to be her parents (117–53). Nevertheless, she was satisfied with her "reunion" and began to look into her "next life"—as a Nepalese girl in the twenty-first century (153).

Unfortunately, Cockell's intriguing and no doubt sincere saga does not withstand critical analysis. First, consider the overwhelming lack of factual information provided by the dreams and hypnosis. Unknown were Mary's surname, either maiden or married, or the names of her husband or children. Similarly, the village's name and even its location were a mystery. Cockell was ignorant of dates as well, including Mary's birth date or even the year of her birth. And so on and on.

She employed circular reasoning. She sent out queries that sought a village with certain sketchy requirements, and when such a village was— not surprisingly—discovered, she adopted it as the one she was looking for. Obviously, if it did not fit she would have looked further. In addition, the technique of retrofitting (after-the-fact matching) was employed. For example, Mrs. Cockell made a sketch of a church after one of her hypnosis sessions, and this was matched with a photo of an actual church, St. Andrew's, in the village of Malahide. But the sketch is simplistic, showing only a gable end and revealing no awareness of the greater overall structure. In addition, it entirely omits the central feature of the church's gable end—a massive gothic window—and there are many other significant omissions and mismatchings. Moreover, St. Andrew's is not the one Mary had actually attended, which was St. Sylvester's Catholic Church, but instead merely one she would have walked by, one belonging to the Church of Ireland.

Rationalizations for errors and omissions abound throughout Cockell's book. "A lot of the remembering was in isolated fragments, and sometimes I would have difficulty making sense of them," she says (6). "I still find it hard to see Mary herself. It was easier to see the surroundings, which is not too surprising as I see through her and the life remembered as her. I feel her personality mostly" (9). Mary's husband was "hard to remember," but then "he seemed to be home less and less" (20). That she lacked even a surname for Mary "was no surprise to me, since I have always been bad at names" (27). Under hypnosis she gave the husband's name, incorrectly, as Bryan; it was John. At one time she thought the family name was O'Neil rather than Sutton (37, 38). When the name of the road Mary lived on was found to be Swords, not Salmons, Road, Cockell noted that both begin with *S* and that the accuracy was "about as close as I usually get when trying to remember names" (66). A village resident "could not quite place the roads" on the map Cockell had drawn, but later found it "to be more accurate than he had expected, given that it had been drawn from dreams" (64–65). Again, when viewing the Catholic church "struck no chords of memory," she "wondered, however, whether the frontage had changed in the intervening fifty years or so: the lawns might once have been a graveyard, and the driveway certainly looked new." She concluded that "so little of what I remembered had stayed intact" (84).

But if Jenny Cockell's story is untrue, where did it come from? The best evidence suggests that such past-life memories are not memories at all. The alleged remembrances made under hypnosis are simply the products of an invitation to fantasize. According to one authority:

> For a long while it was believed that hypnosis provided the person hypnotized with abnormal or unusual abilities of recall. The ease with which hypnotized subjects would retrieve forgotten memories and relive early childhood experiences was astonishing. . . .
>
> However, when the veridicality of such memories was examined, it was found that many of the memories were not only false, but they were even outright fabrications. Confabulations, i.e. making up stories to fill in memory gaps, seemed to be the norm rather than the exception. It seems, literally, that using "hypnosis" to revive or awaken a person's past history somehow or other not only stimulates the person's desire to recall and his memory processes, but it also opens the flood gates of his or her imagination (Baker 1992, 152).

As to the genesis of "Mary," I think we must look to Jenny's unhappy childhood and her consequent tendency to fantasize. An analysis of her autobiographical statements shows her to have many of the traits of a fantasy-prone personality (see Wilson and Barber 1983). For example, (1) she is an excellent hypnotic subject (35, 39); (2) as a child she spent much time fantasizing (16), and (3) had imaginary playmates (15), as well as (4) a fantasy identity (i.e., "Mary"); in addition, (5) her imagined sensations are quite vivid and real to her (36–37), and (6) she not only recalls but *relives* past experiences (36–37); (7) she also has had out-of-body experiences (40, 54–55), and (8) believes she has a variety of psychic abilities (13, 28, 55). Taken together, these traits are strong evidence of fantasy proneness.

As she herself acknowledges, she was forever dreaming: "Sometimes it was about the future, sometimes about the past, but hardly ever about the present." Indeed, she says, "My escape into the past grew as I grew, and it was like a little death in my own life, a death of part of me that replaced part of my life" (16). Such is the admission of a classic fantasizer, whose need to retreat from an unpleasant reality led her to manufacture a reality—one that took on, in a manner of speaking, a life of its own.

References

Baker, Robert A. 1992. *Hidden Memories: Voices and Visions from Within.* Buffalo, N.Y.: Prometheus.

Cockell, Jenny. 1993. *Across Time and Death: A Mother's Search for Her Past Life Children.* New York: Simon and Schuster.

Wilson, Sheryl C., and Theodore X. Barber. 1983. "The Fantasy-Prone Personality" in *Imagery, Current Theory, Research and Application*, ed. Anees A. Sheikh, New York: Wiley, 340–90.

Chapter 21

Photographing the Aura

At psychic fairs and other popular venues, "aura" photographic portraits are all the rage. But are they really what they are claimed to be? According to belief that has persisted since ancient times, the aura is a radiance from the "energy field" that supposedly emanates from and surrounds all living things. It is perceived not by ordinary vision but by clairvoyance. Although "no evidence has been found to prove its existence" (Guiley 1991), the concept has thrived as pseudoscience. For example, in his 1911 book, *The Human Atmosphere*, Dr. Walter J. Kilner claimed he could not only see the aura and use it for medical diagnoses, but he also accepted the validity of nonexistent "N-rays" and clairvoyance. *The British Medical Journal* rightly scoffed.

Today self-professed "medical intuitives" like Caroline Myss (1997) claim to describe the nature of people's physical diseases by reading their "energy field." Thus Myss "can make recommendations for treating their condition on both a physical and spiritual level." She calls this supposedly auric process "energy medicine," but offers no scientific evidence to substantiate her alleged powers. (*New Age* magazine stated Myss no longer gives readings, and quoted me as terming the practice "offensive and dangerous" [Koontz 2000, 66, 102].) The human body does in fact give off certain radiations, including weak electromagnetic emanations (from the electrical activity of the nerves), chemical emissions (some of which may be perceivable, for instance, as body odor), sonic waves (from the physical actions within the body), etc. Paranormalists sometimes equate these radiations with the aura (Permutt 1988, 57–58), but they do not represent a single, unified phenomenon, nor have they been shown to have the mystical properties attributed to auras.

If psychics could actually see the purported energy fields, one wonders why, as Guiley (1991) observes, their composition "is the subject of conflicting opinions." She states: "No two clairvoyants see exactly the same aura. Some say they see the entire aura, divided into different layers or bodies, while others say they see only parts of the aura." In fact, tests of psychics' abilities to see the alleged radiant emanations have repeatedly met with failure. One test, for example, involved placing either one or two persons in a completely dark room and asking the alleged psychic to state how many auras she saw. Only chance results were obtained (Loftin 1990). James Randi conducted another test for a television special, offering $100,000 for successful results. The psychic challenger selected ten people she maintained had clearly visible auras, and agreed that the auras would extend above the screens behind which—unseen by her—the people were to stand. Unfortunately, in choosing which screens supposedly had people behind them, the psychic got only four out of ten correct guesses—less than the five that chance allowed (Steiner 1989).

Once at a psychic workshop, I volunteered as the subject whose aura others were instructed to visualize. I stood in front of a blank wall while the instructor noted how my energy field expanded and contracted as I inhaled and exhaled. Actually, I held my breath for long periods, while raising and lowering my chest and shoulders to simulate breathing. Such is the power of suggestion that some imaginative initiates "saw" the alleged effect despite the negating conditions.

In addition to purportedly seeing auras, some mystics claim they can actually detect them by such means as dowsing. For example, while inspecting a crop circle near Silbury Hill in southern England, I had my auric field checked by a local dowser who had used his divining rod to convince himself the circle was genuine, produced by earth spirits. Although my aura supposedly measured only a few inches, after I had compliantly meditated for a few moments, it expanded to several feet—or so the rhabdomancer claimed (Nickell 1995).

Not surprisingly, there have been various attempts to photograph auras. For example, in the 1890s a French army officer tried to record alleged psychic force fields on photographic plates but with reportedly poor results (Permutt 1988, 89). Claims that auras have been successfully photographed are typically based on a misunderstanding of the simple scientific principles involved. For instance, while infrared photography can produce images of people with auralike bands of radiance

143

around them, these are actually only emanations of body temperature (Nickell 1994; Permutt 1988, 123).

More serious claims that auras could be demonstrated scientifically through Kirlian photography were publicized in the 1970s. In this noncamera technique, a high-voltage, high-frequency electrical discharge is applied across a grounded object. The "air glow" or "aura" that is yielded can be recorded directly onto a photographic plate, film, or paper. Such Kirlian images (named for the Russian inventor of the process, Semyon Kirlian) show fuzzy glows around fingers, leaves, and other objects (Ostrander and Schroeder 1971). Although the Kirlian aura was claimed to present information about the "bioplasma" or "life-energy" of the object, actually it is only "a visual or photographic image of a corona discharge in a gas, in most cases the ambient air." Moreover, experiments have failed to yield any evidence that the coronal pattern is related "to the physiological, psychological, or psychic condition of the sample," but instead only to finger pressure, moisture, and other mechanical, environmental, and photographic factors (some twenty-two in all). Skeptics observed that even mechanical objects, such as coins or paper clips, could yield a Kirlian "aura" (Watkins and Bickel 1986).

Following the Kirlian technique is a development called Aura Imaging photography, introduced in 1992 by Guy Coggins, a California entrepreneur with a background in electronic engineering. Coggins's Aura Camera 6000 is a combined optical-electrical system that produces a Polaroid color photograph of the subject together with his or her "electromagnetic field or aura." Coggins's Progen Company also markets a software program called WinAura that allows one to "see the aura move and change like a movie in real time on your computer or TV screen" and to "print your aura image from your computer printer" (Progen 1999). Coggins concedes that most who purchase and use his device fail to understand how it works. "These people live quite different lives than the rest of us," Coggins told a reporter. "Sometimes, we have trouble explaining to them how to plug the thing in" (Sullivan 1999). Scientists, on the other hand, continue to be skeptical of all claims made about the alleged aura. Observes Sullivan (1999):

> The reason little of the research on energy, auras, and energy healing has been accepted by the scientific community is that it's unpredictable. To be proven as concrete, science demands that an action, per-

Figure 21.1. Author posing for "aura" photograph with hands placed on sensors.

formed in the same way under the same circumstances, must yield the same results. No such luck in this area, Coggins admits.

"None of this is duplicatable. It works once, but maybe not the next time. So there's no way to prove it, according to scientific standards."

But what about Coggins's aura-imaging technology? Can a photograph lie? I was intrigued by the process I observed at a psychic fair at Olcott Beach in western New York (July 17, 1999). There I posed for my very own "Full Body Aura Photograph." Actually, I had two such photos made (at twenty dollars each), and therein lies a story. I was invited to stand facing the camera with my hands on electrical modules wired to both the camera and a computer printer (figure 21.1). I soon received a color Polaroid photograph plus a printout (copyrighted by Progen) showing a simplistic asterisk-rendered outline of a human figure arrayed with letters that indicated color areas ("B" for blue, "G" for green, etc.). These crudely correlated with the areas of colored light in the photo.

The photograph (figure 21.2) showed such an intense "energy field" of yellow-bordered white light that it washed out my facial features. The printout designated this area as "Yellow" and interpreted it (in grammatically unparallel fashion) as "Sunny, Exhilaration." (Small areas of "Green"—"Healing, Teaching"—were shown on either side.) One of the enterprise's "experienced Certified Aura-Imaging Counselors" told me the bright area of light showed I had prominent "spiritual" qualities.

As I reflected on what had transpired, it occurred to me that a single such picture is little more than a novelty, while two would represent the beginning of an investigation. When I returned to the booth for a second portrait, the proprietor seemed discomfited, asking me why I wanted another. I expressed curiosity, wondering aloud whether different moods would affect the outcome. She said it would, jokingly cautioning me not to think about *sex* and—when I asked what would happen—telling me the color red would predominate. In fact, however, while I (blush) thought vividly about the warned-against subject (purely in the interests of science, of course), my aura was depicted in the resulting photo as predominately blue ("Peaceful, Contemplative") and green ("Healing, Teaching"). Since I was accompanied by some college students (summer interns at the Center for Inquiry), I was told that the results were due to the fact that, obviously, I had been "teaching" the students in the interim between photo sessions. My own interpretation was that the radically different photos demonstrated a lack of any consistency that might justify people thinking of their aura as an expression of their inherent individuality. (An accompanying brochure spoke to the reader about "your personal energy field," and Coggins insists, "The aura is individual, like a thumbprint" [Ziegler 1996].) Instead, the disparity seemed attributable to an ever-changing light display that did not seem to correspond to moods—at least not on the occasion I tested the system.

Indeed, a look at the actual process employed—described by Coggins as "intensified Kirlian imaging"—shows it to be not the actual image of the body's unseen image field but the *imitation* of such a field based primarily on something called skin resistance. That is one of the physiological variables measured by a galvanometer as part of a polygraph or "lie detector," whereby an unfelt electrical current passes through the subject's hands and detects sweat-gland activity associated with nervousness.

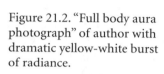
Figure 21.2. "Full body aura photograph" of author with dramatic yellow-white burst of radiance.

Figure 21.3. Second "aura" photo, made only minutes later, with subdued tones of blue and green.

(Cheap lie detectors—as well as the "E-meters" used by Scientologists in their controversial pyschotherapeutic technique called "auditing" [Behar 1999]—are essentially only galvanometers.)

As one source explains the aura camera's technique (while neglecting to mention that the electrical current is induced): "The hand plates on the electronic modules contain sensors that are located at specific acupuncture points on each hand. Each one of the points corresponds to a different area of the body. Coggins said the sensors pick up the electrical current on the skin at each of those locations. This current is called 'skin resistance'" (Sullivan 1999). Next, according to this source:

> The computer plots the information from the sensors. Within the camera is a liquid crystal display [LCD] of different colors. Each electrical frequency plotted by the computer is assigned a different color. The higher frequencies are assigned warmer colors—reds, yellows, oranges. The lower frequencies fall toward the cooler end of the spectrum—blues and purples. Greens and shades like turquoise, aquamarine, and yellow-green fall into the center of the vibrational spectrum. Coggins said he worked with psychics who helped him interpret the frequencies, and the colors they could represent. People with a lot of high energy in their field—red and orange—are described by most clairvoyants as vibrant and passionate (Sullivan 1999).

Finally, "The LCD flashes lights according to the pattern and frequencies plotted by the computer. The Polaroid film is thus exposed to the colored lights, which show up on the photograph in the areas of the body where the corresponding electrical currents were sensed."

This torturous process—involving obtaining dubious electrically stimulated data from the hands, extrapolating it by analogy to the unproven claims of acupuncture to the entire body, translating the electrical frequencies into alleged color equivalents, and then substituting for those alleged equivalents simple flashes of colored lights—can scarcely be called photographing the aura. As is typically the case with photographs of alleged paranormal phenomena, what you see is not what you get.

References

Baker, Robert A., and Joe Nickell. 1992. *Missing Pieces*. Buffalo, N.Y.: Prometheus, 105–07.

Behar, Richard. 1999. The thriving cult of greed and power. *Time*, May 6, 50–57.

The British Medical Journal. 1912. Jan. 6; quoted in the foreword of Kilner 1911 (1984 ed.)

Cavendish, Richard, ed. 1974. *Encyclopedia of the Unexplained.* London: Routledge & Kegan Paul, 48

Guiley, Rosemary Ellen. 1991. *Harper's Encyclopedia of Mystical & Paranormal Experience.* New York: HarperCollins, 40–42.

Kilner, W.J. 1911. *The Human Atmosphere.* (Reprinted as *The Aura.*) York Beach, Me.: Samuel Weiser, 1984.

Koontz, Katy, 2000. The new health detectives. *New Age*, Jan./Feb., 64–67, 102–10.

Loftin, Robert W. 1990. Auras: Searching for the light. *Skeptical Inquirer* 14(4) (summer): 403–09.

Myss, Caroline. 1997. *Why People Don't Heal and How They Can.* New York: Harmony, xi.

Nickell, Joe. 1994. *Camera Clues.* Lexington: Univ. Press of Kentucky, 178–79.

———. 1995. Crop circle mania wanes. *Skeptical Inquirer* 19(3) (May/June): 41–43.

Ostrander, Sheila, and Lynn Schroeder. 1971. *Psychic Discoveries Behind the Iron Curtain.* New York: Bantam, 200–13.

Permutt, Cyril. 1988. *Photographing the Spirit World.* Wellingborough, England: Aquarian.

"Photography." 1960. *Encyclopaedia Britannica.*

Progen Company. 1999. Aura camera promotional literature.

Steiner, Robert. 1989. Live TV special explores, tests psychic powers. *Skeptical Inquirer* 14(1) (fall): 3.

Sullivan, Michele. 1999. Your true colors: Can a camera capture the unseeable? *The Warren (County, Virginia) Sentinel*, March 18.

Watkins, Arleen J., and William S. Bickel. 1996. A study of the Kirlian effect. *Skeptical Inquirer* 10(3) (spring): 244–57.

Ziegler, Daira. 1996. What your aura says about you. *National Examiner*, Aug. 6.

Chapter 22

Mystery of the Holy Shroud

In what *Time* magazine called "a sort of resurrection," the Shroud of Turin controversy has risen once again. It was sparked by exhibition of the reputed burial cloth during April and May 1998, the first public showing in two decades. It also marked the one-hundredth anniversary of the first photograph of the cloth's image—that of a man who appears to have been crucified like Jesus in the Christian gospels (Van Biema, 1998).

Miraculous "Photograph"

The 1898 photographer's glass-plate *negatives* revealed a startlingly realistic *positive* image, with the prominences in highlight and the recesses in shadow. Therefore the image on the cloth, shroud advocates claimed, was "a perfect photographic negative." They insisted no artist could have painted such an image before the concept of photography. (Actually the image is only a quasi negative, the hair and beard being the opposite of the features and giving the effect, when a positive is made, that Jesus was a white-bearded old man. See figure 22.1.)

With these photographs, the modern era of the shroud began, prompting attempts to explain the image. Simple contact imprinting was soon ruled out due to the image's lack of wraparound distortions, and a concept called "vaporography" was disproved when the postulated vapors were shown to produce only a blur. In time "the first Polaroid in Palestine" was ascribed to "flash photolysis," a "theory" that the image was produced by a miraculous burst of radiant energy at the time of Jesus' resurrection (Nickell, 1988).

Figure 22.1. Negative photograph of the frontal image on the Shroud of Turin. A medieval artist reportedly admitted it was his handiwork, and scientific analyses confirm the presence of tempera paint.

"Shroud Science"

With such notions came an unfortunate abuse of science. Whereas the scientific approach is to let the evidence lead to a solution, "shroud science" (or "sindonology") begins with the desired answer and then works backward, dismissing or rationalizing whatever arguments or evidence may be incompatible with it. It was therefore difficult to imagine that it was scientists who were so readily invoking a miracle. Unfortunately, the forty-some members of the Shroud of Turin Research Project (STURP), which conducted the 1978 investigation of the shroud, were woefully unqualified for the task. Many were operating outside their fields, and bad—certainly questionable—science was rampant. That situation continues in sindonology today.

The 1998 exposition was shrewdly timed to begin a week after Easter, and media coverage before and during the religious season was intense. In addition to a spate of new books, including Ian Wilson's *The Blood and the Shroud*, there was a flurry of newspaper and magazine articles as well as TV news segments. Alas, shroud science was well served by shroud journalism, whereby reporters' questions about authenticity were directed primarily to shroud proponents—rather like asking members of the Flat Earth Society about the curvature of the earth. Perhaps the most used word during the shroud media blitz was "mystery." But honest journalists do not engage in mystery mongering. Instead, like all true investigators, they believe mysteries are meant to be carefully and fairly examined. In the case of the Shroud of Turin, the question of authenticity was long ago settled.

The Historical Record

To begin at the beginning, the Shroud of Turin contradicts the Gospel of John, which describes multiple cloths for Jesus' burial, including a separate "napkin" over the face, as well as "an hundred pound weight" of spices—not a trace of which appears on the Turin cloth. And nowhere in the New Testament is there mention of a remarkable portrait of Jesus having been left on his burial garment. In addition, no examples of the Shroud's particular herringbone twill weave date from the first century.

Although Jesus' body would have been ritually washed, as mandated by the Jewish Mishnah, the "body" imaged on the shroud was not cleansed (as shown by the "blood" on the arms). Some sindonologists attempt to circumvent the problem by citing a passage from the Code of Jewish law, but the supposed exception dates from some fifteen centuries after Christ and poorly applies to one who was buried "as the manner of the Jews is to bury" (John 19:40). And even though there have been over forty Holy Shrouds—along with other "relics" of Jesus, including vials of his tears and countless pieces of the True Cross—there is no record of the Turin cloth until the mid-1350s. At that time a French bishop, Henri de Poitiers, was suspicious of its utter lack of provenance, questioning why the early evangelists had failed to mention such a marvel or why it had remained hidden for thirteen centuries. The shroud's owner, a soldier of fortune named Geoffroy de Charny, never explained how he, a man of modest means, had acquired the most holy relic in all of Christendom (Nickell, 1988). According to a later bishop's report to Pope Clement VII, dated 1389, Henri discovered that the shroud originated as part of a phony faith-healing scheme. "Pretended miracles" were staged, said the report's author, Bishop Pierre D'Arcis, "so that money might cunningly be wrung" from unsuspecting pilgrims. "Eventually, after diligent inquiry and examination," he stated, Bishop Henri "discovered the fraud and how the said cloth had been cunningly painted, *the truth being attested by the artist who had painted it*, to wit, that it was a work of human skill and not miraculously wrought or bestowed" (emphasis added).

That the shroud is indeed the work of a medieval artist would explain numerous image flaws. For example, the physique is unnaturally elongated (like figures in Gothic art!). Also, the hair hangs as for a standing rather than recumbent figure, and the imprint of a bloody foot is incompatible with the outstretched leg to which it belongs. Everywhere, the "blood" flows are unrealistically neat. Instead of matting the hair, for instance, they run in rivulets on the outside of the locks. And even *dried* blood (as on the arms) has implausibly transferred. In addition, real blood soaks into cloth and spreads in all directions, rather than leaving picturelike images. As the noted pathologist Dr. Michael Baden observes of the overall shroud image, "Human beings don't produce this kind of pattern" (Baden, 1980).

The shroud exhibits many features that point specifically to artistry. For example, while St. Augustine lamented in the early fifth century that nothing whatsoever was known of Jesus' appearance, the shroud image portrays the traditional, evolved artistic likeness. Also, by the eleventh century, artists were representing Jesus' burial with a double-length linen cloth and the hands crossed over the groin (unlike Jewish burial practice in which they were typically folded on the chest). And from the thirteenth century we find ceremonial or symbolic shrouds bearing full-length embroidered images of Christ's body in this crossed-hands pose.

Scientific Analyses

The question of artistry versus authenticity is especially addressed by scientific examination of the "blood." In 1973, as part of a special commission of scientists and scholars, internationally known forensic serologists subjected the bloodstains to a battery of scientific tests, all of which proved negative: these included chemical analyses, thin-layer chromatography, and neutron activation analysis, as well as attempts to identify blood group and species. In fact, the scientists discovered reddish granules that would not even dissolve in reagents that dissolve blood. Subsequently, the distinguished microanalyst Walter McCrone identified the blood as red ocher and vermilion tempera paint, which explained why it

Figure 22.2. Negative photograph of an image produced by
making a rubbing from a bas-
relief. Such a technique (using
pigment or paint) automatically
converts the usual lights and
darks into a quasi-negative,
shroudlike picture.

was bright red after at least seven centuries. McCrone (who was, he says, "drummed out" of STURP for his efforts) also discovered that on the image—but not on the background—were significant amounts of the red ocher pigment. He first thought this was applied as a dry powder but later concluded it was a component of dilute paint applied in the medieval *grisaille* (monochromatic) technique. (McCrone believes the artist worked freehand; another possibility is shown in figure 22.2.) (McCrone, 1996)

In 1988, the shroud cloth was finally carbon dated. Using accelerator mass spectrometry, laboratories at Zurich, Oxford, and the University of Arizona obtained dates in very close agreement. These were given added credibility by correct radiocarbon dates from a variety of control swatches, including a piece from Cleopatra's mummy cloth. The resulting age span was circa 1260–1390 C.E., or about the time Bishop Henri de Poitiers found the artist who admitted it was his creation.

Rationalizations

Recently, shroud scientists have claimed that microbial contamination may have altered the radiocarbon date; however, for there to be an error of thirteen centuries there would have to be twice as much contamination by weight as the shroud cloth itself! (Pickett, 1996) Another recent claim concerns reported evidence of human DNA in a shroud "blood" sample. Actually, the scientist cited, Victor Tryon of the University of Texas, insists that "Everyone who has ever touched the shroud or cried over the shroud has left a potential DNA signal there." Tryon resigned from the new shroud project due to what he disparaged as "zealotry in science" (Van Biema, 1998, 61).

Still other claims concerned floral evidence. It was alleged that pollen on the shroud proved it came from Palestine, but the source for the pollen was a freelance criminologist, Max Frei, who once pronounced the forged "Hitler Diaries" genuine. Frei's tape-lifted samples from the Shroud were controversial from the outset since similar samples taken by the Shroud of Turin Research Project in 1978 had comparatively little pollen. As it turned out, after Frei's tapes were examined following his death in 1983, they also had very little pollen—although one bore a suspicious cluster on the "lead" (or end), rather than on the portion that had been applied to the shroud. (See *Skeptical Inquirer*, summer 1994, 379–85.) Accompanying the unscientific pollen evidence were claims that faint plant images have been "tentatively" identified on the shroud. These follow previous "discoveries" of "Roman coins" over the eyes and even Latin and Greek words, such as "Jesus" and "Nazareth," that some researchers see—Rorschachlike—in the shroud's mottled stains. The floral images were reported by a psychiatrist who has taken up image analysis and made other discredited claims about the shroud image. Even pro-shroud author Ian Wilson, in his 1998 book *The Blood and the Shroud*, felt compelled to state: "While there can be absolutely no doubting the sincerity of those who make these claims, the great danger of such arguments is that researchers may 'see' merely what their minds trick them into thinking is there."

By such rationalizations and questionable evidence sindonologists promote their agenda. They offer one explanation for the contrary gospel evidence (*maybe* certain passages require clarification), another for the lack of historical record (*maybe* the cloth was hidden away), still another for the artist's admission (*maybe* the reporting bishop misstated the case), yet another for the paint pigments (*maybe* an artist who copied the shroud ritualistically pressed it to the image), and so on. This should be called the "maybe" defense. It is all too characteristic of sindonology, which has failed to produce any scientifically viable hypothesis for the image formation.

Corroborative Evidence

The scientific approach, in contrast, is to allow the preponderance of *prima facie* evidence to lead to a conclusion: the shroud is the handiwork of a medieval artisan. The various pieces of the puzzle effectively interlock and corroborate each other. For example, the artist's admission is supported by the lack of prior record, as well as by the revealingly red and picturelike "blood" that in turn has been identified as tempera paint. And the radio-carbon date is consistent with the time the artist was discovered.

Given this powerful, convincing evidence, it is unfortunate that we must now once again recall the words of Canon Ulysse Chevalier, the Catholic historian who brought to light the documentary evidence of the shroud's medieval origin. As he lamented, "The history of the shroud constitutes a protracted violation of the two virtues so often commended by our holy books: justice and truth."

References

Baden, Michael. 1980. Quoted in Reginald W. Rhein Jr., The shroud of Turin: Medical examiners disagree, *Medical World News*, Dec. 22, 50.

McCrone, Walter. 1996. *Judgement Day for the Turin "Shroud."* Chicago: Micro-scope.

Nickell, Joe. 1988. *Inquest on the Shroud of Turin*, 2nd updated ed. Buffalo: Prometheus. Except as otherwise noted, information for this article is taken from this text.

Pickett, Thomas J. 1996. Can contamination save the shroud of Turin? *Skeptical Briefs*, June, 3.

Van Biema, David. 1998. Science and the shroud. *Time*, April 20, 53–61.

⚛ Chapter 23

The Giant Frog

Like the Lake Utopia Monster (see chapter 19), another reputed New Brunswick lake leviathan is the giant amphibian now displayed at the York Sunbury Historical Society Museum in Fredericton (figure 23.1). Dating to the 1880s, the huge bullfrog reportedly lived in Killarney Lake, some eight miles from Fredericton, where Fred B. Coleman operated a lodge. Coleman claimed he had made a pet of the great croaker and that his guests fed it June bugs, whiskey, and buttermilk. It thus grew to a whopping forty-two pounds, Coleman recalled, and was used to tow canoes and race against tomcats. It was killed, he said, when poachers dynamited the lake to harvest fish, whereupon the distraught raconteur had it stuffed and placed on display in the lobby of his Fredericton hotel. His son's widow donated it to the museum in 1959 ("Coleman" n.d.).

Some local doubters insist Coleman had simply bought a display item that had been used to advertise a cough medicine guaranteed to relieve "the frog in your throat" (Phillips 1982). A former historical society president called it a "patent fake" and said it should have been thrown out years ago, while other officials coyly declined suggestions that it be examined scientifically (Colombo 1988, 50–51; "Coleman" n.d.). *Maclean's* magazine concluded, "The argument about whether it is a stuffed frog or an imitation may never be settled, but as a topic of conversation and a tourist curiosity it has had as long a career as any frog, dead or alive" (McKinney n.d.).

Following my expedition to the museum's third floor, however, I determined that the exhibit was probably not a *Rana catesbeiana*. Did I penetrate the sealed display case to obtain a DNA sample? No, I simply

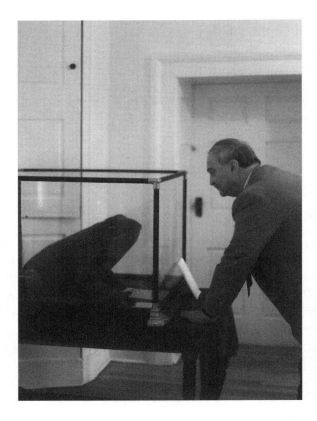

Figure 23.1. Coleman Frog. Since the 1880s, folk have debated which is the greatest whopper: this giant amphibian or the claim that it is authentic.

sweet-talked my way into the museum's files, which were revealing. A 1988 condition report by the Canadian Conservation Institute referred to the sixty-eight-centimeter (almost twenty-seven-inch) artifact as a "Large, possibly stuffed frog," but went on to observe that—in addition to many wrinkles having formed in the "skin"—there was actually a "fabric impression underneath," and indeed "a yellowed canvas" visible through some cracks. There was an overall layer of dark green paint, to which had been added other colors, the report noted. Wax appeared to be "present below the paint layer" and the feet were described as being "a translucent colour, possibly consisting in part of wax." While a taxidermist of the

1880s might possibly have used some of these materials ("Taxidermy" 1910; 1960), the overall effect is of a fabricated item, especially considering the canvas. Its impression showing through the paint suggests the lack of an intervening layer of true skin, for which the fabric was probably used as a substitute.

It should be noted that the largest frog actually known, according to *The Guinness Book of Records* (1999), is the African goliath frog (*Conraua goliath*), a record specimen of which measured a comparatively small 14 ½ inches (sitting) and weighed just eight pounds, one ounce. At almost twice the length and five times the weight, Coleman's pet froggie is no more credible than his other whoppers (his outrageous yarns about the imagined creature).

In the museum file, I also came across a letter stating the policy of the historical society regarding the Coleman Frog. To a man who had objected to exhibition of the artifact, President E.W. Sansom (1961) wrote: "It was agreed . . . that the stuffed frog was of historical interest only as an artificial duplication used for publicity purposes by F.B. Coleman years ago in Fredericton. As such, the majority of those present felt the frog should be retained but only as an amusing example of a colossal fake and deception." And so it remains on display, according to one journalist (Brewer 1973), "as big as life—yea, bigger."

References

Brewer, Jacqueline. 1973. Famous Fredericton frog dates back to city's founding. *Daily Gleaner* (Fredericton, N.B.), March 30.

Coleman frog. n.d. Vertical files, York Sunbury Historical Society Museum and Fredericton Public Library (undated clippings, correspondence, etc.)

Colombo, John Robert. 1988. *Mysterious Canada: Strange Sights, Extraordinary Events, and Peculiar Places.* Toronto: Doubleday Canada.

The Guinness Book of Records. 1999, n.p.: Guinness Publishing, 122.

McKinney, Mary. n.d. Canadianecdote, undated clipping from *Maclean's* in Coleman n.d.

Phillips, Fred H. 1982. Coleman frog a fake? *Daily Gleaner* (Fredericton, N.B.), April 22.

Sansom, E.W. 1961. Letter to J. Winslow, Nov. 20 (in Coleman n.d.).

"Taxidermy." 1910; 1960. *Encyclopaedia Britannica.*

Chapter 24

The Alien Likeness

In a manner similar to the evolution of Jesus' features in art (Nickell 1988, 41–48), or of the popular likeness of Santa Claus (Flynn 1993) the concept of what alien creatures look like has undergone change over time. In the course of graduate work I did in folklore in 1982 and subsequently published (Nickell 1984), I noted (citing Stringfield 1980) that the descriptions of UFO occupants were tending to become standardized, a process that continues at present.

Consider, for example, the development beginning with the origin of the modern UFO era in 1947. (Although many alien encounters were also reported for the pre-1947 period, most of the reports were actually made public after that year, typically with great lapses in time between the alleged date of the encounter and the date of reporting. [Vallee 1969, 179–90] Therefore, there is reason to distrust the accuracy of such reports.) Several sources show the great variety of aliens described in the post-1947 era. (Clark 1993; Cohen 1982; Hendry 1979; Huyghe 1996; Lorenzen and Lorenzen 1977; McCampbell 1976; Sachs 1980; Stringfield 1977, 1980; Story 1980; Vallee 1969) One notes the "little green men" reported in Italy in 1947 (Cohen 1982, 203–05); the beautiful, human-like beings who appeared to the "contactees" of the 1950s (Story 1980, 89); the hairy dwarfs that were common in 1954 (Clark 1993, 177); and the many other varieties of humanoids, monsters, robots, and other alien beings reported in encounters down to the present. The accompanying illustration (figure 24.1) depicts a selection of such beings reportedly encountered from 1947 to the present. (Science fiction examples have not been included.) Prepared for a Discovery channel documentary on

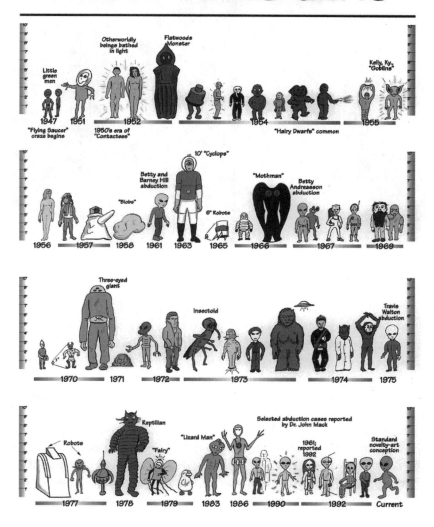

Figure 24.1. Alien Time Line illustrates evolution of popular extraterrestrial likeness.

Figure 24.2. Author's collection of alien toys and novelties shows the standardization of the depiction in popular culture.

alien abductions, this illustration also appeared April 4, 1997, on ABC's *20/20* in a documentary on the "Alien Autopsy" hoax. There I used it to demonstrate that the aliens allegedly retrieved from the 1947 Roswell, New Mexico, UFO crash (actually the crash of a spy balloon) were of a type not popularly imagined until many years later.

That type begins to appear in 1961, the date of the first widely reported alien abduction—the Betty and Barney Hill case. It is the little, big-headed humanoid with large, wraparound eyes. The mythological implication of this type seems to be that the aliens are "time travelers"—in effect, *us* as it is assumed we *will be* in our distant evolutionary future (Nickell 1984). Therefore they have dwindling bodies (because of our inactivity) and large brains (due to increased intelligence). However, some critics are skeptical of all such human/humanoid models. States one early commentator: "While it seems incredible that life does not exist elsewhere in the universe, it is equally incredible that it should resemble man" (Palmer 1951, 64). Nevertheless, due to media influence, this is the type that eventually became standardized. It is the alien image now seen everywhere—on T-shirts, caps, ties, necklaces, posters and books, even the coffee mug on my desk. (See figure 24.2).

References

Clark, Jerome. 1993. *Unexplained.* Detroit: Visible Ink.

Cohen, Daniel. 1982. *The Encyclopedia of Monsters.* New York: Dorsett.

Flynn, Tom. 1993. *The Trouble With Christmas.* Buffalo, N.Y.: Prometheus.

Hendry, Allan. 1979. *The UFO Handbook.* New York: Doubleday.

Huyghe, Patrick. 1996. *The Field Guide to Extraterrestrials.* New York: Avon. (I relied heavily on this source, as well as Vallee 1969.)

Lorenzen, Coral, and Jim Lorenzen. 1977. *Abducted: Confrontations With Beings From Outer Space.* New York: Berkeley Medallion.

Mack, John. 1994. *Abduction: Human Encounters With Aliens.* New York: Ballantine.

McCampbell, James M. 1976. *UFOLOGY: A Major Breakthrough in the Scientific Understanding of Unidentified Flying Objects.* Millbrae, Calif.: Celestial Arts.

Nickell, Joe. 1984. The "Hangar 18" Tales: A Folkloristic Approach. *Common Ground* (England), June.

———. 1988. *Inquest on the Shroud of Turin,* updated edition. Buffalo, N.Y.: Prometheus.

Palmer, Ray. 1951. New report on the flying saucers. *Fate,* Jan., 63–81.

Sachs, Margaret. 1980. *The UFO Encyclopedia.* New York: Perigree.

Stringfield, Leonard H. 1977. *Situation Red: The UFO Siege.* Garden City, N.Y.: Doubleday.

———. 1980. *The UFO Crash/Retrieval Syndrome.* Seguin, Tex.: MUFON.

Story, Ronald D. 1980. *The Encyclopedia of UFOs.* Garden City, N.Y.: Doubleday.

Vallee, Jacques. 1969. *Passport to Magonia: From Folklore to Flying Saucers.* Chicago: Henry Regnery.

Chapter 25

In Search of "Snake Oil"

"Snake oil"—the expression has come to be synonymous with a quack remedy. But questions about the origins of the term provide the basis for an interesting investigation. Although considered quintessentially American, patent medicines actually originated in England. The recipient of the first royal patent for a medicinal compound is unknown, but the second was granted to Richard Stoughton's Elixir in 1712. By mid-eighteenth century, an incomplete list included 202 "proprietary" medicines—those protected by patent or registration. Relatively few of the ready-made medicines were actually patented—which required disclosure of their ingredients—but rather had their brand name registered. Nevertheless, the term *patent medicine* has become generic for all self-prescribed nostrums and cure-alls.

Shipments of patent medicines were halted by the Revolutionary War, and American entrepreneurs took the opportunity to meet the demand. Post-war nationalism and cheaper prices of the nonimported medicines helped American vendors maintain their lead over English suppliers (Munsey 1970). Among the notable patent medicine men and women were Perry Davis, whose painkiller became famous in the 1849 cholera epidemic and was subsequently spread worldwide by missionaries who used it as a cure-all for heathen sufferers; Lydia E. Pinkham, whose portrait on her "Vegetable Compound," first marketed in 1875, made her the most widely recognized American woman of her day; the Kilmer brothers, Andral and Jonas, who moved to Binghamton, New York, in 1879 and were soon selling Swamp Root kidney and liver medicine and other "family remedies" from a palatial eight-story building; the trio of "Doc" Healy, "Texas Charlie" Bigelow, and "Nevada Ned" Oliver, who originated the Kickapoo Indian Medicine Company in 1881; and Mrs. Violet Blossom, who as "Lotus Blossom" ran a medicine show with her husband in the early 1900s and became known as "the queen of pitch doctors" (Holbrook 1959).

Among the most fascinating peddlers were one-time preacher Fletcher Sutherland and his seven daughters, whose hair had a collective length of thirty-seven feet. When the young ladies performed their vocal and instrumental concerts—at such venues as the 1881 Atlanta Exposition and, by 1884, Barnum and Bailey's Greatest Show on Earth—Fletcher Sutherland shrewdly observed that the girls' long hair was a greater attraction than their musical ability. This led him to create the "Seven Sutherland Sisters Hair Grower," a concoction of alcohol, vegetable oils, and water. The fifth daughter, Naomi, married Henry Bailey, a circus employee, who expanded the family sideline into a business that grossed $90,000 the first year. By the time Naomi died unexpectedly in 1893, business was so good that to keep up appearances the remaining sisters hired a replacement. The hair-growing business thrived until 1907, then declined slowly over the next decade when the bobbed-hair fad nearly put an end to sales. Overall, their hair grower and related products brought in more than $2.75 million over a thirty-eight-year period, but the septet squandered it on an opulent lifestyle that included each having a personal maid to comb her luxuriant tresses (Lewis 1991).

The medicine peddlers used a number of tricks and stunts. The larger traveling shows, employing advance men to herald their arrival, entered town with circuslike fanfare, typically with a band leading the procession of wagons. Skits and other diversions were used to attract audiences, who eventually were treated to the "Lecture" (which, when medicine shows expanded into radio, became the commercial). Assistants who moved through the crowds were often garbed as Quakers to lend an air of moral respectability. Native Americans were frequently recruited to promote the notion of "natural" medicine, which was given names like Wright's Indian Vegetable Pills, Seminole Cough Balsam, and various Kickapoo cures (Holbrook 1959, 196–215; Munsey 1970).

A major component of most tonics, "cures," bitters, and other nostrums was alcohol. During the Temperance era, the patent medicines were often sipped—with a wink—"for medicinal purposes," leading the promoters of Old Dr. Kaufmann's Great Sulphur Bitters to advise the public: "Never Use Cheap Rum Drinks Which Are Called Medicine." Interestingly, the manufacturers never felt obliged to disclose the alcohol content of *their* product (Holbrook 1959, 159). The alcohol—as well as the placebo effect—explains why the nostrums often won testimonials from their purchasers, who felt better and so believed they had been helped rather than victimized.

In time, worthless cure-alls came to be known as "snake oil." The origin of the term is uncertain. One source asserts, "There is no such thing as *snakeoil*, though many thousands of bottles containing stuff called *snakeoil* were sold to gullible patrons of carnival sideshows in the nineteenth and early twentieth centuries" (Morris and Morris 1988). Actually, real snake oil was prized for its supposed medicinal properties. In 1880, for example, a newspaper article about a Pennsylvania man—"a celebrated hunter, trapper and snake-tamer by the name of John Geer"—told how he killed rattlesnakes and extracted "oil from their bodies." The article stated: "this oil is very useable and sells readily for $1 per ounce. It is said to have great curative powers" ("Killing Snakes" 1880). Interestingly, the term "snake medicine" was a slang expression for whiskey, used as early as 1865 (Cragie and Hurlbert 1944). I once saw a bottle in a private collection with a label upon which was actually penned "Snake Oil" and that (if memory serves me) may have dated from the mid-nineteenth century or even earlier.

In any event, a cowboy named Clark Stanley, who called himself "The Rattlesnake King," sold a Snake Oil Liniment that was reputedly "good for man and beast." In 1893, at the World's Columbian Exposition in Chicago, Stanley is said to have held crowds spellbound as, dressed in colorful western garb, he slaughtered hundreds of rattlesnakes, processing the juices into the cure-all. A circa 1890s advertisement described Stanley's snake oil as "A wonderful pain destroying compound." It was "the strongest and best liniment known for the cure of all pain and lameness." To be "used external [*sic*] only," it treated "rheumatism, neuralgia, sciatica, lame back, lumbago, contracted muscles, toothache, sprains, swellings, etc." It also, the ad said, "cures frost bites, chill blains, bruises, sore throat, [and] bites of animals, insects and reptiles," in fact being "good for every thing a liniment should be good for." Promising "immediate relief," it sold for fifty cents a bottle (Fowler, 1997, vi, 10–12). Stanley claimed the secret recipe came from a Moki Pueblo Indian medicine man. (Reportedly, some Native Americans, including the Choctaws, did treat rheumatism and other ills with applications of rattlesnake grease.) In

Figure 25.1. "Snake oil" came to refer to any patent medicine, but this bottle is actually embossed, "Known as Snake Oil." (Photo by Joe Nickell)

1917, however, tests of a federally seized shipment of Snake Oil Liniment revealed it to be mostly mineral oil containing about one percent fatty oil (thought to have been beef fat), along with some red pepper (probably to impart a soothing warmth to the skin) and possible traces of turpentine and camphor (perhaps to provide a suitably medicinal smell) (Fowler 1997, 11–12).

The bottle shown in the accompanying photograph (a gift to the author from skeptic Robert Price of Bloomfield, Connecticut) is from one of Stanley's many imitators. While the front of the embossed bottle reads "Known as Snake Oil," the sides inform that it is "Miller's Antiseptic Oil" sold by the "Herb Juice Medicine Co." The exact date is unknown, but the bottle was produced by an automatic glassblowing machine, which means it was manufactured after the turn of the century (see Munsey 1970, 33). Another imitator, probably inspired by the 1909 Centennial of the sixteenth president's birth, called his product Lincoln Oil. As indicated by a handbill in my collection, it supposedly worked from head to toe, curing toothache and corns alike.

Toward the close of the horse-and-buggy era, the sale of patent medicines had become immense and so had the resulting victimization of the American public. A backlash came in the form of a campaign launched in 1905 by *Collier's* magazine against what it called "The Great American Fraud." Although the patent-medicine lobby in the U.S. Congress proved potent (not unlike today's tobacco lobby), the tide was eventually turned and the federal Pure Food and Drug Act became law on January 1, 1907 (Munsey 1970; Holbrook 1959, 3–4). Of course, not all of the tonics and cures were deliberately bogus. Some derived from homespun remedies that—by trial and error—were sometimes found to be effective treatments. Books of "receipts" (recipes) usually included a large section of home remedies (Marquart 1867). Among my own ancestors were a couple of eastern Kentucky folk doctors, James Harrison Murphy (1843–1923) and his wife Martha Baker (1849–1917), who relied on such medicines. Harry gathered the herbs and roots for their remedies, which included a "blood tonic" (that was brewed, sweetened, and mixed with alcohol), along with a vermifuge and horehound tea. Martha administered the nostrums and offered other treatments such as lancing boils and setting broken bones (Nickell 1978).

In addition to folk remedies, quasi-pharmaceutical "receipts," and recipes allegedly obtained from Indian medicine men, there were other sources of patent-medicine formulas. Some proprietors, like Fletcher Sutherland, seemed to rely on sheer inspiration. Mrs. J.H.R. Matteson of Buffalo, New York, went a step further, offering (according to an embossed bottle in my collection) "Clairvoyant Remedies." Then there was simple imitation: the success of Paine's Celery Compound ("A Nerve Tonic") prompted other manufacturers to offer Celery Bitters, Celery Malt Compound, and Celery Crackers, as well as products called Celerena and Celery-Vesce (Holbrook 1959, 52–53).

Implementation of the Pure Food and Drug Act forced many medicines off the market and compelled others to change their advertising or product content, or both. But sale of patent and proprietary medicines continued, including Princess Tonic Hair Restorer (which was guaranteed to be "absolutely harmless"), Dr. Worden's Female Pills (for "Female Diseases and Troubles, Peculiar to the Sex and Women's Delicate System"), a product called Vin Vitae (or "Wine of Life," a "tonic stimulant" that listed among its ingredients port wine and coca eaves, the source of cocaine), Dr. McBain's Blood Pills ("a blood cleanser and purifier"), and

Princess brand Hair Restorer and Bust Developer (both reassuringly described as completely harmless and sporting money-back guarantees). Such products were sold by mail-order companies (Sears 1909), drug and other retail stores, and traveling salesmen. One of the latter was "Snake-Oil Johnnie" McMahon (great-grandfather of former *Free Inquiry* editor Tim Madigan), who sold his wares in New Jersey during the 1920s.

Today, nonprescription medicines are more carefully regulated, but a new form of snake oil is on the rise. Broadly termed "alternative medicine," it includes treatments ranging from the dubious to the bizarre, from acupuncture to zone therapy (Raso 1996). Some of the new versions of snake-oil-like aromatherapy oils and the resurgent homeopathic "remedies" (which supposedly restore the "vital force")—even come in bottles.

References

Craigie, William A., and James R. Hurlbert. 1944. *A Dictionary of American English on Historical Principles*. Chicago: Univ. of Chicago Press, IV: 2161.

Fowler, Gene, ed. 1997. *Mystic Healers and Medicine Shows*. Santa Fe, N.M.: Ancient City.

Holbrook, Stewart H. 1959. *The Golden Age of Quackery*. New York: Macmillan.

Killing snakes for a living. 1880. *The Spectator* (Hamilton, Ontario), Aug. 7, 3. I am most grateful to Ranjit Sandhu for discovering this significant 1880 newspaper article.

Lewis, Clarence O. 1991. *The Seven Sutherland Sisters*. Lockport, N.Y.: Niagara County Historical Society.

Marquart, John. 1867. *Six Hundred Receipts* . . . Reprinted Paducah, Ky.: Troll.

Morris, William, and Mary Morris. 1988. *Morris Dictionary of Word and Phrase Origin*. 2nd ed. New York: Harper & Row, 535.

Munsey, Cecil. 1970. *The Illustrated Guide to Collecting Bottles*. New York: Hawthorn, 65–75.

Nickell, Joe. 1978. "Notes on James Harrison Murphy and His Wife, Martha Baker Murphy," in Lucille N. Haney, *Lineage of John Curren Nickell and Emma Golden Murphy* (Lexington, Ky.: Privately printed, 1987), 71–72.

Raso, Jack. 1996. *The Dictionary of Metaphysical Healthcare*. Loma Linda, Calif.: National Council Against Health Fraud.

Sears, Roebuck and Co. 1909. *Consumer's Guide*. Reprinted New York: Ventura, 1979, 380–403.

Chapter 26

The Haunted Cathedral

Built between 1845 and 1853, Christ Church Cathedral in Fredericton, New Brunswick, is considered "one of the most fascinating ecclesiastical buildings in Canada" (Trueman 1975). Certainly with its imposing spire and lofty interior arches it represents an excellent example of Gothic Revival architecture (figure 26.1). Supposedly, the Anglican sanctuary also has a resident spirit.

Some describe only a vague sense of a presence, while others say a shadowy figure has been sighted—reportedly the ghost of Mrs. John Medley, wife of the first bishop. Just who is alleged to have seen her usually goes unreported, but according to a former assistant curate, the Reverend David Mercer, "She's supposed to come up Church Street and enter by the west door. What she does after that, I really don't know" (Trueman 1975, 85). One source of apparent late vintage attempted to supply the motive: in life the faithful Mrs. Medley had been accustomed to carry her husband's dinner to him at the church, a practice she supposedly rehearsed after she passed into spirithood ("Haunted" 1999). Unfortunately, this charming tale was debunked when I visited the Medleys' graves, located just beyond the east end of the cathedral (figure 26.2). As carved inscriptions made clear, it was the bishop who passed first, in 1892, his widow living on to 1905. Even a local storyteller, who had often repeated the anecdote about the dutiful ghost but who accompanied me to the grave site, quickly conceded that the tale lost rationale in light of this evidence ("Haunted" 1999). Another "it-is-said" source claims Mrs. Medley's alleged visitations are malevolent, resulting from her extreme dislike of her husband's successor (Dearborn 1996), while still another

Figure 26.1. "Haunted" Christ Church Cathedral in Fredericton, New Brunswick, Canada.

Figure 26.2. Graves of Bishop John Medley and his wife, the latter's ghost being reported to haunt the sanctuary.

states that the perambulating spirit merely "surveys the Cathedral, as if in wonderment, and then disappears" (Colombo 1988). Such variant tales are an obvious indication of the human tendency for legend-making.

I talked with two elderly churchgoers (each with about forty-five years' membership) and a young tour guide, none of whom had ever seen a ghost in the church. The latter stated that the notion the cathedral was haunted was not supported by current parishioners and was largely regarded as folklore (Meek 1999). The impetus for ghostly inklings may well have been the cathedral's own "spooky atmosphere" and indeed "haunted air"—an effect stemming from the somber setting and play of subdued light and shadow, and heightened by the presence of a stone cenotaph, its figure of Bishop Medley recumbent in death (Trueman 1975). (See figure 26.3.) Such an atmosphere, admits one writer, is "enough to spark the most dormant imagination" (Dearborn 1996).

Figure 26.3. Stone cenotaph of Bishop Medley, which helps add to "spooky atmosphere" of the cathedral.

References

Colombo, John Robert. 1988. *Mysterious Canada: Strange Sights, Extraordinary Events, and Peculiar Places.* Toronto: Doubleday Canada.

Dearborn, Dorothy. 1996. *Legends, Oddities & Mysteries . . . in New Brunswick.* St. John, N.B.: Neptune, 15–16.

"Haunted Hike" tour guide. 1999. Personal communication. Fredericton, N.B., June 28.

Meek, Hilary. 1999. Personal communication, June 28.

Trueman, Stuart. 1975. *Ghosts, Pirates and Treasure Trove: The Phantoms That Haunt New Brunswick.* Toronto: McClelland and Stewart, 84–85.

Miracle Photographs

On Friday, October 27, 1995, the television program *Unsolved Mysteries* aired a segment, "Kentucky Visions," that included investigative work by the Committee for the Scientific Investigation of Claims of the Paranormal. The popular, prime-time television series had requested CSICOP's opinion of some "miraculous" photographs taken at a recent Virgin Mary sighting at a hillside spot in central Kentucky. This was my first significant case as Senior Research Fellow—or as the narrator termed me, "Paranormal Investigator" (a "P.I." nonetheless).

The photographs were made by a Sunday school teacher who had visited the Valley Hill site (near Bardstown, Kentucky) with eight girls from her class. I did not see the photographs until the day I was brought on location for filming, but I was sent color photocopies of them in advance. The lack of reproductive quality put me at more of a disadvantage with some photos than with others. I did recognize that the claimed "faces of Jesus and Mary" in one photo were simply due to random, out-of-focus patterns of light and shadow caused by mishandling of the film pack. (More on that later.) I also recognized in another photo the now common effect at Marian apparition sites, a phenomenon known as the "golden door." This is an arched-door shape, filled with golden light and believed by some to be the doorway to heaven mentioned in Revelation 4:1. In fact, as explained in an earlier *Skeptical Inquirer* (winter 1993), it is simply an artifact of the Polaroid OneStep camera, which when flooded with bright light (as when pointed at the sun or a halogen lamp), produces a picture of the camera's own aperture (Nickell 1993a) (figure 27.1). This was codiscovered by Georgia Skeptics members Dale Heatherington

Figure 27.1. "Golden door" photograph.

and Anson Kennedy, who tutored me in making such photos. (Together we have wasted much Polaroid film, all in the interest of scientific experimentation.)

I telephoned Kennedy about two of the other "miracle" effects, and he was already familiar with one of them. Sight unseen, simply from my description of the alleged "angel wings," he diagnosed light leakage into the Polaroid film pack. My subsequent experimentation confirmed his explanation and showed how the leakage could have occurred (figure 27.2).

Fortunately, my experimentation also provided an explanation for the remaining effect—one that had at first puzzled both Kennedy and me as well as some professional photographers and film processors I consulted. The effect was that of a *chart* superimposed on one picture. The chart was slightly out of focus but nevertheless unmistakable. One of the girls at the site thought she could see in the blurred printing the name of

Figure 27.2. "Angel wings" effect.

a deceased friend. Where had the chart come from? It appeared to have resulted from a double exposure, although the Polaroid OneStep camera should not ordinarily permit that to occur. Suddenly, I realized that the card atop the film pack, which protects the film from light and which is ejected when the pack is first loaded into the camera, has a chart printed on its underside! Indeed, that was clearly the mysterious chart in question, somehow appearing in mirror image in the photograph taken by the Sunday school teacher. But how had it gotten onto one photo? My subsequent experiments showed it was possible to produce such an effect by light leakage (the same culprit that produced the "angel wings"). The light had leaked in between the card and the first potential photograph, bouncing off the white card and onto the light-sensitized surface of the film, thus making an exposure of a portion of the chart. In this way it was superimposed on the first photograph made from that pack (figure 27.3).

Figure 27.3. Detail of "miracle" chart superimposition.
(Experimental photos by Joe Nickell)

Taken together, the evidence from all four photographs, some of which had multiple effects, provided corroborative evidence that the film pack was somehow mishandled and admitted light, maybe by the front having been pulled down with the thumb on being inserted into the camera, or even by someone having sat on the pack. Since the other major effect, the golden door, was due to the construction of the camera, there was therefore no indication of hoaxing with any of the pictures.

On the television program, my comments were edited down to very brief but sufficient explanations. The treatment of the photographs was uneven from a skeptical point of view. The "faces" were greatly enhanced to make them look more realistic. Commendable was the use of an effective graphics technique whereby the chart was placed on the screen beside the chart-bearing photo, then flopped so as to superimpose it on the photo.

Skeptics who watched the segment with me laughed loudly at the conclusion of my interview when the narrator commented, "Rational explanations may satisfy *some* people, but. . . ." This comment was followed by various "miracle" claims that went unchallenged. I had not only explained how the "golden door" photos are made, but I showed several of them for the *Unsolved Mysteries* camera (again see figure 27.1); however, this was omitted from the program even though such photos were described as "mysterious." Also omitted were my explanations for silver rosaries supposedly turning to gold—either due to tarnishing or the rubbing off of the silver plating to expose the copper or brass beneath (Nickell 1993b). I included an explanation for a new claim: glass-beaded rosaries were supposedly turning, momentarily, a golden color; I theorized that the faceted beads were reflecting the golden light of the sun. Much ado was made about people reportedly seeing the sun pulsate, spin, or exhibit other phenomena—all arguably due to optical effects resulting from staring at the sun, which I discussed at some length in my *Looking for a Miracle* (1993b). Many pilgrims also had claimed to see showers of golden flakes, which I attributed to their having looked at the bright sun (even though some insisted they had not looked *directly* at the sun), or to a dappling of sunlight through the canopy of tree leaves, or to the power of suggestion—or a combination. All of my comments about such other phenomena, including faith healing, ended up on the cutting-room floor.

The program did end on a rather skeptical note, with program host Robert Stack stating: "It is interesting to note that the local Catholic church has declined to recognize Valley Hill as anything out of the ordinary. The rest of us will have to decide for ourselves." Unfortunately, they will have to decide without the benefit of all of the skeptical evidence. That's why I sometimes refer to the television show as "Unsolving Mysteries."

References

Nickell, Joe. 1993a. Miracles in Kentucky. *Skeptical Inquirer* 17(2) (winter): 120–22.

———. 1993b. *Looking for a Miracle: Weeping Icons, Relics, Stigmata, Visions and Healing Cures,* 177–78, 196–97. Amherst, N.Y.: Prometheus.

Chapter 28

The Gypsies' "Great Trick"

Everyone knows what fortune-telling is supposed to be, but sometimes it might best be defined as "the art of absconding with fortunes." For example, in 1995 a London gypsy who called herself "Mrs. Marina" persuaded a man to hand over his life's savings, some £3,000. The thirty-five-year-old postman, whom police described as "intelligent but unsophisticated," contacted the woman about his severe depression. She informed him that his stomach was harboring evil and instructed him to return with a tomato, a photo of his fiancée, and £350 in cash. As the *Evening Standard* (London) reported: "In the darkened flat, the tomato was swapped for another without the man's knowledge. When she cut it open, a hair was extracted—a sign, the frightened man was told, that the evil was still present. By now in a state of near-panic, he promised to return with his entire savings of £3,000." This time the credulous postman was shown an egg filled with blood, whereupon he fainted. When he revived, the money he had clutched to his stomach was gone. "The evil has been removed," the soothsayer claimed. "You can go." When the man later attempted to get his money back, she told him she had burned it and buried the ashes in a cemetery. She later claimed to police that the money was "payment for services" but did eventually return it to avoid facing charges (Delgado 1995).

Typically the practitioners of the egg/tomato trick are *gypsies*, the term having derived from "Egyptian" due to a mistaken notion of their ancestry. They were actually exiled from northwestern India in the first millennium A.D. and in the Middle Ages sought asylum in Romania, hence their other designation as *Romanies* or (as they prefer) *Roma* ("Gypsies"

1960; Popp 1997). They constitute an ethnic group who "essentially live outside the cultures of the countries in which they choose to reside" and who often treat nongypsies as "fair game for their fortune-telling, curse-lifting and other superstitious ministrations" (Randi 1995). According to William Lindsay Gresham in his fascinating book on carnivals, *Monster Midway* (1953):

> The gypsies call fortunetelling *pen dukkerin*. It is the traditional trade of gypsy women the world over and throughout history. But along with it goes another art called *hokkani boro*—the great trick. A credulous patron (usually a housewife), after having her fortune told, is initiated by the gypsy into the magic of making money double itself when the proper spell is chanted over it. The money is wrapped in a handkerchief and must be "dreamed on"—placed under the pillow at night. Next morning, when the gypsy comes again, lo and behold, the sum is twice that which was tied into the handkerchief. This time the housewife takes all her savings, sometimes even borrows from relatives and neighbors, and has the gypsy tie it up and chant over it. So much money must have more time to double itself—usually three weeks, and the gypsy exacts an oath that the owner will not tamper with the bundle until the spell has had a chance to work.
>
> The gypsy never returns and the bundle, when opened, naturally contains a roll of wrapping paper, cut into the size of dollar bills. This is *hokkani boro*, old when the pyramids were new, and still good for taking off modest scores, although it has landed more than one Romany *chi* in the *staripen* (pokey to you) and in frontier days in Tennessee, got one old gypsy woman burned at the stake for pulling this trick.

Continues Gresham:

> Another Romany name for this dodge is *hakk'ni panki*, from which *hanky-panky*, as a synonym for trickery of any sort, probably stems.[10]
> There is a counting rhyme among English children which goes:
>
> > *Eckery, ackery, ookery an,*
> > *Fillisy, follasy, Nicholas John. . . .*
>
> which is pure Romany double-talk:
>
> > *Ekkeri, akai-ri, u kair—an.*
> > *Fillissin, follasy. Nakelas ja'n. . . .*
>
> It means, literally:
>
> > *First, here, you begin.*
> > *Castle, gloves; go on, you can't play!*

180

The interesting thing is that this nonsense rhyme in Romany is the traditional spell uttered over the handkerchief containing the money! Children have retentive memories and a great many of them down the centuries, listening at the keyhole while the gypsy crone enchanted the cash, must have heard this time-honored formula.

Increasingly, fortune-telling is practiced by the *gorgio* (nongypsies)— a trespass the true Roma may find hard to forgive (Gresham 1953). In any event, "the great trick" remains part of their legacy. As Gresham indicates, it is sometimes performed without the egg or tomato. Such was the case in Toronto in 1971. A sixty-two-year-old woman was persuaded to withdraw her "cursed" money from the bank—some $9,300—which the fortune-teller placed in a red cloth and "blessed." The cloth was sewn shut and the woman told not to open it for at least two weeks. Thereupon she discovered $35 and pieces of paper ("Woman" 1971).

Quite often the *hokkani boro* is facilitated by use of an egg or tomato— or both—and the techniques are extremely varied. For example, a quite sinister tomato was the device used to bilk one woman of over $20,000. She had visited a soothsayer named "Sister Bella," who duly divined that the credulous woman was threatened by an evil force. To counter it, she was instructed to return the following day with a handkerchief and a fresh tomato. Passing the tomato over the woman's body, Sister Bella then wrapped it in the handkerchief and instructed the woman to crush it with her foot. Out of the bloody pulp stared an ominous black lizard—a sure sign of the predicted evil. Sister Bella explained that such evil—perhaps cancer or other disaster—resulted from money that had a lingering curse, possibly from ill-gained dollars passed onto her. "Take all your money except a few hundred dollars out of the bank," instructed Sister Bella. "This money I will convert from evil to good by special magic venerated for over three thousand years." The gypsy sewed the money in a pillowcase and instructed her client to place the bag in her safe deposit box for three months. When the bundle was finally opened, it contained not the purified $22,000, but a mere $22 and strips of paper (Rachleff 1971).

In 1997, several instances of the scam were reported in New York State alone. In one case, a Romanian native and "psychic astrologer" pled guilty to grand larceny for bilking a Massapequa resident of $2,000 out of an intended $20,000. Police secretly videotaped the "exorcism," which involved candles and chanting, followed by the breaking of an egg that the victim, a widow, had kept under her bed. A "chicken embryo" reportedly emerged, whereupon the psychic screamed, "You have to sacrifice the money. All of the evil that is in your body is in there" ("Jail" 1997).

Later that year, an Aurora resident was defrauded of $9,600 and an Elgin woman was cheated of cash and jewelry totaling $14,000. Police warned Hispanic residents about the "group of gypsy con artists posing as Spanish-speaking fortunetellers and palm readers," who had absconded with almost $30,000 the previous year. Renting an apartment for a week to ten days, the scam artists asked clients to bring an egg or tomato. "When the item is broken or cut open," a newspaper reported, "either a worm, a skeleton or a spider is found inside, symbolizing bad luck" ("Fortuneteller" 1997). This was a prelude to having the clients bring their valuables to be blessed. Later they would return for them only to find instead an empty apartment or, alternately, the victims would open a bag to find only scraps of paper.

Interestingly, somewhat ironically, and perhaps predictably, while I was working on this historical sketch, a Buffalo, New York, Roma woman using the name "Sister Ana" was arrested for allegedly stealing over $3,600 from a twenty-eight-year-old single mother. According to her, the mystic performed a ritual to remove "an evil curse" from her, employing lighted candles and incantations and passing an egg over her body (Michel 1998). She was then directed to step on the egg and saw therein an ugly mass. It was so repulsive she did not examine it closely, but she told the arresting officer it resembled a mixture of chicken parts, hair, and the like (Rinaldo 1998). The officer, Detective Tom Rinaldo, a friend of CSICOP, is a fraud expert and author and a member of the Board of Directors of Professionals Against Confidence Crime. He said of the mystic, "She acted in disbelief when we came to her house. I told her, 'You're a psychic. You should have known we were coming.'"

Given that it is useful for the fortune-teller to demonstrate and dramatize the "evil" that attends the unsuspecting client, why are eggs and tomatoes specifically employed? One reason is the symbolism and lore associated with them. For example, eggs are obvious symbols of fertility and continuing life. The ancient Greeks and Romans exchanged colored eggs at spring festivals, a custom later appropriated by Christians and—eggs being emblems of resurrection—associated with the Easter season. Many popular superstitions are linked to eggs. For example, small, yolkless eggs supposedly bode ill, especially if brought into the house, whereas two yolks in a single egg represent good luck for the one who received it.

And dreaming about spoiled eggs supposedly foretells death in the family. Eggs have also been used in divination, one approach being to read the shapes of the white dripped into water (much like tea-leaf reading), and in other occult practices. Reportedly the Mayan Indians used the yolk of an egg to undo the spell of an "evil eye." The medicine man repeatedly passed an egg in front of the bewitched person's face. He then broke the shell and stared at the yolk as though it were the actual Evil Eye, before burying it in a hidden place (DeLys 1989; Hole 1961).

Tomatoes are also the subject of superstitions. "Some Italians," reports *The Encyclopedia of Superstitions*, "put a large red tomato on the mantel to bring prosperity to the house. When placed on the windowsill, or in any opening, it wards off evil spirits, and protects the occupants of the house" (DeLys 1989). Eggs and tomatoes are also common objects that can be brought to a session by the client himself, thereby dispelling any suspicion that the object is specially prepared. Of course, that is exactly what happens. As already indicated, the usual method is to prepare an egg or tomato in advance and then switch it for the client's, using "misdirection" (as magicians say) or an even simpler method, as I demonstrated for a Discovery Channel special.

Titled "The Science of Magic," the documentary was hosted by Harry Anderson, star of the TV series *Night Court* and a magician in his own right. The day before the film crew arrived to tape the segment (which aired on November 30, 1997), I prepared an egg in the small laboratory connected to my office. I used an awl to poke a hole in the end of the egg and then, inserting the tool, scrambled the contents. Through the small opening I worked a hairball, added some ink with an eyedropper, and finally squirted in some theatrical "blood." I then covered the opening with a small piece of tape and dabbed over it with some white correction fluid. With the cameras rolling, I had my "victim"—Center for Inquiry Library Director Tim Binga—select an egg from a bowl. I passed the egg over his body, as if to draw out any evil influences, then turned him around to repeat the procedure. As he was facing away, I took the opportunity to place the egg in one of my coat pockets, while simultaneously withdrawing the prepared egg from another. When I broke it into a dish, Tim responded to the repulsive mass with a look that may earn him a nomination for "Best Performance of an Eyebrow."

Skeptics wishing to make such a demonstration can follow a similar procedure. Alternately, depending on the desired effect, an egg may be emptied by making a hole at each end and blowing out the (scrambled) contents; the shell may then be refilled with blood (as in the London postman case) or other material. Or a tomato can be prepared by making a slit in the bottom and inserting objects (like the rubber lizard "Sister Bella" produced). Magicians can produce these and other effects very convincingly, even without using a prepared egg or tomato or making any switch.

Magical entertainment and pretended soothsaying aside, it seems predictable that "the great trick" will be repeated again and again. It is to be hoped that a detective like Tom Rinaldo will, in each instance, also be in the practitioner's future.

References

Delgado, Martin. 1995. Police powerless as voodoo con girl makes thousands. *Evening Standard* (London), July 6.

DeLys, Claudia. 1989. *What's So Lucky About a Four-Leaf Clover?* New York: Bell, 247–50.

Fortuneteller scam returns . . . 1997. *Daily Herald* (reprinted in *CON-fidential Bulletin*, Oct.,15).

"Gypsies." 1960. *Encyclopaedia Britannica.*

Gresham, William Lindsay. 1953. *Monster Midway.* New York: Rinehart, 113–15.

Hole, Christina, ed. 1961. *The Encyclopedia of Superstitions.* New York: Barnes and Noble, 149–50.

Jail may be in cards for psychic. 1997. *New York Newsday,* June 20(reprinted in *CON-fidential Bulletin*, Aug. 1997, 6).

Michel, Lou. 1998. Self-proclaimed west side psychic didn't predict own arrest. *Buffalo News*, Oct. 11.

Popp, Christine. 1997. Rescuing rich gypsy tradition (article reprinted in *CON-fidential Bulletin*, Dec.,13).

Rachleff, Owen S. 1971. *The Occult Conceit.* Chicago: Cowles, 172–76.

Randi, James. 1995. *The Supernatural A–Z.* London: Brockhampton, 148.

Rinaldo, Tom. 1998. Interview by author, Nov. 11.

Woman, 62, claims fortune teller swindled her out of $9,300. 1971. *Toronto Daily Star*, Oct. 20.

Chapter 29

Magnetic Hill

Located in eastern New Brunswick, near Moncton, is Magnetic Hill, Canada's third most-visited natural tourist attraction (after Niagara Falls and the Canadian Rockies). Nineteenth-century farmers going to market noticed a mysterious stretch of road where a wagon going uphill would run against the hooves of the horse pulling it. In 1933, an ice-cream stand with a gas pump opened at the top of the hill, sparking more interest in the site (then known variously as Fool Hill, Magic Hill, and Mystery Hill). Sightseers were invited to drive down the slope, place their vehicle in neutral, and experience being drawn back uphill! Truckers said the place must be magnetic, and the name stuck (Cochrane 1998; "Magnetic" 1997).

Visitors to Magnetic Hill—the drivers and passengers of up to seven hundred vehicles daily during the peak summer season—offer priceless quotes: "Do you stay in your car, or does it go up the hill by itself?" "I have an expensive watch. The magnet won't hurt it, will it?" And "Do you leave the magnet on all the time, or does it get turned off at night?" (Cochrane 1998). Souvenir magnets are sold in the gift shop of the adjacent theme park. In fact, of course, the place is no more magnetic than various similar sites—including two each in Ontario and Québec (Colombo 1988), as well as one in central Florida (Wilder 1991). As the very helpful staffers at Magnetic Hill are quick to admit, the mysterious effect is essentially due to an optical illusion. This is created, says one source, "by a hill on top of a hill, which makes people believe that they are actually travelling uphill when they are, in fact, going downhill" (Cochrane 1998).

Figure 29.1. Magnetic Hill. Driver proceeds from point A along an apparently continuous downhill course to B, places vehicle in neutral and removes foot from brake pedal. Vehicle seems mysteriously drawn backward, but in fact the distance from B to C is a slightly downward incline, and momentum propels the vehicle back toward A (but never higher than B, due to the law of the conservation of energy).

A more precise explanation is obtained by using a simple carpenter's implement. I was permitted to "walk" my four-foot level along the route, observing the bubble frequently. This demonstrated that the course is not a straight incline but a dipped one, although higher at the top. In other words, proceeding downhill, after the initial incline the course seems to almost level off, continuing in a gentle downslope, but in fact it actually turns gently upward. (See figure 29.1). Therefore, from the point designated for vehicles to stop and be placed in neutral, they will begin to roll backward. The effect seems quite mysterious, since the driver is conscious of having driven downhill, and trees on either side of the road help hide the true horizon.

But myths die hard. One Torontonian returned annually, claiming the magnetic force helped relieve his arthritis, and an American tourist insisted he could feel the magnet pulling on the nails in his shoes. One visitor insisted, "If it was only an optical illusion, my car wouldn't actually do it!" (Trueman 1972)

References

Cochrane, Alan. 1998. 65 years of magic. *Times & Transcript* (Moncton, N.B.), Aug. 8.

Colombo, John Robert. 1988. *Mysterious Canada: Strange Sights, Extraordinary Events, and Peculiar Places.* Toronto: Doubleday Canada.

Magnetic Hill. 1997. Advertising flyer, Moncton, N.B.

Trueman, Stuart. 1972. *An Intimate History of New Brunswick.* 1970; reprinted Toronto: McClelland and Stewart, 109–14.

Wilder, Guss. 1991. Spook Hill: Angular illusion. *Skeptical Inquirer* 16.1 (fall): 58–60.

Chapter 30

Phantom Ship

In 1999, at Nova Scotia's Mahone Bay, I investigated the twin riddles of the Teazer Light and the Oak Island "Money Pit." (The latter, one of the world's greatest unsolved mysteries, is discussed in "The Secrets of Oak Island" chapter of this book.) The Teazer Light is an example of "ghost lights" or "luminous phenomena" (see Corliss 1995)—in this case, the reputed appearance of a phantom ship in flames. On June 26, 1813, the *Young Teazer*, a privateer's vessel, was cornered in Mahone Bay by British warships. Realizing they were doomed to capture and hanging, the pirates' commander had the ship set ablaze, whereupon—at least according to legend—all perished (Blackman 1998). Soon after, however, came eyewitness reports that the craft had returned as a fiery spectral ship. It has almost always been observed on foggy nights, according to marina operator (and private investigator) Jim Harvey (1999), especially when such nights occur "within three days of a full moon" (Colombo 1988, 32).

In the late evening of July 1 (approximately three days after the full moon), I began a vigil for the Teazer Light, lasting from about 11:00 P.M. until 1:00 A.M. Unfortunately, the phantom ship did not appear, although that came as no surprise since one of the last reported sightings was in 1935 (Colombo 1988). I wondered if the diminishing of apparition reports might be due, at least in part, to encroaching civilization, with its accompanying increase in light pollution (from homes, marinas, etc.) obscuring the phenomenon.

In researching the Teazer Light, I came across the revealing account of a local man who had seen the fiery ship with some friends. They shook their heads in wonderment, then went indoors for about fifteen minutes. When they came out again, "[T]here, in exactly the same place, the moon was coming up. It was at the full, and they knew its location by its relation to Tancook Island." The man appreciated the sequence of events: "It struck him then that there must have been a bank of fog in front of the moon as it first came over the horizon that caused it to appear like a ship on fire, and he now thinks this is what the Mahone Bay people have been seeing all these years. If the fog had not cleared away that night he would always have thought, like all the other people, that he had seen the *Teazer*" (Creighton 1957).

References

Blackman, W. Haden. 1998. *The Field Guide to North American Hauntings.* New York: Three Rivers, 65–66.

Colombo, John Robert. 1988. *Mysterious Canada: Strange Sights, Extraordinary Events, and Peculiar Places.* Toronto: Doubleday Canada.

Corliss, William R. 1995. *Handbook of Unusual Natural Phenomena.* New York: Gramercy, 1–87.

Creighton, Helen. *Bluenose Ghosts,* 1957. Reprinted Halifax, N.S.: Nimbus, 1994, 118–20.

Harvey, Jim (Oak Island Marina). 1999. Interview by Joe Nickell, July 2.

Chapter 31

The Cryptic Stone

During an investigative tour of Canada's maritime provinces in 1999 (Morris 1999), my final adventure (before ferrying two hundred miles across the Atlantic to the coast of Maine to begin the drive back to Buffalo) focused on the intriguing case of the Yarmouth Stone, now located in the Yarmouth County, Nova Scotia, Museum. This is a four-hundred-pound boulder bearing an inscription that has been variously "translated" since it came to light in 1812 (figure 31.1). In that year, a Dr. Richard Fletcher claimed to have discovered the stone near the head of Yarmouth Harbour.

The stone began to receive serious attention in 1875 when an antiquarian convinced himself the markings were Norse runes that read "Harkko's son addressed the men" (Phillips 1884). But in 1934, another amateur runeologist (said by one critic to be "able to find runes in any crevice or groove in any stone and decipher them" [Olessen n.d.]) decided the "runes" actually read "Leif to Eric Raises [this Monument]" (Archives 1999).

As qualified runic scholars disparaged the imaginative "translations" and debunked a Viking source for the inscription (Goldring 1975), others came forward to "identify" the apparent writing as an "old Japanese" dialect, or the work of early Greeks, Hungarians, or others, including Nova Scotian Micmac Indians. Zoologist-cum-epigrapher (decipherer of ancient texts) Barry Fell thought the writing ancient Basque, which he interpreted as "Basque people have subdued this land," but he later changed his mind to favor a Norse source (Archives 1999; Surette 1976; Colombo 1988, 44–45). (Fell believed America was extensively visited by

Figure 31.1. Yarmouth Stone. Discovered in 1812, these markings have been described as representing a mysterious—possibly Viking—inscription, an accident of nature, or a deliberate hoax. (Photo by Joe Nickell)

Old World peoples far in advance of Columbus, but critics accuse him of lacking "a scientific, skeptical, or deductive approach" [Feder 1996, 101]). An editorial in the Yarmouth *Vanguard* expressed the view of many local skeptics when it asked regarding the inscription, "Why don't we just say it was left by aliens?" ("Runic" 1993)

I began my own investigation of the stone by consulting Viking archaeologist Birgitta Wallace Ferguson (1999) and Nova Scotia Museum ethnologist Ruth Holmes Whitehead (1999) who concluded, respectively, that the inscription was neither runic nor Micmac. It appears, in fact, to represent no known alphabet (Ashe et al. 1971) and is "not translatable" since, reportedly, "the characters were taken from a number of different alphabets" (Goldring 1975). Therefore, it was probably "made by the later English, either for amusement or for fraudulent purposes" (Webster n.d.).

There has long been speculation that the markings were mere fissures, glacial striations, or the product of some other natural agency (Nickerson 1910; Surette 1976), possibly subsequently enhanced, but that view has been challenged (Wickens 1967). The museum's curator, Eric Ruff, graciously gave me full access to the stone, and I proceeded to do a rubbing (using Japanese art paper and a lithographic crayon) as well as an oblique-light examination (used to enhance surface irregularities). I saw no significant evidence of similar natural markings elsewhere on the stone.

Using a stereomicroscope removed from its base, I examined the inscription at considerable length and was able to determine the successive stages of alterations the inscription had undergone, "enhancements" confirmed by knowledgeable sources. According to an early account, the original carving was done somewhat "delicately" and "barely penetrated the layers of quartz" (Farish [1857?]). Later, the characters were traced over with white paint, and still later—in the 1930s—a well-meaning curator further altered the markings by rechiseling them (Ruff 1999)—their dashed-line appearance suggesting the use of a slotted screwdriver or narrow chisel pounded, punchlike, with a hammer or mallet.

The superficiality of the original carving, together with the diminutive size of the inscription and the stone's location—in a marshy area, in a cove, at the head (rather than mouth) of the harbor—does not inspire confidence that the inscription was meant to command the attention of others. (Fell, for example, believed it was intended as a warning sign to other explorers that the land had already been claimed [Surette 1976].) Thus, scrutiny must fall back upon the original "discoverer," Dr. Richard Fletcher. A retired army surgeon, Fletcher had moved to the area in 1809 and lived there until his death a decade later. His descendants say he had a reputation as "a character," and there is a family legend that he had probably carved the inscription himself (Ruff 1999). According to one direct descendant, "It was always believed in the family, that he had done it as a joke" (quoted in Goldring 1975). So it would appear that the Yarmouth Stone is but another in a series of fakes that includes the Grave Creek, West Virginia, sandstone disc of 1838; the Davenport, Iowa, "Moundbuilder" tablets of 1877; and the notorious Kensington, Minnesota, rune stone of 1898 (Feder 1996, 114–15, 131).

Indeed, a second Yarmouth-area artifact was the Bay View Stone "discovered" in 1895 but since lost (Ruff 1999). It bore a similar inscription to that of the Yarmouth Stone but "was proven to be a hoax perpetrated by a local hotel owner and displayed outside the hotel for several years" (MacInnis 1969).

References

Archives of Yarmouth County Museum. 1999. Display text for artifact No. 1993: 3; file Y MS 13 (including letters, clippings, etc.).

Ashe, Geoffrey, et al. 1971. *The Quest for America.* New York: Praeger, 162–63.

Colombo, John Robert. 1988. *Mysterious Canada: Strange Sights, Extraordinary Events, and Peculiar Places.* Toronto: Doubleday Canada.

Farish, G.J. [1857?] Quoted in Goldring 1975.

Feder, Kenneth L. 1996. *Frauds, Myths, and Mysteries,* 2nd ed. Mountain View, Calif.: Mayfield.

Ferguson, Birgitta Wallace. 1999. Telephone interview by Joe Nickell, June 17.

Goldring, Charles Spencer. 1975. The Yarmouth "runic stone" explained. *The Vanguard* (Yarmouth, N.S.), Aug. 13; letter to editor, Aug. 27.

MacInnis, George A. 1969. Vinland map hoax? *Light-Herald* (Yarmouth, N.S.), May 1.

Morris, Chris. 1999. Skeptic shoots holes in Maritimes tales. *Globe and Mail* (Toronto), June 30.

Nickerson, Moses H. 1910. A short note on the Yarmouth "runic stone." *Nova Scotia Historical Society,* vol. 17, 51–52.

Olessen, Tryggvi. n.d. Quoted in Goldring 1975.

Phillips, Henry, Jr. 1884. Runic inscription Near Yarmouth, Nova Scotia. *Yarmouth Herald,* July 23 (reprint in Archives 1999).

Ruff, Eric. 1999. Interview by Joe Nickell, July 3 (citing conversation with Katryn Ladd some twenty-five years before).

The "runic stone"—why don't we just say it was left by aliens? 1993. Editorial, *The Vanguard* (Yarmouth, N.S.), Aug. 17.

Surette, Allan. 1976. Runic stone? Another explanation. *Light-Herald* (Yarmouth, N.S.), May 12.

Webster, K.G.T. n.d. Quoted in Goldring 1975.

Whitehead, Ruth Holmes. 1999. Interview by Joe Nickell, July 1.

Wickens, A. Gordon. 1967. The runic stone. *The Vanguard* (Yarmouth, N.S.), Feb. 8.

Chapter 32

Communicating with the Dead?

Thanks to modern mass media, old-fashioned spiritualism is undergoing something of a revival. Witness James Van Praagh's best-selling *Talking to Heaven* (1997) and the talk-show popularity of Van Praagh and other mediums like Rosemary Altea, George Anderson, and John Edward. Like Van Praagh before him, Edward was featured on the June 19, 1998, *Larry King Live* television show. King promoted Edward's forthcoming video and book, both titled *One Last Time*—"meaning," King explained, "saying good-bye to someone who is gone."

Although purported communication with spirits of the dead is ancient (for example, the biblical Witch of Endor conjured up the ghost of Samuel at the request of King Saul [1 Sam. 28:7–20]), modern spiritualism began in 1848 at Hydesville, New York (as mentioned in Chapter 3). Two young girls, Maggie and Katie Fox, pretended to communicate with the ghost of a murdered peddler. Although four decades later they confessed how their "spirit rappings" had been faked, in the meantime spiritualism had spread like wildfire across the United States and beyond. The great magician and escape artist Harry Houdini (1874–1926) spent the last years of his life crusading against phony spirit mediums and exposing their bogus "materializations" and other physical phenomena such as spirit photography.

A case I investigated in Lexington, Kentucky, in 1985 illustrates the dangers fake mediums risk in producing such phenomena. Laboratory analyses of certain "spirit precipitations" (figure 32.1) revealed the presence of solvent stains, and a recipe for such "precipitations" from the book *The Psychic Mafia* (Keene 1976)—utilizing a solvent to transfer images from printed photos—enabled me to create similar spirit pic-

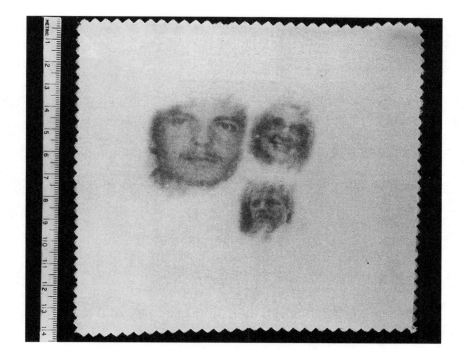

Figure 32.1. Alleged "spirit precipitations" on cloth, produced at a 1985 séance.

tures (figure 32.2). With this evidence, as well as affidavits from a few séance victims, I was able to obtain police warrants against the medium, who operated from the notorious Indiana spiritualist center, Camp Chesterfield (Nickell with Fischer 1988).

Today's mediums—whether charlatans, fantasy-prone personalities, or a bit of both—tend to eschew such physical phenomena. On my visits to New York's spiritualist community, Lily Dale, I have been told that all such productions are now effectively prohibited there due to fakery in the past. Anyone claiming to produce authentic physical phenomena—like trumpet voices, slate writing, or apports (objects allegedly transported by spirits)—must pass the scrutiny of a committee. As a consequence, the dark-room séance is becoming a thing of the past.

Like the mediums at Lily Dale (figure 32.3), Van Praagh, Edward, and most others now limit themselves to the other major category of spiritualist offerings: "mental phenomena," the purported use of "psy-

Figure 32.2. Images produced experimentally by author.

chic ability" such as clairvoyance (inner sight), clairaudience (perceived voices), and clairsentience (extrasensory feelings) to obtain messages from the spirit realm. Because such mediums avoid the tricks of producing physical phenomena, it is more difficult to expose spiritualist charlatans— that is, to distinguish between mediums who practice intentional deception and those who may be self-deceived (believing they really communicate with the dead). What *can* be done, however, is to focus not on the medium's motives but on his or her ability, such as by setting up suitable scientific tests (e.g. to measure supposed clairvoyance) or by analyzing a medium's readings.

When I appeared on radio programs to debate James Van Praagh (on "The Stacy Taylor Show," San Diego, May 19, 1998) and Dorothy Altea (on "The Gil Gross Show," New York, June 15, 1998), I began by inviting each of the two to contact a deceased relative whom I named. Both declined my very open-minded invitation, saying they had nothing to prove to skeptics. (At one point I remarked to Van Praagh that I believed I could contact spirits as well as he—meaning not at all. He missed

Figure 32.3. A medium giving readings at an outdoor service at Lily Dale, the western New York spiritualist colony.

my point and challenged me to do a reading for him! I responded that I visualized the spirit of Abraham Lincoln, who was telling me that Van Praagh had never contacted anyone "over there." Van Praagh did not think this was funny.)

I did obtain a transcript of John Edward's "spirit" pronouncements on *Larry King Live*, and the results are revealing. They suggest that if Edward really does communicate with the dead, the spirit world must be populated with entities who have little to do but heed the call of self-promoting mystics. And while they seem able to appear virtually on demand, irrespective of distance, they must have lost many of their other faculties—being plagued with poor vision, impaired speech, and faulty memory.

Consider the reading Edward gave to the very first caller on *Larry King Live*, a woman who wanted to contact her mother. "O.K., Linda," says the glib Edward, "the first thing I want to talk about is, I know you're looking for your mom, but I'm getting an older male who's also there on the other side. I feel like this is somebody who would be above you, which means it's like a father figure, or an uncle, and he passes from either lung cancer or emphysema, tuberculosis; it's all problems in the chest area." Edward continues: "O.K., that's the first thing. And I feel like there's a J- or a G-sounding name attached to this." Happily for Edward, Linda responds, "That's my mother." Unfortunately, despite the "hits" the woman is willing to credit, Edward is wrong on both counts, since he was not talking about the mother but some "father figure" Linda is unable to recognize. Edward does not correct the error but proceeds. "She's got a very dominant personality" (as most mothers are no doubt perceived by their offspring), and again Linda offers, "That's my mother. Her first name starts with 'G' and she had emphysema." Thus far, Linda's persistent credulity notwithstanding, Edward has scored only one very weak hit but two clear misses, a foreshadowing of his overall performance.

Edward frequently asks questions—a ploy used by other self-styled mediums and psychics. By the information being provided in interrogative form, it may be considered a hit if correct but otherwise will seem an innocent query. Questioning also keeps the reader from proceeding very far down a wrong path. And so Edward asks, "Does the month of August have a meaning for her, or the eighth of a month?" When Linda replies, "Not that I know of," Edward uses another standard ploy, telling her to "write this down" and becoming even more insistent. This positive reinforcement diverts attention from the failure and gives the caller (or sitter) an opportunity to discover a meaning later. Repeatedly, Edward offers data that is subject to many interpretations. With Linda he returns to an earlier point, insisting that her mother's spirit "is telling me that there's a father figure that's there, so *I don't know if your father's passed* [emphasis added] but there's a father-type figure." Still, Linda is unable to make the connection, replying, "No, my father—I just spoke to him on my son's phone." Edward helpfully suggests "a father-in-law" or at least "a male figure who's there," but Linda still doesn't seem able to verify the claim. Edward is bailed out of his dilemma by Larry King who interrupts, "But the important thing is, how is she doing?" This gives Edward the opportunity to tell Linda, "Your mom is fine"—offering what I call a "moot statement" (one that cannot be proved or disproved).

In all, Edward gave eighteen brief readings on the show, offering (apart from a few ramblings) some 125 statements or pseudostatements (i.e. questions). As I score them, there were four instances of Edward being unable to make contact or supply an answer and twenty-four unverified and sixteen moot statements. I counted forty-one misses. There were about the same number of hits, forty-two (only 33.6 percent of the total). Or perhaps I should say *apparent* hits: most, thirty-four, of these were weak hits (as when Edward envisioned "an older female," with "an M-sounding name," either an aunt or grandmother, he said, and the caller supplied "Mavis" without identifying the relationship). Just six of the statements seemed worthy of being termed *moderate* hits. (For example, Edward told a caller, "there's a dog who's passed also," and she responded by saying her mother "had a dog that passed." I rated this only a moderate hit since dogs are common pets.) And there were just two statements I felt might be deserving of the unqualified label "hit." (Edward asked a caller, who was seeking her husband, "Did you bury him with cigarettes?" and when she responded in the affirmative, queried, "Was this the wrong brand?" The information does seem rather distinctive, but in both instances was phrased as a question and the second one was, of course, a follow-up.)

As these results indicate, John Edward was incorrect about as often as he was right. And considering the weaknesses of his ostensible hits, his success seems little better than might be obtained from guessing. By taking advantage of human nature, simple probabilities, the opportunities for multiple interpretations, and the technique of asking questions as a means of directing the reading, among other techniques, mediums like John Edward may give the impression they are communicating with the dead. The evidence, however, indicates otherwise.

References

Keene, M. Lamar. 1976 (as told to Allen Spraggett). *The Psychic Mafia.* New York: St. Martin.

Nickell, Joe, with John F. Fischer. 1988. *Secrets of the Supernatural.* Buffalo, N.Y.: Prometheus, 47–60.

Van Praagh, James. 1997. *Talking to Heaven.* New York: Dutton.

Chapter 33

Jesus Among the Clouds

According to a Texas newspaper, a Fort Worth woman has obtained a remarkable photograph of Jesus. As reported in the *Arlington (Texas) Morning News*, the woman, a University of Dallas student, took the picture in 1992. She claims she was fleeing an abusive husband, traveling with her two-year-old son on a flight between Albuquerque and Seattle. Soon storm clouds appeared and a voice instructed her to take a photograph through the airplane window. Later, when her film was processed, there was a cloudlike shape of a robed figure. "I knew it was Christ," declared the religious woman. Curiously, she seems not to have been very impressed with the picture at the time but rather put it away in a locked jewelry box on a closet shelf. However, she claims the photo recently fell to the floor (from within a locked box?) while she was rummaging in the closet for something else. Since then she has been telling others—including newspaper, radio, and television reporters—about her experiences (Fields 1997).

I spotted the distinctive picture in some clippings a staff member was sorting for me, and it was (as the saying goes) deja vu all over again. That is because the robed—and headless!—figure in the clouds is ubiquitous. I have seen it in one photo after another over the years, like a visual urban legend. In my opinion, supported by a CSICOP computer comparison, each of the photos is a derivative of a common source. Small differences are explainable by the contrast effects of multigenerational copying. In one incarnation, the picture was labeled "Cloud Angel" and circulated by Betty Malz, author of several religious books. It was accompanied by the following brief narrative:

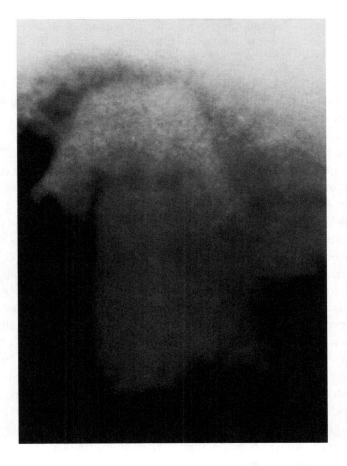

Figure 33.1. Figure-in-the-clouds photograph has had a lengthy history, as "Jesus," an "angel" and (as early as 1974) a "ghost."

A couple flying for their first airplane ride, on their honeymoon, took a whole roll of photos out the window of the plane. They were fascinated by the topside clouds, so much like Cool Whip, or Dairy Queen ice cream! The pilot announced on the intercom that they were flying into turbulence that would last about twenty minutes. Bill and his wife prayed aloud, "Oh Lord, protect us, send the Angels of the Lord to hold this plane upright and keep us safe." Almost immediately the choppy wind subsided. The second officer got on the intercom and announced, "It is amazing. The monitor showed turbulence for twenty minutes and it was over in two minutes." Returning home they found this photo when they picked up their prints at Anderson Pharmacy.

Unfortunately, Ms. Malz had "not kept background material" on her publications, and the alleged honeymooning couple remain unidentified. The date is unknown as well, but the event and picture are referred to in Malz's *Angels Watching Over Me*, first printed in 1986.

The photo is also consistent with verbal descriptions of a "Hugo Christ" picture of 1990. (We have been unable to locate a single copy of this picture, although it was reproduced by the hundreds in the Gastonia, North Carolina, area—over a thousand copies reportedly being circulated by Wal-Mart's photo lab alone.) It was described as "a robed figure, arms outstretched, floating among sinister dark clouds" and was alleged to have been taken at the peak of Hurricane Hugo ("Experts" 1990). On the other hand, a computer imaging expert said of it at the time: "It's a picture we've seen many, many times before. It was made in a darkroom." He explained that the image he examined lacked the three-dimensional qualities of a genuine photograph ("Experts" 1990). Moreover, after the picture was shown on the television program *A Current Affair,* a Montgomery, Alabama, woman stated that twenty years previously, her sister in New Bern, North Carolina, had given her a photo exactly like it. "I knew what they were saying on TV was a lie," the woman declared ("Jesus in Clouds" 1990). And the *Charlotte (North Carolina) Observer* ran an article questioning the photo's authenticity, reporting that "experts said it was a fake and had been circulating throughout the United States for decades" ("Images" 1990).

What is clearly the same figure as the one published in the *Arlington Morning News* appeared as a frontispiece in Peter Haining's 1974 *Ghosts: The Illustrated History*. It is attributed to a Florida man. On the other hand, the same picture illustrates chapter 19 of Hans Holzer's *America's Restless Ghosts,* which states that it was "taken in 1971 during a terrible storm in rural Pennsylvania" by a woman named Marjorie Brooks. She is described as a "friend and associate" of an "ordained spiritual minister," the Reverend Cecilia Hood, who actually sent the photograph to Holzer. Holzer says: "There was a terrible flood and the sky was very dark. Suddenly Miss Brooks observed a figure in white in the sky and took this picture. Was it a way those from the other side wanted to reassure her of her safety?" (Holzer 1993) Whether or not this reported 1971 date represents the original appearance of the Jesus/Angel/Ghost-in-the-Clouds photograph, it is roughly consistent with the statement of the Montgomery woman that she had seen the "Hugo Christ" picture some twenty years before its reputed late-1989 origin. Even so, she said it supposedly originated in North Carolina rather than Pennsylvania.

Obviously this record is incomplete, but it is sufficient to suggest that we have not seen the last of the reappearing picture. Not all newspapers have been as willing as *The Charlotte Observer* to mention the picture's many antecedents—certainly not the *Arlington Morning News*, whose editors we repeatedly contacted but who always asked for more evidence, clearer photos, more time, etc., but who ultimately never felt obliged to join us in an effort to provide a corrective to the initial story by their religion editor.

References

Experts call "Hugo Christ" photo fake. 1990. *(Charleston) Evening Post,* Charleston, S.C., April 12.

Fields, Valerie. 1997. Woman believes photograph reveals Jesus Christ's image.*Arlington (Texas) Morning News,* May 10.

Haining, Peter. 1974. *Ghosts: An Illustrated History.* London: Sidgwick and Jackson.

Holzer, Hans. 1993. *America's Restless Ghosts.* Stamford, Conn.: Longmeadow.

Images remind us Christ is coming. 1990. *The Charlotte (North Carolina) Observer,* April 22.

Jesus in clouds. 1990. *The Charlotte (North Carolina) Observer,* April 20.

Chapter 34

Alien Implants

Science fiction author Whitley Strieber continues to promote the notion of extraterrestrial visitations. His *Communion: A True Story* (1987) told of his own close encounter—actually, what psychologist Robert A. Baker has diagnosed as "a classic, textbook description of a hypnopompic hallucination" (or "waking dream") (Baker and Nickell 1992). Now, several money-making books later, Strieber offers *Confirmation: The Hard Evidence of Aliens Among Us*. The evidence is threefold: UFO sightings (*yawn*), close encounters (*been there, done that*), and—the hard evidence, quite literally—alien implants!

Implants are the latest rage in UFO circles, and Strieber marshals the diagnostic, radiographic, surgical, photographic, and analytic evidence that supposedly indicates—but admittedly does not prove—extraterrestrials are implanting devices in human beings. To put Strieber's claims into perspective, we should first look at the development of the implant concept.

The notion of induced mind/body control is pervasive, with paranormal entities typically having some means of monitoring mortals as a prelude to control. Examples range from mythological beings—like Cupid, whose magical arrows infected men's hearts with love, and Morpheus, who formed sleepers' dreams—to superstitious belief in angelic guidance, demonic possession, voodoo hexes, and zombie slaves. Folklore told of abductions to fairyland from which people returned with addled wits or sapped vitality. Popular literature brought such examples as Bram Stoker's *Dracula* (1897) and the mesmerizing Svengali in George du Maurier's *Trilby* (1894). Science fiction helped develop the alien-take-over concept, with such movies as *The Invasion of the Body Snatchers* (1956). A 1967 *Star Trek* TV episode, "Errand of Mercy," featured a "mind-sifter," a device used by the alien Klingons to probe prisoners' thoughts during interrogations (Okuda and Okuda 1997).

Meanwhile, Kenneth Arnold's 1947 "flying saucer" report touched off the modern era of UFOs and with it an evolving mythology. By the 1950s, "contactees" were claiming to receive messages from the Space People. Then in 1961 came the first widely publicized abduction case, that of Betty and Barney Hill. (Their psychiatrist concluded the couple had shared their dreams rather than having had an actual experience.) (Klass 1974) With the publicizing of the Hill case—notably by John G. Fuller's *The Interrupted Journey* in 1966 and NBC television's prime-time movie "The UFO Incident" in 1975—claims of alien abductions and "medical" examinations began to proliferate. So did another phenomenon, the abduction guru: a self-styled alien researcher and often amateur hypnotist who elicits fantasy abduction tales from suitably imaginative individuals (Baker and Nickell 1992, 203).

Reports of alien implants may have begun with the alleged abduction of a Massachusetts woman, Betty Andreasson, which supposedly took place in early 1967. However, the case was not publicized widely until 1979, when Raymond E. Fowler published his book *The Andreasson Affair*. Andreasson, who seems to have had a predisposition to fantasize, claimed the aliens had removed an apparently implanted device, in the form of a spiked ball, by inserting a needle up her nose. Fowler speculated that the BB-size implant could have been "a monitoring device" (Fowler 1979, 191). About this time, the concept of "psychotronic technology"—i.e., mind control by means of physical devices—entered ufology (Sachs 1980, 200, 262).

Andreasson's abduction report was followed by that of a Canadian woman named Dorothy Wallis. She described a similar implant under hypnosis, which seemed to explain an earlier "compulsion" to meet with the aliens (Klass 1989, 122). When we appeared together on *The Shirley Show* (which aired April 15, 1993), I suggested that Mrs. Wallis's story appeared to imitate Andreasson's. She countered that her abduction came first, but I observed that she did not come forward until about 1983 and that Andreasson's much earlier publication gave the latter the stronger claim (Nickell 1995; Wray 1993). In time, David Jacobs, a historian-turned-abduction-researcher, found the Andreasson/Wallis-type implant to be stereotypical among abductee claimants.

> The object is as small as or smaller than a BB, and it is usually smooth, or has small spikes sticking out of it, or has holes in it. The function of this device is unknown: it might be a locator so that the targeted individual can be found and abducted; it might serve as a monitor of hormonal changes; it might facilitate the molecular changes needed for transport and entrance; it might facilitate communication. . . . Sometimes nosebleeds occur after this procedure. Both child and adult abductees have seen physicians for nosebleed problems, and have discovered odd holes inside their noses. (Jacobs 1992, 95–96)

Alas, Jacobs relates,"Several abductees have reported that a ball-shaped object either dropped out of their nose or was expelled when they blew their nose. All of these expulsions happened before they knew they had been abducted; in each case they thought they had inexplicably inhaled something and discarded the object or lost it" (96).

Actually, one of these items did survive and was thoroughly investigated by the Center for UFO Studies (CUFOS) in the late 1980s. Possessed by a self-claimed abductee, the "implant" had supposedly been stuck up the man's nose by his extraterrestrial abductors but was later dislodged when he caught a cold and blew his nose. CUFOS investigator Don Schmitt accompanied UFO historian Jerome Clark, editor of CUFOS's journal *International UFO Reporter*, to meet the man in an Illinois restaurant. As Clark relates the incident, after brief exchanges, the man unwrapped the object. "Don and I stared at it incredulously. *It was a ball bearing.*" Despite the obvious identification, the CUFOS team sought the man's X-rays, which "showed nothing out of the ordinary," Clark states. Nevertheless, CUFOS went on to have the alleged implant scientifically examined, whereupon it proved to be "an utterly ordinary terrestrial artifact" (Clark 1992).

In contrast to Jacobs's similar, but generally unavailable, brain/nasal implants are the current devices. The change in the type and location of implants is remarkable. Since 1994, alleged implants have been surgically recovered, but they've become remarkably diverse: one looks like a shard of glass, another a "triangular" (or possibly "star-shaped") piece of metal, still another a carbon fiber, and so on. None was located in the brain or nasal cavity, instead being recovered from such extremities as toe, hand, shin, external ear, etc.; some were accompanied by scars while others were not (Linderman 1998; Strieber 1998, 171–247).

Indeed, so varied are the implants, their sites, and other characteristics that they recall a similar craze of yore. During the witch mania of the fifteenth through seventeenth centuries, inquisitors identified certain "witch's marks" that could be almost anything. As one writer explains, "Papillomas, hemangiomas, blemishes, warts, welts, and common moles were seized upon as authentic witch's marks, and these marks invariably determined the destiny of the suspect" (Rachleff 1971).

Several disparate implants are described in the best-selling *Abduction: Human Encounters With Aliens* by Harvard psychiatrist John E. Mack. For example, two small nodules that appeared on an abductee's wrist were surgically removed and analyzed in a pathology laboratory. The lab found the tissue unremarkable (Mack 1994, 27–28). Another implant was supposedly placed at the base of an abductee's skull. Under hypnosis, the man—who believes he has an alternate identity as a humanoid named Orion—described a small, pill-shaped object with protruding wires that, he said, would make it easier for the aliens "to follow me." Astonishingly, Mack makes no mention of any subsequent attempt to locate and remove the reported implant (Mack 1994, 172).

Many of the removals have been performed by "California surgeon" Roger Leir. Actually Dr. Leir is not a physician but a podiatrist (licensed to do minor surgery on feet). His office includes UFO magazines for patients to read and displays "bug-eyed alien dolls" (Chan 2001). Leir was accompanied by an unidentified general surgeon (who did not want to be associated with UFO abduction claims). The latter performed all of the above-the-ankle surgeries. A critic of implant claims, Dr. Virgil Priscu, a department head in an Israeli teaching hospital, observes that a foreign object can enter the body unnoticed, as during a fall, or while running barefoot in sand or grass—even as a splinter from a larger impacting object (Priscu 1998). Such foreign objects may become surrounded by a membrane, like several of the "implants" removed by Dr. Leir and others (Lindemann 1998); depending on the material, they may also degrade over time, leaving only a small bit of "reaction" tissue in place of the foreign object—"No mystery, no 'implants,'" says Dr. Priscu. He challenged Dr. Leir's associate, a hypnotherapist named Derrel Sims, to provide specimens, or at least color slides of them, for analysis at a forensic medical institute but reported he received no cooperation. Dr.

Priscu also noted the lack of the scientific peer-review process in the case of implant claims. Although he is himself an admitted UFO believer, he states, "I also firmly believe that meticulous research by competent persons is the way to the truth" (Priscu 1998).

In *Confirmation*, Whitley Strieber describes several of the implants, including one removed from his own external ear by a physician. It turned out to be collagen, the substance from which cartilage is formed (Strieber 1998, 228). Strieber admits that the promised "hard evidence" provided by implants is not so hard after all: "I hope this book will not cause a rush to judgement," he writes, "with skeptics trying to prove that evidence so far retrieved is worthless while UFO believers conclude that it is proof. Both approaches are a waste of time, because the conclusive evidence has not yet been gathered" (Strieber 1998, 255). A similar admission comes from ufologist David E. Pritchard, an M.I.T. physicist who, with Mack, hosted the 1992 Abduction Study Conference at M.I.T. (Pritchard emphasized that the conference was merely held there; it was *not* an M.I.T. conference.) Pritchard gave a presentation on a suspected implant, a tiny object with a collagen sheen that he acknowledged *might* have grown in the alleged abductee. (It had supposedly been implanted in the man's penis but worked itself out over time.) Pritchard conceded: "I don't have anything conclusive. What I have is just what you usually get in this business: it will provide more beliefs for the believers and will be instantly skeptified by the skeptics, and it's not very good evidence if it won't move the lines at all. The point is to convince the jury."(Bryan 1995, 50–51).

Of course, it is not skeptics but implant advocates who have the burden of proof—a burden they have emphatically failed to meet. Indeed, the implant concept—like the larger alien abduction phenomenon itself—lacks proof that it has an objective reality. Instead, the evidence indicates it is simply part of an evolving UFO mythology. Its theme of entities exerting influence over humans is one seen in many variants, ranging from ancient mythical lore to modern science fiction and persisting in some form in popular culture. There have always been individuals—fantasizers as well as paranoid schizophrenics—who have heard voices that directed or controlled them, voices that are expressions of hopes and fears. Therefore it seems safe to predict that there will be further claims of "hard evidence" of extraterrestrial visitation. We may also expect that misperceptions and exaggerations of natural phenomena, as well as hoaxes, will abound.

References

Baker, Robert A., and Joe Nickell. 1992. *Missing Pieces: How to Investigate Ghosts, UFOs, Psychics, and Other Mysteries.* Buffalo, N.Y.: Prometheus, 227.

Bryan, C.D.B. 1995. *Close Encounters of the Fourth Kind.* New York: Knopf, 50–51.

Chan, Cecilia. 2001. Out of this world: Doctor's sideline is extraterrestrial investigations. *Daily News* (Woodland Hills, Calif.), March 18.

Clark, Jerome. 1992. Abduction artifact. *Fate*, April, 19–22.

Fowler, Raymond E. 1979. *The Andreasson Affair.* Englewood Cliffs, N.J.: Prentice-Hall.

Jacobs, David. 1992. *Secret Life: Firsthand Documented Accounts of UFO Abductions.* New York: Simon & Schuster.

Klass, Philip J. 1974. *UFOs Explained.* New York: Vintage, 299.

———. 1989. *UFO Abductions: A Dangerous Game.* Buffalo, N.Y.: Prometheus.

Linderman, Debra L. 1998. Surgeon tells first results of implant analysis. Excerpted from CNI News, vol. 15.8 (Feb. 26, 1996).

Mack, John E. 1994. *Abduction: Human Encounters with Aliens.* New York: Ballantine.

Nickell, Joe. 1995. *Entities: Angels, Spirits, Demons, and Other Alien Beings.* Amherst, N.Y.: Prometheus, 211.

Okuda, Michael, and Denise Okuda. 1997. *The Star Trek Encyclopedia.* New York: Pocket, 141, 303.

Priscu, Virgil. 1998. Rebuttal to Derrell Sims the implant guy! Internet posting to the UFO Folklore Center. http://www.shoah.free-online.co.uk/801/Abduct/sims.html

Rachleff, Owen S. 1971. *The Occult Conceit.* Chicago: Cowles, 108.

Sachs, Margaret. 1980. *The UFO Encyclopedia.* New York: Perigee.

Strieber, Whitley. 1985. *Communion: A True Story.* New York: William Morrow.

———. 1998. *Confirmation: The Hard Evidence of Aliens Among Us.* New York: St. Martin's.

Wray, Shannon. 1993. Notes of interview with Dorothy Wallis for *The Shirley Show*, n.d. (faxed to Joe Nickell March 31; show taped April 1).

Chapter 35

Sleuthing a Psychic Sleuth

On February 7, 1996, I appeared on the *Mark Walberg Show,* a television program produced in New York City. Among other guests—who included an alien abductee and her hypnotherapist, a UFO conspiracy theorist, and a pair of ghost hunters—there were two "psychics," one of whom claimed to assist police departments. He was Ron Bard from southern New York State.

Walberg asked, "Ron, how did you discover this ability?"

Bard replied, "Well, it's been in my family for quite a few generations. I've solved over 110 murder cases and returned 150 missing children in my career so far," he boasted.

"And how did you help them . . . ?"

"The one that stands in my mind most," Bard replied, "was two girls found in plastic bags in Harrison, New York. Anybody can call the Chief of Harrison Police Department and find this out for fact," he challenged.

I resolved to do just that.

Bard continued: "They found two girls in plastic bags. We went to the scene. The girls weren't identifiable. We identified the girls, found an unmarked key in the pocket, went to the south Bronx, unlocked the door—there is a lot of putting the evidence together inevitably—the key worked in the lock and that's how we found the murderer" (Bard 1996).

This certainly sounded like an amazing case of psychic power. Unfortunately, an examination of news stories relating to the case (Gannett 1984) and the testimony of the Harrison police chief (Dorio 1996a, 1996b) paint quite a different picture. The first newspaper account was March 9, 1984. It reported that "the bound, frozen bodies of two unidentified women, possibly teenagers"—each in a green trash bag tied at the top with rope—had been discovered near Harrison High School. "One of the women was white, the other black," the newspaper reported. "Both had their hands tied behind their backs with twine, and were curled up, almost in a fetal position." A detective was quoted as saying that the young women appeared to have been dumped at the site after being killed—the cause of death not yet having been determined. Subsequent reports told of the difficulty police were having in learning the identities of the two victims, neither of whom was carrying identification. The victims had been fully clothed, and there was no evidence of sexual abuse. They had died from suffocation. An item found in one of the plastic bags—which police would not identify at the time—led them to a particular area of the Bronx. The item was a key that had been made in a store on Southern Boulevard, so the police search was focused on that vicinity.

In just over a month, police circulars bearing descriptions and morgue photos of the victims, together with articles in a Spanish-language newspaper, had brought forth the parents of one young woman and the mother of another—each looking for a missing child. They identified their respective daughters as Daisy Rivera, 20, and Iris Comacho, 15, both from the Bronx and both Hispanic. The key in Miss Rivera's possession fit the door to her apartment. Before that, according to an April 15 newspaper account, police thought the key might have belonged to the murderer.

Eventually, after a five-month investigation of the case, in the aftermath of a drug raid in Yonkers, police were able to arrest three men for the murders. Eyewitnesses named those responsible and told how one man had ordered the older of the two females killed because he thought she was an undercover agent, and the teenage girl because she had said something that offended him. Each of the three killers was convicted and sentenced to two consecutive sentences of twenty-five years to life—the maximum under New York law (Gannett 1984).

Only a couple of news reports relating to the case referred to a psychic. And although no name was given, it was not Ron Bard but his mother (Dorio 1996a). "She" was described in the news reports as a "volunteer psychic." Her involvement had been permitted by the lieutenant in charge of the case, who spoke of what he considered her accuracy in the case. One account attributes to him the statement that she helped both to identify the bodies and hone in on the murderer, while another account quotes him as saying, "She helped primarily for identification." In fact, she helped in neither way.

If the psychic had indeed helped in the identification, the lieutenant would have to have withheld that information from his own detectives. We know this because a major detective on the case was the current Harrison police chief, Louis Dorio, who insists that "the identification was done by sheer police work, not a psychic" (Dorio 1996b). Indeed, the lieutenant himself admitted that "what she told us didn't really lead to things, but after we discovered answers, we could confirm what she told us." This, in fact, is the major technique used by so-called "police psychics" and it is called *retrofitting* (discussed in chapter 17). The alleged clairvoyant tosses out several "clues," like "water" and "the number 7." Typically, these are merely puzzling to the police, but after they solve the crime by ordinary if often dogged detective work, the psychic retroactively fits the "clues" to the now-known facts. Credulous police officers may even assist in this. The psychic does not even need many of the "clues" to be counted as hits; the rest will be conveniently forgotten, or dismissed as the natural consequence of an imperfect "power," or heroically interpreted.

Chief Dorio gave the following account of the Harrison murder investigation:

> I was one of the primary investigators on what we refer to as the "Bag Murder Case" in 1984. As such, I never worked with Mr. Bard. I did meet his mother a couple of times and she provided some visions or whatever on things that at the time were of no use to our investigation. Some of the things she said, a true believer may give credence to; for example, she held a key and said, "I see a red door." That information did not help in the investigation as our area of search was the south Bronx and there are thousands of red doors. After we found the residence (through investigation), it did turn out to have a red apartment door. That is an example of the information supplied. (Dorio 1996a)

In other words, the psychic was using the technique of retrofitting. Chief Dorio continued: "This case was solved by information cultivated and investigated by those of us who were involved. Our arrest and convictions were due to diligent police work, not visions" (Dorio 1996a). He added somewhat sarcastically, "I do not remember seeing Mr. Bard on the witness stand during the trial," and he concluded, "I would strongly deny that any involvement by Mr. Bard solved this case" (Dorio 1996a).

This is in sharp contrast to the statements and claims made on the *Mark Walberg Show* by Ron Bard. The case that he cited as apparently his best, "the one that stands in my mind most," was one that as far as the police and reporters knew was solely his mother's. It is true that on the TV show he said "we," instead of just "I," which we may now see as a possible reference to his mother's involvement. If he did in fact collaborate with her on the case, it is curious that he has so completely distorted the basic facts—stating for example, that a key led to the discovery of the murderer when in fact it did not. The bottom line is that neither Bard nor his mother helped solve the double homicide. If this is one of the best cases he can cite, his other cases must be poor indeed.

References

Bard, Ron. 1996. Interviewed on the *Mark Walberg Show,* New York City, Feb. 7.

Dorio, Louis A. 1996a. Letter to Joe Nickell, Feb. 20.

———. 1996b. Follow-up letter to Joe Nickell, n.d., together with annotated newspaper clippings. (See Gannett 1984.)

Gannett Westchester Newspapers. 1984. Various clippings from March to September (inclusive) supplied and annotated by Harrison, N.Y., police chief Louis A. Dorio.

Chapter 36

Adventure of
the Weeping Icon

On Tuesday, September 3, 1996, at the request of *The Toronto Sun*, I headed to Canada to investigate the world's latest "weeping icon." I was to meet with reporters at the newspaper's King Street offices and from there to be escorted to a Greek Orthodox Church in Toronto's East York district. Church officials had promised the *Sun* they could examine the icon at 11:00 P.M., and I was enlisted for that purpose. In addition to my overnight bag, I also packed a "weeping icon kit" consisting of a camera and close-up lenses, a stereomicroscope removed from its base, and various vials, pipettes, bibulous paper, and other collection materials.

As we arrived in the neighborhood, however, I saw not the nearly deserted church I had expected to be awaiting our special appointment but rather traffic congestion and a line of pilgrims stretching far off into the night. I waited outside with my conspicuous case while reporters went to learn that the promise of an examination had been retracted. I determined to proceed anyway and do the best I could. A *Sun* reporter of Greek extraction feared I might start a riot, but his colleague, Scot Magnish, who had brought me there, was only concerned for my safety. (It was not wise for *him* to go inside, given rumored responses to his critical article on the phenomenon published in the latest edition of the newspaper.) After stuffing some essentials from my kit into my pockets, I handed Scot my case, turned, and bounded up the steps of the little church two at a time. Behind me, *Sun* photographer Craig Robertson rushed to keep up. We passed a lady who shouted the admission price ("two dollars fifty cents") at us; I shouted back, *"Toronto Sun!"* and kept going.

Figure 36.1. Author peers over shoulder of priest—once defrocked for working in an Athens brothel—as he illuminates a "weeping" icon at a Greek Orthodox church in Toronto. (Photo courtesy *Toronto Sun*)

Inside, the church was swelteringly hot. Nevertheless, people milled about for a time after viewing the controversial icon of the Madonna and Child, while new pilgrims passed before it. A table filled with candles and a crude sign, "PLEASE DO NOT TOUCH THE ICON OF VIRGIN MARY," kept the curious at bay. An attendant refused my request for a sample of the tears and pretended to ignore me when I asked again in a louder voice.

A hanging oil lamp partially obscured the face of the Madonna, but by moving my head from side to side and thus catching the light on the surface of the picture, I made several important discoveries. First, the icon was a fake—not an original wood-panel painting at all but merely a color photographic *print*. In addition, the "tears" did not emanate from the eyes but from somewhere near the top of the Virgin's head, and so by definition the image was not "weeping." Moreover, one of the four rivulets was smeared and from its appearance looked "suspiciously oily" (as I told the *Sun*).

The latter point was quite significant since real tears, or even mere water, would quickly dry in the hot atmosphere of the church. But a non-drying oil (such as olive oil) would remain fresh and glistening indefinitely—just the trick for "weeping" icons and one apparently more commonly used than the hidden tubes and special chemicals so often proposed by theorists. During the quarter of an hour or so that I observed the image, there was no fresh flow of "tears"—just the same unchanging rivulets I saw at the beginning. (There were also fine droplets between the streaks as if spattered on, possibly from the oil lamp that almost touched the print.)

At length, I persuaded the priest, the Reverend Ieronimos Katseas, to provide a better view—at least for the photographer. Katseas pulled the lamp away with one hand while holding a candle close to the Madonna's face with the other. Photographer Robertson clicked away, producing the accompanying photograph.

In the subsequent article by Magnish and two colleagues, I was quoted as saying that the phenomenon was "more carnival sideshow than miracle" and that I was troubled by the withdrawal of the promise to allow the icon to be examined. "It would seem to me a miracle could withstand a little skepticism," I stated, complaining further about being kept at a distance and being refused a sample of the "tears" (Magnish et al. 1996).

In the meantime, reporters learned that Katseas had been embroiled in considerable earlier controversy. It turns out that he had also preached at a Greek Orthodox Cathedral in Queens, New York, when an icon there—that of a mid-nineteenth nun, St. Irene—began crying and drawing hundreds of thousands of pilgrims, some as far away as India and Japan. More than a year later, after I had investigated that icon with New York Area Skeptics and concluded that the phenomenon was bogus (Nickell 1993), the icon was stolen at gunpoint. Supposedly, Katseas refused to cooperate in producing the key to the Plexiglas case that housed it and was pistol-whipped, after which the bandits broke the lock and made off with the "miraculous" icon. It was subsequently returned—minus $800,000 in gems and golden jewelry that decorated it—under conditions that still remain controversial (Christopoulos 1996).

Katseas was also defrocked in 1993 when it was learned he had previously worked in a brothel in Athens. A church document on the priest's excommunication states that a New York ecclesiastical court found him guilty of slander, perjury, and defamation, as well as being "in the em-

Figure 36.2. On a later occasion, author collects samples of oil from icon under media scrutiny.

ploy of a house of prostitution" (Goldhar 1996). In fact, in 1987 sworn testimony before a Greek judge, Katseas admitted he had been so employed (Magnish et al. 1996).

A rumor I heard from neighborhood residents was soon confirmed by a newspaper report, namely that the Toronto icon began weeping after the East York church found itself financially strapped with an accumulated debt from mortgages of almost $271,000. In the interim, in June, the church dispatched Father Archimandrite Gregory from Colorado with instructions to evict Katseas from the church, but the matter became mired in the courts. After the icon began "weeping," Gregory cast doubt on the phenomenon, stating in a letter, "It would not be surprising if this were a hoax, in order to attract people to spend money" (Goldhar 1996). Such revelations and opinions, however, had no effect on some pilgrims. Said one woman: "I don't care if there's a pipe and a hose behind that picture. I don't care if the Virgin Mary jumps right out of the painting. You either believe in miracles or you don't. I believe" (DiManno 1996).

On the other hand, a woman living in the neighborhood stated, "We all need something to believe in, but this is preying on those who really need a miracle" (Goldhar 1996).

On August 27, 1997, I was invited back to the church—this time by attorneys for the parent church authority. With a police guard and under scrutiny from the Canadian news media (figure 36.2), I examined the icon (which was dismantled from the frame it had acquired by a carpenter hired for the purpose) and took samples of the oil for the Metropolitan Toronto Police Fraud Squad for testing (Kudrez 1997). Some time later, at a forensic conference in Nova Scotia, I learned that the oil had indeed been found to be a nondrying oil, but that—of course—no one could say who put it on the icon, so the case fizzled.

References

Christopoulos, George. 1996. Priest's 2nd "miracle" $800GS from "crying" N.Y. icon stolen. *Toronto Sun*, Sept. 8.

DiManno, Rosie. 1996. Moolah everywhere as the pious mob weeping Madonna. *Toronto Star*, Sept. 4.

Goldhar, Kathleen. 1996. Church of "weeping" Virgin headed by defrocked priest. *Toronto Star*, Sept. 4.

Kudrez, Anastasia. 1997. Crying foul. *Buffalo News*, Aug. 29.

Magnish, Scot, Philip Lee-Shanok, and Robert Benzie. 1996. Expert unmoved by crying icon's "tears." *Toronto Sun*, Sept. 4.

Nickell, Joe. 1993. *Looking for a Miracle*. Amherst, N.Y.: Prometheus, 54–55.

Chapter 37

The Secrets of Oak Island

It has been the focus of "the world's longest and most expensive treasure hunt" and "one of the world's deepest and most costly archaeological digs" (O'Connor 1988, 1, 4), as well as being "Canada's best-known mystery" (Colombo 1988, 33) and indeed one of "the great mysteries of the world." It may even "represent an ancient artifact created by a past civilization of advanced capability" (Crooker 1978, 7, 190). The subject of these superlatives is a mysterious shaft on Oak Island in Nova Scotia's Mahone Bay. For some two centuries, greed, folly, and even death have attended the supposed "Money Pit" enigma.

The Saga

Briefly, the story is that in 1795 a young man named Daniel McInnis (or McGinnis) was roaming Oak Island when he came upon a shallow depression in the ground. Above it, hanging from the limb of a large oak was an old tackle block. McInnis returned the next day with two friends who—steeped in the local lore of pirates and treasure troves—set to work to excavate the site. They soon uncovered a layer of flagstones and, ten feet deeper, a tier of rotten oak logs. They proceeded another fifteen feet into what they were sure was a man-made shaft, but tired from their efforts, they decided to cease work until they could obtain assistance. However, between the skepticism and superstition of the people who lived on the mainland, they were unsuccessful.

The imagined cache continued to lie dormant until early in the next century, when the trio joined with a businessman named Simeon Lynds from the town of Onslow to form a treasure-hunting consortium called

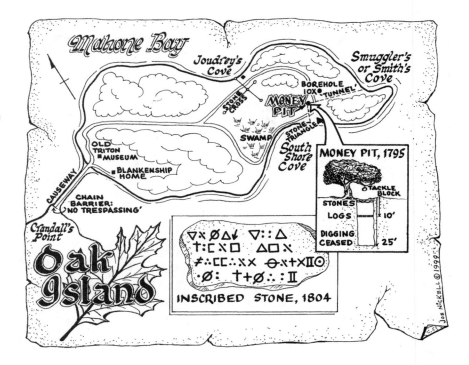

Figure 37.1. Oak Island "treasure map." (Illustration by Joe Nickell)

the Onslow Company. Beginning work about 1803 or 1804 (one source says 1810), they found oak platforms "at exact intervals of ten feet" (O'Connor 1978, 10), along with layers of clay, charcoal, and a fibrous material identified as coconut husks. Then, at ninety feet (or eighty feet, according to one alleged participant) they supposedly found a flat stone bearing an indecipherable inscription. (See figure 37.1). Soon after, probing with a crowbar, they struck something hard—possibly a wooden chest!—but discontinued for the evening. Alas, the next morning the shaft was found flooded with sixty feet of water. Attempting to bail out the pit with buckets, they found the water level remained the same, and they were forced to discontinue the search. The following year, the men attempted to bypass the water by means of a parallel shaft from which they hoped to tunnel to the supposed treasure. But this shaft suffered the same fate, and the Onslow Company's expedition ended (O'Connor 1978, 9–16; Crooker 1993, 14; Harris 1958, 12–22).

Again the supposed cache lay dormant until in 1849 another group,

220

the Truro Company, reexcavated the original shaft. Encountering water, the workers then set up a platform in the pit and used a hand-operated auger to drill and remove cores of material. They found clay, bits of wood, and three links of gold chain—supposed evidence of buried treasure. The Truro Company sank additional nearby shafts, but these too were inundated with water, and work ceased in the fall of 1850. Other operations continued from 1858 to 1862, during which time one workman was scalded to death by a ruptured boiler (O'Connor 1988, 17–31).

The Oak Island Association followed and attempted to intersect the "tunnel" that presumably fed water to the pit. When that 120-foot shaft missed, another was sunk and, reportedly, a three-by-four-foot tunnel was extended about eighteen feet to the "Money Pit" (as it was then known). However, water began coming in again. A massive bailing operation was then set up to drain the pits, when suddenly there was a loud crash as the Money Pit collapsed. It was later theorized that the imagined chests had fallen into a deep void and that the pit may have been booby-trapped to protect the treasure (O'Connor 1988, 29). The Association's work was followed in 1866 by the Oak Island Eldorado Company but without significant results (Harris 1958, 203).

Decades elapsed and in 1897 the Oak Island Treasure Company (incorporated four years earlier) apparently located the long-sought "pirate tunnel" that led from Smith's Cove to the Money Pit. They drilled and dynamited to close off the tunnel. Subsequent borings were highlighted by the discovery of a fragment of parchment upon which was penned portions of two letters (possibly "ri"). They also found traces of a chalklike stone or "cement" (Harris 1958, 91–98). In this same year, Oak Island's second tragedy struck when a worker was being hoisted from one of the pits and the rope slipped from its pulley, plunging him to his death.

After that company ran out of funds, most of the moveable assets were sold at a sheriff's sale in 1900. The new century brought continued searches, with the digging of innumerable drill holes, shafts, and tunnels—so many that "The entire Money Pit area has been topographically demolished, changing completely its original appearance and rendering old maps and charts useless" (Crooker 1978, 190). In 1965, there came yet another tragedy when four men died in a shaft after being overcome either by swamp gas (methane) or by carbon monoxide fumes from the pump's engine (O'Connor 1988, 143–45).

In 1966, a Florida building contractor named Dan Blankenship teamed up with Montréal businessman David Tobias to continue the quest. The partners began an extensive drilling operation, sinking some sixty boreholes the following year alone, and in 1968 enlisted a number of investors in what they named Triton Alliance. Unfortunately, mechanical problems, land disputes, the stock market crash of 1987, and other troubles, including the eventual falling out of the two partners, stopped their projected $10 million "big dig" (Randle 1995). Once open to tourists, the site sank into neglect.

Over the years, the fabled treasure has been the target of dowsers, automatic writers, clairvoyants, channelers, tarot-card readers, dream interpreters, psychic archaeologists, and assorted other visionaries and soothsayers, as well as crank inventors of devices like a "Mineral Wave Ray" and an airplane-borne "treasure smelling" machine—not one having been successful (Preston 1988, 62; O'Connor 1988, 121–36; Finnan 1997, 166–70).

An Investigative Approach

The more elusive the treasure has proved, the more speculation it has engendered. Given the "immense amount of labor" presumably required to construct the pit and the accompanying "flooding tunnel" that served as a "booby trap," presumption of a pirates' hoard has begun to be supplanted by such imagined prizes as the French crown jewels, Shakespeare's manuscripts, the "lost treasure" of the Knights Templar, even the Holy Grail and the imagined secrets of the "lost continent" of Atlantis (Sora 1999, 7–38, 101; Crooker 1978, 153).

But is there a treasure at the bottom of the "Money Pit?" My research into the mystery of Oak Island dates back many years, and I opened a file on the case in 1982. However, except for periodic updates, I put it on hold, largely because the solution seemed to lie in the same direction as those of some other mysteries (Nickell 1980; 1982a; 1982b). However, my interest was revived in 1998 when I was invited to give a presentation at a forensic conference in Nova Scotia. And the following year, when I was asked to address another such conference in nearby New Brunswick, I resolved to place Oak Island on my itinerary (Nickell 1999).

In planning my trip, I attempted to contact Triton's David Tobias, who did not return my call, but I did reach Jim Harvey at the Oak Island Inn and Marina on the nearby mainland. A retired Royal Canadian

Mounted Police officer and licensed private investigator, Harvey is in charge of security for Oak Island, and he was adamant that it is no longer open to visitors. Making not-so-veiled references to the legendary temper of Dan Blankenship, the other Triton partner who still lives on the island, Harvey suggested it would not be safe for me to trespass on the island, although he offered for hire his cabin cruiser for a guided circumnavigation.

Harvey may have had in mind an incident of many years ago involving an altercation between Blankenship and another island resident, Frederick Nolan. According to one source: "One day Blankenship had approached with a rifle in hand and an ugly situation had begun to develop. Eventually the police were called in to calm everybody down and confiscate the gun" (Finnan 1997, 93).

So it was with some trepidation that on the afternoon of July 1, 1999, after arriving at the village of Western Shore and checking in at the Oak Island Inn, I drove to the causeway leading to Oak Island. This land bridge connecting the island to the mainland was constructed in 1965 so that a great excavating machine could be transported to the "treasure" area. Today it is chained off and marked "PRIVATE / NO HUNTING OR TRESPASSING / DANGER."

Apparently this posting did not apply to two local men who were fishing off the causeway. One came over and spoke to me at some length, saying of my proposal to walk across and talk to Mr. Blankenship, "He won't shoot you, but he will probably turn you back." Grabbing my camera I started across, only to be confronted by a barking dog. Soon, however, I was petting the creature when its owner arrived. Blankenship was at first standoffish, having read a Canadian Press article about the "professional skeptic" who was heading to Oak Island (see Nickell 2000). I soon mollified him, and he graciously invited me to his home (much to the later surprise of several locals). I was there until nearly 11:00 p.m., being shown artifacts, photos, papers, and a video made by a camera lowered into a borehole—the fruits of almost thirty-five years of treasure hunting that had earned Blankenship the title of "Oak Island's most obsessive searcher" (O'Connor 1988, 145). The video reveals the interior of a "tunnel," graced with an apparent upright timber and what some imagine to be "chests," a "scoop," and other supposedly man-made artifacts. Blankenship (1999) told me he had located the site of the borehole by dowsing. He spoke of his falling out with Tobias, saying that his former

Figure 37.2. Offshore view of Oak Island showing site of Borehole 10X. The "Money Pit" lies just beyond.

partner dismissed the video and even cast doubt on its authenticity. Dan Blankenship struck me as a sincere man, and he certainly treated me in a gentlemanly fashion, even sparing me a walk back across the causeway in the dark, insisting on driving me instead. The next day, Jim Harvey took me on our prearranged boat trip, permitting me to view the remainder of the island. (See figure 37.2).

The more I investigated the Oak Island enigma, the more skeptical I became. Others had preceded me in supplying what I came to regard as the two main pieces of the puzzle, although apparently no one had successfully fitted the pieces together. One concerned the nature of the "money pit" itself, the other the source of certain elements in the treasure saga, such as the reputed cryptogram-bearing stone.

Manmade or Natural?

Doubts begin with the reported discovery in 1795 of the treasure shaft itself. While some accounts say that the trio of youths spied an old ship's pulley hanging from a branch over a depression in the ground (Harris

1958, 6–8), that is "likely an apocryphal detail added to the story later" and based on the assumption that some sort of lowering device would have been necessary in depositing the treasure (O'Connor 1988, 4). Nevertheless, some authors are remarkably specific about the features, one noting that the "old tackle block" was attached to "a large forked branch" of an oak "by means of a treenail connecting the fork in a small triangle" (Crooker 1978, 17). Another account (cited in Finnan 1997, 28) further claims there were "strange markings" carved on the tree. On the other hand, perhaps realizing that pirates or other treasure hoarders would have been unlikely to betray their secret work by leaving such an obvious indicator in place, some versions of the tale agree that the limb "had been sawed off" but that "the stump showed evidence of ropes and tackle" (Randle 1995, 75).

225

Similarly, the notion that there was a log platform at each ten-foot interval of the pit for a total of nine platforms, is only supported by *later* accounts, and those appear to have been derived by picking and choosing from earlier ones so as to create a composite version of the layers. For example, the account in the *Colonist* (1864) mentions that the original treasure hunters found only flagstones at two feet ("evidently not formed there by nature") and "a tier of oak logs" located "ten feet lower down" (i.e., at twelve feet). They continued some "fifteen feet farther down," whereupon—with no mention of anything further of note—they decided to stop until they could obtain assistance. James McNutt, who was a member of a group of treasure hunters working on Oak Island in 1863, described a different arrangement of layers and was the only one to claim that at fifty feet was "a tier of smooth stones . . . with figures and letters cut on them" (quoted in Crooker 1978, 24).

In 1911 an engineer, Captain Henry L. Bowdoin, who had done extensive borings on the island, concluded that the treasure was imaginary. He questioned the authenticity of various alleged findings (such as the cipher stone and piece of gold chain), and attributed the rest to natural phenomena (Bowdoin 1911). Subsequent skeptics have proposed that the legendary Money Pit was nothing more than a sinkhole caused by the ground settling over a void in the underlying rock (*Atlantic* 1965). The strata beneath Oak Island are basically limestone and anhydrite (Crooker 1978, 85; Blankenship 1999), which are associated with the formation of solution caverns and salt domes (Cavern 1960; Salt Dome 1960). The surface above caverns, as well as over faults and fissures, may be characterized by sinkholes.

Indeed, a sinkhole actually appeared on Oak Island in 1878. A woman named Sophia Sellers was plowing when the earth suddenly sank beneath her team of oxen, forming a hole about eight feet across and more than ten feet deep. Ever afterward known as the "Cave-in Pit," it was located just over a hundred yards east of the Money Pit and directly above the "flood tunnel" (O'Connor 1988, 51). "Today," states D'Arcy O'Connor (1988, 52), "the Cave-in Pit is a gaping circular crater one hundred feet deep and almost as many feet across. And the water in it still rises and falls with the tide."

Geologist E. Rudolph Faribault found "numerous" sinkholes on the mainland opposite Oak Island, and in a geological report of 1911 concluded there was "strong evidence" to indicate that the purported artificial structures on the island were "really but natural sink holes and cavities." Further evidence of caverns in the area came in 1975 when a sewage disposal system was being established on the mainland. Approximately 3,000 feet north of the island, workmen excavating with heavy machinery broke through a rock layer and discovered a 52-foot-deep cavern below (Crooker 1993, 144). Fred Nolan insists that earlier, in 1969, while drilling on Oak Island, Triton broke into a cavern near the fabled treasure shaft at a depth of 165 feet. "Blankenship and Tobias figured that the cavern was man-made," said Nolan, "but it isn't, as far as I'm concerned" (Crooker 1993, 165). And Mark Finnan (1997, 111), writing of "the unique geological nature of Oak Island," states as a fact that "naturally formed underground caverns are present in the island's bedrock." These would account for the flood "booby-traps" that were supposedly placed to guard the "treasure" (Preston 1988, 63).

Today, of course, after two centuries of excavation, the island's east end is "honey-combed with shafts, tunnels and drill holes running in every imaginable direction" (Crooker 1978, 190), complicating the subterranean picture and making it difficult to determine the nature of the original pit. In suggesting that it was a sinkhole, caused by the slumping of debris in a fault, one writer noted that "this filling would be softer than the surrounding ground, and give the impression that it had been dug up before" (Atlantic 1965). Fallen trees could have sunk into the pit with its collapse, or "blowdowns" could periodically have washed into the depression (Preston 1988, 63), later giving the appearance of "platforms" of rotten logs. In fact, just such a pit was discovered in 1949 on the shore of Mahone Bay, about five miles to the south of Oak Island,

when workmen were digging a well. The particular site was chosen because the earth was rather soft there. Reports O'Connor (1988, 172–73):
"At about two feet down a layer of fieldstone was struck. Then logs of
spruce and oak were unearthed at irregular intervals, and some of the
wood was charred. The immediate suspicion was that another Money
Pit had been found."

The treasure seekers and mystery mongers, however, are quick to
dismiss any thoughts that the "shaft" and "tunnels" could be nothing
more than a sinkhole and natural channels. Why, the early accounts would
then have to be "either gross exaggerations or outright lies," says one writer
(O'Connor 1988, 173). For example, what about the reported "pick marks
found in the walls of the pit"? (O'Connor 1988, 173) We have already
seen—with the oak-limb-and-pulley detail—just how undependable are
such story elements. Then what about the artifacts (such as the fragment
of parchment) or the coconut fiber (often carried on ships as dunnage,
used to protect cargo) found at various depths? Again, the sinkhole theory
would explain how such items "worked their way into deep caverns under the island" (Preston 1988, 63).[12]

Secrets Revealed

Assuming the "shaft" is a natural phenomenon, there still remains the
other major piece of the Oak Island puzzle: how do we explain the presence of such cryptic elements as the cipher stone allegedly discovered in
the pit in 1803, a large equilateral triangle (made of beach stones and
measuring ten feet on each side) found in 1897, or a megalithic cross
that Fred Nolan discovered in 1981? (Again see map, Figure 37.1; Finnan
1997, 36, 68–69, 79–82.)

By the early 1980s, I had become aware of parallels between Oak
Island's Money Pit and the arcana of the Freemasons (Nickell 1982).
Theirs is not, they insist, a "secret society" but a "society with secrets."
Carried to North America in the eighteenth century, Masonry has been
defined as "a peculiar system of morality veiled in allegory and illustrated by symbols" (*Masonic Bible* 1964, 26). One of the essential elements of any true Masonic group is "a legend or allegory relating to the
building of King Solomon's Temple" ("Freemasonry" 1978). And an allegory of the "Secret Vault," based on Solomon's fabled depository of

227

certain great secrets, is elaborated in the seventh or "Royal Arch" degree. Among the ruins of the temple, three sojourners discover the subterranean chamber wherein are found three trying-squares and a chest, identified as the Ark of the Covenant, including the key to a cipher (*Masonic* 1964, 12, 37, 63; Lester 1977, 150; Duncan 1972).

No doubt many readers have encountered Secret Vault symbolism—which pertains to lost secrets, buried treasure, and the grave (Macoy 1908, 445; *Revised* 1975, 64 n.22)—without recognizing it as such. For example, Sir Arthur Conan Doyle, a Freemason, not only employed Masonic allusions in several of his Sherlock Holmes stories (Bunson 1994, 84) but penned three tales that evoke Masonry's hidden vault itself. For instance, Holmes uncovers dark secrets in "The Adventure of Shoscombe Old Place." Beneath an old chapel on the Shoscombe property, accessed by stumbling through "loose masonry" (an obvious pun) and proceeding down a steep stairway, Holmes finds himself in a crypt with an "arched . . . roof" (evoking the Royal Arch degree of Masonry). Accompanied by his client—a "Mr. Mason"!—Holmes finds the key to a series of strange mysteries. Similarly allusive Holmes stories are "The Red-Headed League" (featuring a client who sports a Masonic breastpin), and the suggestively titled "The Musgrave Ritual."

In addition to the Sherlockian Secret Vault allegories, there are several examples of the genre that many people have taken at face value, believing them true accounts. One, for example, is the tale of Swift's Lost Silver Mine of eastern Kentucky. In his alleged *Journal*, one "Jonathan Swift" explored the region prior to Daniel Boone, marking a tree with "the symbols of a compasses, trowel and square"—Masonic emblems—and discovering and mining silver (which geologists doubt exists in the region). Leaving to seek backers, Swift says he stored the treasure in a cave and "walled it up with masonry form." Later he became blind and unable to find his fabled treasure (although still capable of writing in his journal). This evokes Masonic ritual wherein a candidate must enter the lodge in *complete blindness* [i.e. blindfolded] to begin his quest for enlightenment (Nickell 1980).

Another such lost-treasure story is found in the purported Beale Papers, which tell a tale of adventure and include unsolved ciphers. Supposedly "Thomas Jefferson Beale" went west in 1817 with a company of men, accidentally discovered a fabulous lode of gold and silver "in a cleft of the rocks" (an expression from the Master Mason Degree), converted some of the treasure to "jewels" (Freemasonry's term for officers' emblems), and "deposited" the trove in a stone-lined "vault" (using language from the Select Masters' degree). The Beale papers were published by a Virginia Freemason named James Ward "with the hope that all that is dark in them may receive light" (evoking the Masonic concept of *lux e tenebris* or "light out of darkness"). (Nickell 1982b)

Then there is the "restless coffins" enigma of the Chase Vault of Barbados. According to proliferating but historically dubious accounts, each time the vault was opened between 1812 and 1820, the coffins were discovered in a state of confusion. The accounts say that after they were reordered, the vault was closed and the stone door "cemented" by "masons" (*cement* in Masonic parlance being that which unites the brethren [Macoy 1908, 454]). Yet the coffins would again be found in disarray upon the next opening. At least two of the men involved in the alleged activities were high-ranking Freemasons. In 1943, another restless-coffins case occurred on the island, this time specifically involving *a party of Freemasons* and the vault being that of *the founder of Freemasonry in Barbados*! (Nickell 1982a)

It now appears that another such tale is the legend of Oak Island, where again we find unmistakable evidence of Masonic involvement. There are, of course, the parallels between the Money Pit story and the Masonic Secret Vault allegory. The "strange markings" reportedly carved on the oak adjacent to the Pit suggest *Masons' Marks*, inscribed signs by which Masons are distinguished (Waite 1970, xx; Hunter 1996, 58). The three alleged discoverers of the Pit would seem to represent the *Three Worthy Sojourners* (with Daniel McInnis representing the *Principal Sojourner*) who discover the Secret Vault in the Royal Arch degree (Duncan 1972, 261). In that ritual, the candidate is lowered on a rope through a succession of trap doors, not unlike the workmen who were on occasion hauled up and down the (allegedly platform-intersected) Oak Island shaft. The tools used by the latter—notably spades, pickaxes, and crowbars (O'Connor 1988, 2; Harris 1958, 15)—represent the three *Working Tools* of the Royal Arch Mason (Duncan 1972, 241). Indeed, when in 1803 the Onslow Company workers probed the bottom of the Pit with a crowbar and struck what they thought was a treasure chest (before water inundated the shaft), their actions recall the Royal Arch degree in which the Secret Vault is located by a sounding blow from a crowbar (Duncan 1972, 263). The parallels go on and on. For example, the soft stone (or "cement"), charcoal, and clay found in the Pit (Crooker 1978, 24, 49) are consistent with the *Chalk, Charcoal and Clay* cited in the Masonic degree of Entered Apprentice as symbolizing the virtues of "freedom, fervency and zeal" (Lester 1977, 60; Hunter 1996, 37).

Then there are the artifacts. Of course, many of these—like the old branding iron found in the swamp or a pair of wrought-iron scissors recovered near the Money Pit (Crooker 1993, 175, 176)—are probably nothing more than relics of the early settlers. Some are actually suspicious, like the links of gold chain found in the Pit in 1849. One account holds that they were planted by workers to inspire continued operations and thus their employment—something that reportedly happened on other occasions, sometimes simply for mischief (O'Connor 1988, 177–78). Other artifacts are more suggestive, like the cipher stone (again see figure 37.1) that disappeared about 1919. Its text has allegedly been preserved, albeit in various forms and decipherments (Rosenbaum 1973, 83). For instance, zoologist-turned-epigrapher Barry Fell thought the inscription was ancient Coptic, its message urging people to remember God lest they perish (Finnan 1997, 148–49). In fact, the text as we have it has been correctly deciphered (and redeciphered and verified by several investigators, me included). Written in what is known as a simple-substitution cipher, it reads, "FORTY FEET BELOW TWO MILLION POUNDS ARE BURIED" (Crooker 1993, 23). Most Oak Island researchers consider the text a hoax—reportedly an 1860s fabrication to lure investors (O'Connor 1988, 14)—but as Crooker (1993, 24) observes, an inscribed stone *did* exist, "having been mentioned in all the early accounts of the Onslow company's expedition." Significantly, a cipher message (with key), found in the Secret Vault, is a central aspect of Freemasonry's Royal Arch degree (Duncan 1972, 248–49).

Other artifacts (Finnan 1997, 67, 80, 83) that appear to have ritualistic significance are the stone triangle and great "Christian Cross" as well as "a handworked heart-shaped stone"—Masonic symbols all. Crooker (1993, 179) notes that "a large amount of time and labor" were spent in laying out the cross, but to what end? Could it have been part of a Masonic ritual? An "old metal set-square" found at Smith's Cove may simply be an innocent artifact, but we recall that three small squares were among the items found in the Secret Vault (Duncan 1972, 243). Indeed, the square is one of the major symbols of Freemasonry that, united with a pair of compasses, comprises the universal Masonic emblem.

Explicitly Masonic, I believe, are certain inscribed stones on the island. These include one discovered at Joudrey's Cove by Gilbert Hedden in 1936. It features a *cross* flanked by the letter "H," said to be a modification of the Hebraic letter for Jehovah, and a prime Masonic symbol known as a *Point Within a Circle*, representing mankind within the compass of God's creation (Morris n.d., 47; Finnan 1997, 66, 151). (This symbol, along with several others, can also be found as one of the cryptographic characters in the text of the cipher stone—again see figure 37.1). Another clearly Masonic stone is a granite boulder found near the Cave-in Pit in 1967. Overturned by a bulldozer it bore on its underside the letter "G" in a rectangle (what Masons term an *oblong square*). G denotes the Grand Geometer of the Universe—God, the central focus of Masonic teachings—and is "the most public and familiar of all symbols in Freemasonry," observes Mark Finnan (1997, 152). He continues: "The presence of this symbol on Oak Island and its location in the east, seen as the source of light in Masonic teachings, is further indication that individuals with a fundamental knowledge of Freemasonry were likely involved."

Indeed, the search for the Oak Island treasure "vault" has been carried out largely by prominent Nova Scotia Freemasons. I had an intimation of this years ago, but it fell to others—especially Finnan, who gained access to Masonic records—to provide the evidence. Freemasonry had come to Nova Scotia in 1738 and, concludes Finnan (1997, 145), "it is almost a certainty that organizers of the first coordinated dig . . . were Masonicly associated." Moreover, he states: "Successive treasure hunts throughout the past two hundred years often involved men who were prominent members of Masonic lodges. Some had passed through the higher levels of initiation, and a few even held the highest office possible within the Fraternity."

They include A.O. Creighton, the Oak Island Association treasurer who helped remove the cipher-inscribed stone from the island about 1865, and Frederick Blair, whose family was involved in the quest as far back as 1863. Blair, who formed the Oak Island Treasure Company in 1893, was a "prominent member" of the lodge in Amherst, Nova Scotia. Treasure hunter William Chappell was another active Mason, and his son Mel served as Provincial Grand Master for Nova Scotia from 1944 to 1946 (Finnan 1997, 145–46). Furthermore, discovered Finnan (1997, 146): "The independently wealthy Gilbert Hedden of Chatham, New Jersey, who carried out the treasure search from 1934 to 1938, and Professor

Edwin Hamilton, who succeeded him and operated on the island for the next six years, were also Freemasons. Hamilton had at one time held the office of Grand Master of the Grand Lodge of Massachusetts. Hedden even made it his business to inform Mason King George VI of England about developments on Oak Island in 1939, and Hamilton corresponded with President Roosevelt, another famous Freemason directly associated with the mystery." (Roosevelt actually participated in the work on Oak Island during the summer and fall of 1909.) Other Masonic notables involved in Oak Island were polar explorer Richard E. Byrd and actor John Wayne (Sora 1999, 12; Hamill and Gilbert 1998).

Significantly, Reginald Harris, who wrote the first comprehensive book on Oak Island at the behest of Frederick Blair, was an attorney for Blair and Hedden. Himself a thirty-third-degree Mason, Harris was provincial Grand Master from 1932 to 1935. Among his extensive papers were notes on Oak Island, scribbled on the backs of Masonic documents and sheets of Masonic letterhead. The papers show that at least one Oak Island business meeting was held in the Masonic Hall in Halifax, where Harris had an office as secretary of the Grand Lodge (O'Connor 1988, 93; Harris 1958, vii; Finnan 1997, 143; Rosenbaum 1973; 154).

One investigator, Ron Rosenbaum (1973, 154), discovered that among Harris's papers were "fragments of a Masonic pageant" that were apparently "designed to accompany the rite of initiation into the thirty-second degree of the Masonic Craft." The allegory is set in 1535 at the Abbey of Glastonsbury, where the prime minister is attempting to confiscate the order's fabulous treasures. But one item, the chalice used at the Last Supper—the Holy Grail itself—is missing, and secret Masons are suspected of having hidden it for safekeeping. The allegory breaks off with them being led to the tower for torture.

Given this draft allegory by Harris, it may not be a coincidence that some recent writers attempt to link the Holy Grail to Oak Island. They speculate that the fabled chalice is among the lost treasures of the Knights Templar, precursors of the Freemasons (Sora 1999, 180, 247–51). In any event, the evidence indicates a strong Masonic connection to the Oak Island enigma. Others have noted this link but unfortunately also believed in an actual treasure of some sort concealed in a man-made shaft or tunnel (Crooker 1993; Finnan 1997; Sora 1999; Rosenbaum 1973). Only by understanding both pieces of the puzzle and fitting them together correctly can the Oak Island mystery finally be solved.

In summary, therefore, I suggest first that the "Money Pit" and "pirate tunnels" are nothing of the sort but are instead natural formations. Secondly, I suggest that much of the Oak Island saga—certain reported actions and alleged discoveries—can best be understood in light of Freemasonry's Secret Vault allegory. Although it is difficult to know at this juncture whether the Masonic elements were opportunistically added to an existing treasure quest or whether the entire affair was a Masonic creation from the outset, I believe the mystery has been solved. The solution is perhaps an unusual one—but no more so than the saga of Oak Island itself.

References

Atlantic Advocate. 1965. Article in Oct. issue, cited in Crooker 1978, 85–86.

Blankenship, Daniel. 1999. Author interview, July 1.

Bowdoin, H.L. 1911. Solving the mystery of Oak Island. *Collier's Magazine*, Aug. 18. Cited and discussed in Harris 1958, 110–20; O'Connor 1988, 63–66.

Bunson, Matthew E. 1994. *Encyclopedia Sherlockiana.* New York: Barnes & Noble.

Creighton, Helen. 1957. *Bluenose Ghosts.* Reprinted Halifax, N.S.: Nimbus, 1994, 42–59, 118–20.

Crooker, William S. 1978. *The Oak Island Quest.* Hantsport, N.S.: Lancelot.

———. 1993. *Oak Island Gold.* Halifax, N.S.: Nimbus.

Duncan, Malcolm C. 1972. *Duncan's Masonic Ritual and Monitor.* Chicago: Ezra A. Cook, 217–65.

Faribault, E. Rudolph. 1911. *Summary Report of Geological Survey Branch of the Department of Mines.* Quoted in Furneaux 1972, 110.

Finnan, Mark. 1997. *Oak Island Secrets*, rev. ed. Halifax, N.S.: Formac.

"Freemasonry." 1978. *Collier's Encyclopedia.*

Furneaux, Rupert. 1972. *The Money Pit Mystery.* New York: Dodd, Mead.

Hamill, John, and Robert Gilbert. 1998. *Freemasonry.* North Dighton, Mass.: J.G. Press, 228, 241, 245.

Harris, R.V. 1958. *The Oak Island Mystery.* Toronto: Ryerson.

Hunter, C. Bruce. 1996. *Masonic Dictionary*, 3rd ed. Richmond, Va.: Macoy.

Lester, Ralph P. ed. 1977. *Look to the East!* rev. ed. Chicago: Ezra A. Cook.

Macoy, Robert. 1908. *Illustrated History and Cyclopedia of Freemasonry.* New York: Macoy.

Masonic Heirloom Edition Holy Bible. 1964. Wichita, Kans.: Heirloom Bible Publishers.

Morris, W.J. n.d., *Pocket Lexicon of Freemasonry.* Chicago: Ezra A. Cook.

Nickell, Joe. 1980. "Uncovered—The Fabulous Silver Mines of Swift and Filson," *Filson Club History Quarterly* 54 (Oct.): 325–345.

———. 1982a. Barbados' restless coffins laid to rest. *Fate*, Part I, 35.4 (April): 50–56; Part II, 35.5 (May): 79–86.

———. 1982b. Discovered: The secret of Beale's treasure, *Virginia Magazine of History and Biography* 90, no. 3 (July): 310–24.

———. 2000. Canada's mysterious Maritimes. *Skeptical Inquirer* 24 (Jan./Feb.): 15–19.

O'Connor, D'Arcy. 1988. *The Big Dig.* New York: Ballantine.

Preston, Douglas. 1988. Death trap defies treasure seekers for two centuries. *The Smithsonian.* June, 53–63.

Randle, Kevin D. 1995. *Lost Gold & Buried Treasure.* New York: M. Evans and Co., 75–107.

Revised Knight Templarism Illustrated. 1975. Chicago: Ezra A. Cook.

Rosenbaum, Ron. 1973. The mystery of Oak Island. *Esquire* 79 (Feb.): 77–85, 154–57.

Sora, Steven. 1999. *The Lost Treasure of the Knights Templar.* Rochester, Vt.: Destiny.

Waite, Arthur Edward. 1970. *A New Encyclopedia of Freemasonry*, vols. 1 and 2. New York: Weathervane.

234

Chapter 38

Enigma of the Crystal Tears

Gosh, I thought, after watching an episode of the then-new Fox TV series, *Psi Factor: Chronicles of the Paranormal*. Those Office of Scientific Investigation and Research (O.S.I.R.) types sure seem cool. "Case file 20168," they would begin. They would make sure their phone calls went out over "secure lines"—real "secret agent-y" stuff! And the equipment O.S.I.R. uses, like Magnetometers—wow! According to the *Psi Factor* Web page, these are used because "Fluctuations in the magnetic spectrum are common in coincidence with anomalous activity." Really? I don't think there's evidence that ghosts have magnetic personalities, but I've always wanted to talk like that. I began to dream of the possibilities. . . .

Suddenly, I perceived a dark shape approaching. Was it real or—? I broke off in mid-thought to reach for an O.S.I.R. Spectral Photometer, a "sophisticated device" that is used to "determine whether unusual phenomena is [*sic*] real or if the phenomenon is a purely subjective experience." It showed I was right: I was dreaming. Then I realized I wasn't in a *Psi Factor* episode; and the dark shape wasn't the host, "actor/writer/producer/musician Dan Aykroyd, a lifelong student of the paranormal." It was actually Barry Karr, CSICOP's executive director, leaning over me. Apparently I had fallen asleep at my desk again. I raised my head, pushed aside my Maltese Falcon paperweight, and asked, "What is it, shweetheart?"

"Martini lunch again?" he asked. I let that pass. "Here's the video from New York you've been expecting," he said, and walked off.

"Oh, yeah." Now it was coming back to me. I had agreed to look into the case of a young Lebanese girl who "miraculously" produced "crystal tears" from her eyes. A Brazilian TV production company—the largest in South America—was doing the story and wanted our view. They had rushed the video from their New York office.

Now I knew why I was thinking of Aykroyd. Episodes of his new Fox TV series *Psi Factor* are "fictionalized" from "closed cases" taken from the files of O.S.I.R., a group whose "methods and technical support run the gamut, from state-of-the-art science to folklore and mystic philosophy." Their "lab facilities" (and tarot-card divination quarters?) are located in "Central California." (Where better to mix science with mystic philosophy?) (*Psi Factor* Web page, 1996) It's pretty easy to see why they use the term "fictionalized." One episode features a meteorite that has brought with it some huge eggs. These hatch into gargantuan *fleas* that kill a team of NASA scientists. (*Psi Factor* 1996) (Does NASA know about this?) Aykroyd hosts the show, which is coproduced by his brother, another man, and a magician named Christopher Chacon. Chacon—to finally get to the point—is supposedly a professional conjurer who investigates paranormal claims. One of these was an earlier case of "crystal tears" that was featured on TV's *Unsolved Mysteries* in 1990. It gives us a chance to assess Chacon's critical acumen—or lack thereof.

The program heralded "a woman named Katie," whom her psychiatrist— paranormal enthusiast Berthold Schwarz—described as "a great, classical physical medium" and "a medical marvel." She demonstrated a wide variety of alleged psychic phenomena, notably producing "apports"—such as a "glass stone, resembling a diamond" that supposedly materialized from her eye. Schwarz gushed his approval and stated he could not envision trickery being involved, although Katie's effects seemed to skeptics to be on a par with the efforts of a beginning conjurer. For example, the glass gem was never seen in her eye; rather, she covered her eye with her hand and then opened her fingers, whereupon the object fell from between them. Seen in slow motion, the effect was entirely consistent with the object having been hidden between her fingers. Indeed, at the behest of CSICOP, magician Bruce Adams demonstrated the trick for the *Unsolved Mysteries* program. However, before approaching CSICOP, the producer of the program had sought out Christopher Chacon. He responded to Katie's effects by stating: "From my observations I don't feel that she is, at present, utilizing magical abilities to produce the materials that she is producing. I don't think she is skilled in those particular aspects of sleight of hand or illusion." (Chacon 1990)

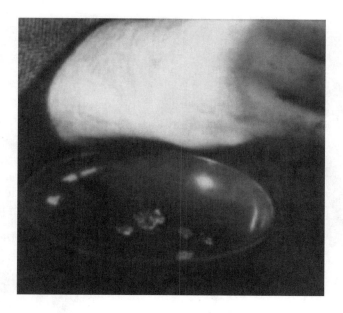

Figure 38.1. "Crystal tears"—actually, natural quartz crystals known as "Herkimer diamonds"—are obtained.

I don't know whether or not Chacon works for O.S.I.R., but if Dan Aykroyd and his *Psi Factor* are relying on Chacon's critical skills, they might wish to reconsider. (Incidentally, Chacon's segment was not aired but was instead replaced by the one featuring CSICOP's duplication of Katie's major effects.) (*Unsolved Mysteries* 1990)

I have presented this 1990 case not only for the light it sheds on the new television series but also because it serves as a useful introduction to the case at hand—that of the girl who produces "crystal tears." As shown on a Globo International documentary, a twelve-year-old girl named Hasnah, who lives in Lebanon's fertile Bekaa Valley, has the apparent ability to produce small crystal stones from her eyes. No sleight of hand is involved, since the camera zooms in close as the girl's father gingerly pulls down her lower eyelid and a crystal comes into view. It then pops out, whereupon it is shown to be a hard, faceted rock whose sharp points can cut paper. Her father believes the appearing crystals represent "a gift from Allah." Lebanese ophthalmologists say the stones are "crystal rocks," but otherwise they are reportedly unable to explain the phenomenon.

Figure 38.2. The author demonstrates how the lower eyelid is pulled out and a crystal inserted.

Figure 38.3. A tug on the lower lid causes the crystal "tear" to come into view. (Photos for the author by Tom Flynn)

Hasnah, who claims to produce up to seven crystals a day, showed a collection of the allegedly apported rocks. From their rhomboidal shape and other properties, I recognized them as types of natural quartz crystals that are generally known as "Herkimer diamonds." With the television crew being expected to arrive here the following day, I hastily made some phone calls and soon had acquired a handful of the gemstones. (See figure 38.1.)

Although such stones are indeed sharp—and I could see a dark red spot inside the girl's eyelid that probably represented a wound from one of them—I decided to duplicate the effect. All that was necessary was to pull out the lower eyelid to form a pouch and drop in a small crystal so that it rested, only a bit uncomfortably, out of sight (figure 38.2). A tug on the lower lid causes the stone to come into view (figure 38.3) and then pop out of the eye. This I demonstrated at an appropriate time for the television camera, allowing their reporter to actually do the extraction himself. The effect was indistinguishable from the Lebanese "miracle."

The final product appeared on the Globo program "Fantastico," described by one correspondent (who sent e-mail to Barry Karr) as "one of the most popular programs in Brazil." He remembered the appearance of a CSICOP magician but not the name. (How fleeting is fame!) He found it an "interesting report" and offered a prediction that actually came true: that we would receive a number of subscription orders from it (Karr 1996). Maybe soon we can buy some of that fancy O.S.I.R. equipment to play with.

References

Chacon, Christopher. 1990. Unused outtake for *Unsolved Mysteries*. Oct. (Copy in CSICOP Video Archive.)

"Fantastico." 1996. Brazil: Globo International Television, Oct. 13.

Karr, Barry. 1996. Personal communication, Oct. 15.

Psi Factor: Chronicles of the Paranormal. 1996. "File no. 33130," Nov. 2.

Psi Factor Web page. 1996. http://www.psifactor.com/. The World Wide Web. Nov. 4.

Unsolved Mysteries. 1990. Oct. (Copy in CSICOP Video Archives.)

Chapter 39

Death of the
Fire-Breathing Woman

Spontaneous human combustion (SHC) cases continue to spark controversy (so to speak), largely due to the efforts of nonscientist authors and journalists. These include self-styled British paranormal researchers Jenny Randles and Peter Hough (*Spontaneous Human Combustion* 1992), Pennsylvania school bus driver Larry Arnold (*Ablaze!* 1995), English coal-miner-turned-constable John E. Heymer (*The Entrancing Flame* 1996), and—more recently—the producers of A & E network's TV series, *The Unexplained.* The continued lack of scientific evidence for SHC (Benecke 1998) keeps proponents desperately looking for cases they can attribute to the alleged phenomenon—cases that are often quite disparate. They assign instances of unusual burning deaths to SHC rather like one might blame freak auto accidents on the Highway Gremlin. (For a discussion, see Nickell and Fischer 1987 and Nickell 1996.)

The case of Jeannie Saffin, included in Heymer (1996, 179–88) and Arnold (1995, 208–9), is quite instructive. Because the source of the body's ignition is not obvious in Saffin's death, paranormalists are especially quick to propose SHC. In doing so, of course, they engage in a logical fallacy called *argumentum ad ignorantiam* (literally, "arguing from ignorance"), since one cannot prove a cause from a lack of facts. The case also illustrates how crucial details may be omitted and how accounts become exaggerated over time; therefore, it demonstrates the consequent need to return to original sources.

Jean Lucille "Jeannie" Saffin was a sixty-one-year-old English woman with the mental age of a child, due to brain damage from a forceps delivery at birth. Her mother having died the previous year, she lived with her eighty-two-year-old father and a brother at the family home in Edmonton, north London. On Wednesday, September 15, 1982, a hot, humid day, Jeannie was sitting with her father in the kitchen. The windows were open. Suddenly, at about 4:15 p.m., Jack Saffin's attention was directed to his daughter—who was ablaze. He shouted to his son-in-law, Don Carroll, who had been doing some work in the house and was just returning from upstairs, and the two men put out the fire with water. Carroll phoned for an ambulance, which arrived quickly, and Jeannie was transported to North Middlesex Hospital. She was later transferred to the burn unit at Mount Vernon Hospital, where she died nearly eight days later at 8:10 a.m. on September 23. The cause of death was listed as "bronchopneumonia due to burns."

241

To proponents of SHC, however, the case is a spine-tingling mystery. In a chapter devoted to Jeannie Saffin's death, Heymer expresses "puzzlement about the source of her burns" (1996, 186), and he includes a statement by Don Carroll, who says "there was nothing alight in the kitchen except the pilot light on the grill." Even so, Carroll insists that he saw "flames coming out of her mouth and her midriff." Indeed, he says, "the flames were coming from her mouth like a dragon and they were making a roaring noise." Yet, he insists, "Her clothes did not burn much at all" (Carroll 1994). Heymer emphasizes the latter point, insisting it is "a mystery how she came to be burned *inside unburned clothes*" (original emphasis; Heymer 1996, 187).

Arnold essentially repeats the claims, obtaining his information largely from Heymer and apparently doing little actual investigation of his own. He writes: "As the men battled to save Lucille [*sic*], the son-in-law swore that 'she had flames roaring from her mouth like a dragon.'" He adds: "Ambulance men . . . noticed there was *no* smoke damage in the kitchen; that her clothing was *not* burned. Only a portion of her red nylon cardigan only [*sic*] had melted" (Arnold 1995, 208–09).

Certainly the case sounds impressive—at least until we go back to original sources, whereupon we obtain quite a different picture. First, regarding the allegedly unburned clothing, there is the signed statement Don Carroll gave to authorities soon after his sister-in-law's death. In that account from twelve years earlier, he noted that "Her clothes were in ribbons and were charred black. She was black as well. She started to try to pick her clothes off herself but I told her to stop" (Carroll 1982). In addition, a typed account by Constable Leigh Marsden stated: "The clothes were still burning when I got there. I pulled off the rest of her clothes. She and her clothes were burning. I put it out with a towel" (Marsden 1982). The ambulance attendants supposedly reported that Jeannie Saffin's clothing had not burned, but what they actually wrote was that she was "wearing nylon clothes, not on fire" (Heymer 1996, 186)—obviously meaning "no longer on fire," *not* "unburned." It is disingenuous to state, as Heymer does, that the nylon cardigan was "melted not burned" (Heymer 1996, 186). In addition to the cardigan, her clothing consisted of a cotton apron and dress (Marsden 1982; Heymer 1996, 196).

As to Mr. Carroll's statements about the fire, the flames probably did appear to come from Ms. Saffin's midriff. That may have been where the nylon cardigan began burning. Also, flaming blobs of melting nylon may have caused the burns on the victim's "front of left thigh" and, after she stood up, on her "left buttock" and "patches on the right knee"—as related in the autopsy report. Since damage is greatest above a flame rather than below it, it is not surprising that there were also "Full to partial thickness burns on the face, neck, both shoulders, front of upper chest" and "patchily distributed on the abdomen" as well as "affecting both hands" (see "Post-Mortem" 1982). ("Full thickness burns" mean the skin is destroyed down to the underlying fat.)

As to the flames issuing from her mouth "like a dragon," that claim is not supported by the medical evidence. A report from Mount Vernon Hospital to the coroner's office stated that when the victim arrived at the burn unit "There was soot in her nose, but the back of the mouth appeared undamaged" (Whitlock 1982). This was confirmed by the autopsy. Except for the bronchopneumonia (with the inflammation of the trachea and bronchi) there was "no evidence of natural disease"; neither, it may be added, was there any indication of *internal* combustion. To the contrary, the autopsy report confirmed "Total body *surface* burns being about 30–40%" (emphasis added; Post-Mortem 1982).

But what of Don Carroll's description of the flames being expelled from Ms. Saffin's mouth and "making a roaring noise?" (Carroll 1994) That may have been the effect on Carroll—especially after twelve years' reflection. Those details are absent from his original statement to the police. However, Carroll does say in his later statement that, at the hospital, despite her head being swathed in bandages, "I could see into Jeannie's mouth and the inside of her mouth was burnt" (Carroll 1994). It is possible that Ms. Saffin was breathing excitedly so that the flames attacking her face were partially drawn into, then expelled from her mouth. Heymer (1996, 195) agrees with this possibility. As to the alleged "roaring," although a doctor reportedly told Carroll he must be mistaken (Arnold 1995, 208), and even though he is admittedly technically deaf, "Even so, I heard the sound of the flames coming from Jeannie," he says (Carroll 1994). Possibly due to expectation and the interrelationship of the senses, he simply thought the flames roared.

The medical evidence makes clear that the fire was not internal but, instead, that Jeannie Saffin suffered external burning as a result of her clothing catching fire. As usual, SHC proponents are unable to imagine how that could have occurred. But a clue comes from Carroll's original report in which he states, "I made a point of checking on the gas cooker and saw that it was not on and saw that my father-in-law had his pipe in his hand and I checked it and saw that it was fresh tobacco which had not been lit" (Carroll 1982). At first sight this seems to rule out the pipe, and indeed there is no further mention of it—by Carroll (1994), Heymer (1996), or Arnold (1995). Yet Her Majesty's coroner for Greater London (Western District), John Burton, told Arnold, "we usually find some smoking material, particularly in the immobile or elderly victim" (Burton 1996). The pipe represents just the type of smoking material one looks for, and Carroll's insistence that it was freshly filled and unlit nevertheless begs the question, did the elderly Mr. Saffin previously knock the hot ashes from his pipe, and in the process, did an ember land in Jeannie Saffin's lap? To this very plausible scenario we must add the fact that the kitchen window and door were open, as was the back door, so that there was the potential for a draft. This could easily have caused the smoldering clothing to flare up.

Only minor mysteries remain in the Saffin case, and we may clear them up as well. Jeannie Saffin was sitting on some newspapers in a wooden Windsor chair and SHC proponents wonder why the paper suffered no fire damage (Heymer 1996, 185). The simple answer is that Ms. Saffin's body actually protected the papers; obviously the flames did not extend to her buttock until she stood up and moved away from the chair. Proponents also wonder why there was no smoke damage to the room (Heymer 1996, 186–87). The obvious answer would be that smoke was minimized because the fire was confined to the victim, and the open windows and draft effectively helped dispel what smoke there was. Finally, paranormalists wonder whether it was "normal" that the victim was not in pain—either at the time of the accident or subsequently (Heymer 1996, 187, 194). In fact, at the time of the fire, while she failed to cry out, she had "whimpered," according to her father (Saffin 1982). Her mental condition, her body's production of endorphins (pain-reducing chemicals), the subsequent shock, and her eventual semiconscious state may all have played a part in minimizing Jeannie Saffin's response to pain.

A & E's *The Unexplained* series included the Saffin case in its hour-long discussion of SHC (airing September 18, 1997). My brief comments on the cases were included, and overall, the presentation might have been considered balanced. Unfortunately, at the closing of the program, the narrator spoke of "an acupuncturist with remarkable talents. Through meditation and practice, he had learned to harness the electrical currents in his body." Suiting action to words, the supposed marvel crumpled a newspaper that—with a wave of his hand (and a bit of editing to cover the delay)—burst into flames. Alas, it appears the producers were snookered by a well-known magic trick billed variously as the "Yogi's Gaze" (Miller 1978) and "Fire by mental power" (Premanand 1994). Ironically, the feat depends on the secret combining of two chemicals that do, actually, spontaneously combust.

References

Arnold, Larry E. 1995. *Ablaze! The Mysterious Fires of Spontaneous Human Combustion.* New York: M. Evans & Co.

Benecke, Mark. 1998. Spontaneous human combustion: Thoughts of a forensic biologist. *Skeptical Inquirer* 22.2 (March/April 1998): 47–51.

Burton, John. 1996. Letter from Coroner's Court to Larry Arnold, June 27.

Carroll, Don. 1982. Signed witness statement made to Constable Lee Marsden, Oct. 2.

———. 1994. Statement of Nov. 20, published in Heymer 1996, 180–82.

Heymer, John E. 1996. *The Entrancing Flame: The Facts of Spontaneous Human Combustion.* London: Little, Brown.

Marsden, Lee. 1982. Constable's typed notes, Saffin case, n.d.

Miller, Hugh. 1978. *The Art of Eddie Joseph.* England: Supreme Magic Co.

Nickell, Joe. 1996. Investigative Files column, Not-so-spontaneous human combustion. *Skeptical Inquirer,* 20.6 (Nov./Dec.): 17–20.

Nickell, Joe, and John F. Fisher. 1987. Incredible cremations: Investigating spontaneous combustion deaths. *Skeptical Inquirer,* 11.4 (summer): 352–57.

"Post-Mortem Examination." 1982. Department of Forensic Medicine, Charing Cross Hospital, Sept. 28.

Premanand, B. 1994. *Science versus Miracles.* India: Indian CSICOP.

Randles, Jenny, and Peter Hough. 1992. *Spontaneous Human Combustion.* London: Robert Hale.

Saffin, John. 1982. Signed witness statement made to Constable Lee Marsden, Oct. 2.

Whitlock, Michael. 1982. Report as Registrar in Plastic Surgery, Mt. Vernon Hospital, to Mr. R. Wilde, Coroner's Officer, Uxbridge, Oct. 27.

Chapter 40

Comatose "Miracle Worker"

As we begin the new millennium, the media have been pointing to "millennial madness" as the source for a wide range of divine claims. Yet the faithful have been seeking miracles and finding them—or so they believe—in unlikely forms and places for years. These include apparitions of the Virgin Mary (for example in the Bosnian village of Medjugorje, beginning in 1981), bleeding statues and crucifixes (e.g., in Quebec in 1985), and miraculously appearing images, such as the portrait of Mary seen in a splotch on a tree in Los Angeles in 1992 (Nickell 1993; 1997). More recently, there are reported healings and other "miraculous" phenomena attending a comatose teenage girl in Worcester, Massachusetts.

Pilgrims currently stream to the home of Audrey Santo, who has been bedridden since 1987, when at the age of three, a near-drowning left her in an unresponsive condition. Visitors to the home chapel, converted from a garage, report healings after being shown statues that drip oil and communion wafers that bear smears of blood. Skeptics may not be guilty of excessive doubt when they wonder how and why a tragic figure who cannot heal herself is able to heal others. The Catholic Church is often skeptical of such extracanonical phenomena as well. It has distanced itself from Medjugorje (where six children supposedly conversed with the Virgin Mary), and the local bishop proclaimed the Medjugorje affair a fraud.

Interestingly, a year after Audrey's accident, her mother, Linda Santo, spent $8,000 to take her to Medjugorje in hopes of a miracle. As even a sympathetic priest admitted, "On a rational level, this was an extremely absurd idea. It was absurd. It should not have been done. It was medically wrong. And I think from all kinds of angles, sane people would say it was even spiritually wrong" (Sherr 1998). Expecting her daughter to be cured, Linda Santo bought her sandals so that she could walk. But as it happened, instead of being helped, Audrey suffered a sudden cardiac arrest. She was revived but had to be returned home by air ambulance at a cost of $25,000—a bill her grandmother mortgaged her home to pay. Linda Santo's response to the near-fatal incident was to blame it on the proximity of a Yugoslavian abortion clinic (Harrison 1998; Sherr 1998).

Skepticism of miracle claims is often warranted. For example, newsmen from the Canadian Broadcasting Corporation were able to borrow one of the Quebec "bleeding" statues and have it scientifically analyzed. The blood had been mixed with pork fat so that when the room warmed from pilgrims' body heat, the mixture would liquefy and run like tears. A more innocent explanation was afforded the tree-splotch "Virgin" in Los Angeles: a tree expert determined a fungus was responsible. However, there seems little incentive for church prelates to adopt a critical stance. Clerics who debunked a perambulating and weeping statue in Thornton, California, in 1981, for example, were denounced for their efforts by religious believers who called them "a bunch of devils" (Nickell 1993, 67–68). Nonetheless, in the Santo case, the Worcester bishop appointed a theologian and two psychologists to form an investigating commission. Their preliminary report was issued on January 21, 1999, and I appeared that evening on *The NBC Nightly News with Tom Brokaw* to offer a brief skeptical view of the case.

Among other things, the commission members showed skepticism toward claims that Audrey is a "victim soul" (one who suffers for others). Stating that this is not "an official term in the Church," the report noted that "It was used in some circles in the 18th and 19th century when there was a fascination with suffering and death." It remained to be determined, the commission concluded, that Audrey demonstrated "cognitive abilities" or "at the age of three was, and presently is, capable of making a free choice to accept the suffering of others." In fact, doctors say that Audrey exhibits "akinetic mutism"—a comalike state. Except for her eyes, which restlessly blink and wander, the tragic teenager remains virtually motionless. When ABC's *20/20* reporter Lynn Sherr placed her hand in Audrey's, she received, she thought, a slight squeeze, but when she tried again there was no response (Sherr 1998).

Nevertheless, Linda Santo rejects the idea that her daughter is unresponsive: "She cannot speak, but she knows everything. She is not in a coma . . . she's in that room with her Jesus seven days a week, adoring him, waiting on him, serving him, and he's blessing her." She even says that Audrey appears to people—"in person or in dreams"—and when she does so, "is moving and speaking" (Harrison 1998). Linda Santo also believes that Audrey has worked many miracles. She cites the case of a young man injured in a motorcycle accident whose doctors had reportedly said he would never be able to walk again; yet on the same day his mother had gone to see Audrey, he began to walk without his crutches. Actually, according to his personal physician, there had been a good likelihood—a 75 percent chance—that he would indeed walk (Sherr 1998).

On the *20/20* segment, titled "The Miracle of Audrey" (first broadcast October 4, 1998), Lynn Sherr asked, "Is this fourteen-year-old child a miracle worker, a messenger of God? Or is this all a cruel hoax, exploiting a sick and innocent girl?" Elsewhere a spokesman for the bishop confessed to having qualms about a disabled child being placed on public display. On one anniversary of Audrey's accident, she was exhibited at a Worcester stadium with some ten thousand people in attendance. At the Santo home a window was added to Audrey's bedroom, through which pilgrims could stare at the "miracle" girl and pray for her to intercede with God on their behalf. (The window was reminiscent of one in a mobile-home carnival exhibit through which spectators could view "Siamese" twins as they watched TV.)

In preparing the *20/20* segment, a producer called *Skeptical Inquirer* magazine and discussed with me the phenomenon of weeping icons. Of those that were not due to simple condensation or "sweating," I said, approximately one hundred percent were fakes, judging by my experience. That includes oil-yielding icons, which typically involve a nondrying oil (like olive oil) that can stay fresh-looking indefinitely. We discussed the possibility of using surveillance cameras to monitor the Santo statues, but I pointed out that if trickery were involved, it was unlikely that such an investigative technique would be permitted. As Lynn Sherr would subsequently report on camera, "We wanted to do our own test with a surveillance camera in the [home] chapel, but the family prefers to let the commission finish its work first."

Unfortunately, the commission members seemed woefully ill-prepared to investigate trickery. Sherr asked commission member Dr. John

Madonna, "Did you see any way that anybody was pouring oil or making the oil appear on those objects?" He replied: "No. Especially after we did our examination behind the pictures and under the statues and so forth and found that there was no way that these objects were being fed the oil." Another member, Dr. Robert Ciotone, stated, "We found nothing, no source of the oil." Actually, the conditions under which the statues and other objects yield oil are consistent with the surreptitious application of a nondrying oil. According to Sherr, "Although no one claims to have seen an object actually start to spout oil"—a very significant fact—"the commissioners were astounded when a religious icon they brought along oozed oil that night." Of course no surveillance cameras were monitoring the icon during that time.

Linda Santo did permit *20/20* to take a sample of the oil. It proved to be 75 percent olive oil, "the rest unidentifiable," according to Sherr (1998). She added, "Other independent tests have all yielded different results—in other words nothing conclusive." In fact, analysis of one sample by a Pittsburgh laboratory revealed it to be 80 percent vegetable oil and 20 percent chicken fat, according to *The Washington Post*, which ordered the test (Weingarten 1998).

While noting that the source of the oil was not yet explained, the commission's report did correctly conclude, "One cannot presume that the inability to explain something automatically makes it miraculous." (In other words, the commissioners were duly noting the logical fallacy of an argument *ad ignorantiam*—literally an appeal "to ignorance.") The report added, "We must be careful not to identify this oil as 'holy oil'"—that is, oil blessed by a Catholic priest and used to anoint the ill—and insisted it not be used or offered as such. Prior to this, the Santos distributed packets of oil-soaked cotton balls, often receiving money and other gifts in return.

Taken together, the evidence relating to the oil exudations raises strong suspicions. First, there is the lack of any scientific proof for the alleged phenomenon: not a single case of a weeping effigy has ever been scientifically verified. In fact, the history of such reported occurrences is a litany of deception, including self-deception. In the Santo case, there is no mere misperception, since the presence of copious amounts of oil—including the "spontaneous" filling of chalices—has been well established. Moreover, the fact that the oil has not been observed to flow strongly suggests prior application. And the varying test results seem less consistent with a genuine phenomenon than with an attempt to adulterate the oil in hopes of confounding the analysis. The presence of chicken fat—which, along with common vegetable oil, is readily available in a home kitchen—seems particularly telling.

Even the timing of the phenomenon is suspicious, beginning long after Audrey's accident and following other traumas including her father's several-years desertion of the family and her mother's diagnosis of breast cancer. According to Lynn Sherr (1998), "[J]ust as it seemed that God wasn't listening, the Santos believe he sent them a sign. With no warning and no logic, they say oil suddenly coated a religious portrait in their living room." This was a picture of the Image of Guadalupe—itself a faked "miracle" picture! (Nickell 1993, 29–34)—and it occurred after national media attention had focused on several other instances of "weeping" images.

The phenomena that accompany the Santo oil exudations are also suspect, in part because cases of bogus weeping images have often been attended by other easily faked miracles (Nickell 1993). In this case, there are "bleeding" pictures and communion wafers. Especially troubling are reports that stigmata—wounds imitating Jesus' crucifixion—have "mysteriously" appeared on Audrey's body, and on Good Fridays she has reportedly been seen to lie with her arms outstretched, as if crucified. According to one reporter, "Her parents say they cannot explain how their daughter, who cannot normally move herself, becomes positioned in this way" (Harrison 1998).

Although we live in a scientific age, there has been a resurgence in magical thinking, resulting in a revival of religious fundamentalism, the rise of the "New Age" movement, and an increase in "miracle" claims. The appeal is widespread, although it may be especially strong among the economically disadvantaged, where human despair and superstition may coexist. (The Santo phenomena, for example, take place in the midst of Portuguese immigrant families.) People seem to hunger for some tangible religious experience, and wherever there is such profound want there is the opportunity for what may be called "pious fraud." Money is rarely the primary motive, the usual impetus being to seemingly triumph over adversity, renew the faith of believers, and confound the doubters. An end-justifies-the-means attitude may prevail, but the genuinely religious and the devoutly skeptical may agree on one thing—that the truth must serve as both the means and the end. Ultimately, neither science nor religion can be served by dishonesty.

References

Harrison, Ted. 1998. Miracle child. *Fortean Times*, Dec., 40–41.

Nickell, Joe. 1993. *Looking for a Miracle*. Amherst, N.Y.: Prometheus.

———. 1997. In the eye of the beholder. *Free Inquiry* (spring), 5.

Sherr, Lynn. 1998. The Miracle of Audrey. *20/20* (ABC News transcript no. 1848), Oct. 4.

Weingarten, Gene. 1998. Tears for Audrey. *Washington Post*, July 19.

Chapter 41

Extraterrestrial Autopsy

It keeps going and going and. . . . The Roswell crashed-saucer myth was given renewed impetus by a controversial television program, "Alien Autopsy: Fact or Fiction?" that purported to depict the autopsy of a flying saucer occupant. The "documentary," promoted by a British marketing agency that formerly handled Walt Disney products, was aired August 28 and September 4, 1995, on the Fox television network. Skeptics, as well as many ufologists, quickly branded the film used in the program a hoax.

"The Roswell Incident," as it is known, is described in several controversial books, including one of that title by Charles Berlitz and William L. Moore. Reportedly, in early July 1947, a flying saucer crashed on the ranch property of William Brazel near Roswell, New Mexico, and was subsequently retrieved by the United States government (Berlitz and Moore 1980). Over the years, numerous rumors, urban legends, and outright hoaxes have claimed that saucer wreckage and the remains of its humanoid occupants were stored at a secret facility—e.g., a (nonexistent) "Hangar 18" at Wright Patterson Air Force Base—and that the small corpses were autopsied at that or another site (Berlitz and Moore 1980; Stringfield 1977).

UFO hoaxes, both directly and indirectly related to Roswell, have since proliferated. For example, a 1949 science fiction movie, *The Flying Saucer,* produced by Mikel Conrad, purported to contain scenes of a captured spacecraft; an actor hired by Conrad actually posed as an FBI agent and swore the claim was true. In 1950, writer Frank Scully reported in his book *Behind the Flying Saucers* that the United States government had in its possession no fewer than three Venusian spaceships, together with the bodies of their humanoid occupants. Scully, who was also a *Variety* magazine columnist, was fed the story by two confidence men who had hoped to sell a petroleum-locating device allegedly based on alien technology. Other crash-retrieval stories followed, as did various photographs of space aliens living and dead: one gruesome photo portrayed the pilot of a small plane, his aviator's glasses still visible in the picture (Clark 1993). (For other Roswell hoaxes, see "The Roswell Legend" chapter in this book.)

Sooner or later, a Roswell "alien autopsy" film was bound to turn up. That predictability, together with a lack of established historical record for the bizarre film, is indicative of a hoax. So is the anonymity of the cameraman. But the strongest argument against authenticity stems from what really crashed at Roswell in 1947. According to recently released Air Force files, the wreckage actually came from a balloon-borne array of radar reflectors and monitoring equipment launched as part of the secret Project Mogul and intended to monitor acoustic emissions from anticipated Soviet nuclear tests. In fact, materials from the device match contemporary descriptions of the debris (foiled paper, sticks, and tape) given by rancher Brazel's children and others (Berlitz and Moore 1980; Thomas 1995).

Interestingly, the film failed to agree with earlier purported eyewitness testimony about the alleged autopsy. For example, multiple medical informants described the Roswell creatures as lacking ears and having only four fingers with no thumb (Berlitz and Moore 1980), whereas the autopsy film depicts a creature with small ears and five fingers in addition to a thumb. Ergo, either the previous informants are hoaxers, or the film is a hoax, or both.

Although the film was supposedly authenticated by Kodak, only the leader tape and a single frame were submitted for examination, not the entire footage. In fact, a Kodak spokesman told the *Sunday Times* of London: "There is no way I could authenticate this. I saw an image on the print. Sure it could be old film, but it doesn't mean it is what the aliens were filmed on."

Various objections to the film's authenticity came from journalists, UFO researchers, and scientists who viewed the film. They noted that it bore a bogus, nonmilitary code mark ("Restricted access, AO1 classification") that disappeared after it was criticized; that the anonymous

254

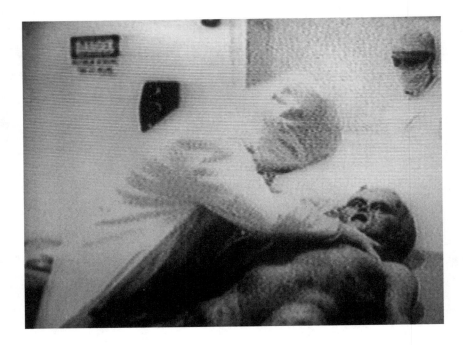

Figure 41.1. Scene from "Alien Autopsy" television program purports to show the postmortem of an extraterrestrial being from the Roswell "UFO crash."

photographer's alleged military status had not been verified; and that the injuries sustained by the extraterrestrial were inconsistent with an air crash. On the basis of such objections, an article in the *Sunday Times* of London advised: "RELAX. The little green men have not landed. A much-hyped film purporting to prove that aliens had arrived on earth is a hoax" (Chittenden 1995).

Similar opinions on the film came even from prominent Roswell-crash partisans: Kent Jeffrey, an associate of the Center for UFO Studies and author of the "Roswell Declaration" (a call for an executive order to declassify any United States government information on UFOs and alien intelligence) stated "up front and unequivocally there is no (zero!!!) doubt in my mind that this film is a fraud" (1995). Even arch Roswell promoter Stanton T. Friedman said, "I saw nothing to indicate the footage came from the Roswell incident, or any other UFO incident for that matter" ("Alien or Fake?" 1995).

Still other critics found many inconsistencies and suspicious elements in the alleged autopsy. For example, in one scene the "doctors" wore white, hooded anticontamination suits that could have been neither for protection from radiation (elsewhere the personnel are examining an alien body without such suits), nor for protection from the odor of decay nor from unknown bacteria or viruses (either would have required some type of breathing apparatus). Thus it appears that the outfits served no purpose except to conceal the "doctors'" identities. American pathologists offered still more negative observations. Cyril Wecht, former president of the National Association of Forensic Pathologists, seemed credulous but described the viscera in terms that might apply to supermarket meat scraps and sponges: "I cannot relate these structures to abdominal contexts." Again, he said about contents of the cranial area being removed, "This is a structure that must be the brain, if it is a human being. It looks like no brain that I have ever seen, whether it is a brain filled with a tumor, a brain that has been radiated, a brain that has been traumatized and is hemorragic." (Wecht 1995). Much more critical was the assessment of nationally known pathologist Dominick Demaio, who described the autopsy on television's *American Journal* (1995): "I would say it's a lot of bull." Houston pathologist Ed Uthman (1995) was also bothered by the unrealistic viscera, stating, "The most implausible thing of all is that the 'alien' just had amorphous lumps of tissue in 'her' body cavities. I cannot fathom that an alien who had external organs so much like ours could not have some sort of definitive structural organs internally." As well, "the prosectors did not make an attempt to arrange the organs for demonstration for the camera." Uthman also observed that there was no body block, a basic piece of equipment used to prop up the trunk for examination and the head for brain removal. He also pointed out that "the prosector used scissors like a tailor, not like a pathologist or surgeon" (pathologists and surgeons place the middle or ring finger in the bottom scissors hole and use the forefinger to steady the scissors near the blades). Uthman further noted that "the initial cuts in the skin were made a little too Hollywood-like, too gingerly, like operating on a living patient," whereas autopsy incisions are made faster and deeper. Uthman faulted the film for lacking what he aptly termed "technical verisimilitude."

The degree of realism in the film has been debated, even by those who believe the film is a hoax. Some, like Kent Jeffrey (1995), thought

255

the autopsy was done on a specially altered human corpse. On the other hand, many—including movie special-effects experts—believed a dummy had been used. One suspicious point in that regard was that significant close-up views of the creature's internal organs were consistently out of focus ("Alien or Fake?" 1995). *American Journal* (1995) also featured a special effects expert who doubted the film's authenticity and demonstrated how the autopsy "incisions"—which left a line of "blood" as the scalpel was drawn across the alien's skin—could easily have been faked. (The secret went unexplained but probably consisted of a tube fastened to the far side of the blade.)

In contrast to the somewhat credulous response of a Hollywood special effects filmmaker on the Fox program, British expert Cliff Wallace of Creature Effects provided the following assessment:

> None of us were of the opinion that we were watching a real alien autopsy, or an autopsy on a mutated human, which has also been suggested. We all agreed that what we were seeing was a very good fake body, a large proportion of which had been based on a lifecast. Although the nature of the film obscured many of the things we had hoped to see, we felt that the general posture and weighting of the corpse was incorrect for a body in a prone position and had more in common with a cast that had been taken in an upright position.
>
> We did notice evidence of a possible molding seam line down an arm in one segment of the film but were generally surprised that there was little other evidence of seaming, which suggests a high degree of workmanship.
>
> We felt that the filming was done in such a way as to obscure details rather than highlight them and that many of the parts of the autopsy that would have been difficult to fake, for example the folding back of the chest flaps, were avoided, as was anything but the most cursory of limb movement. We were also pretty unconvinced by the lone removal sequence. In our opinion the insides of the creature did not bear much relation to the exterior, where muscle and bone shapes can be easily discerned. We all agreed that the filming of the sequence would require either the use of two separate bodies, one with chest open, one with chest closed, or significant redressing of one mortal. Either way the processes involved are fairly complicated and require a high level of specialized knowledge.

Another expert, Trey Stokes—a Hollywood special effects "motion designer," whose film credits include *The Abyss, The Blob, Robocop Two,*

Batman Returns, Gremlins II, Tales from the Crypt, and many others—provided an independent analysis at CSICOP's request. Interestingly, Stokes's critique also indicated that the alien figure was a dummy cast in an upright position. He further noted that it seemed lightweight and "rubbery," that it therefore moved unnaturally when handled, especially in one shot in which "the shoulder and upper arm actually are floating rigidly above the table surface, rather than sagging back against it" as would be expected (Stokes 1995).

CSICOP staffers (Executive Director Barry Karr, *Skeptical Inquirer* Assistant Editor Tom Genoni Jr., and I) monitored developments in the case. Before the film aired, CSICOP issued a press release, briefly summarizing the evidence against authenticity and quoting CSICOP Chairman Paul Kurtz as saying, "The Roswell myth should be permitted to die a deserved death. Whether or not we are alone in the universe will have to be decided on the basis of better evidence than that provided by the latest bit of Roswell fakery. Television executives have a responsibility not to confuse programs designed for entertainment with news documentaries."

257

References

Alien or fake? 1995. *Sheffield Star* (England), Aug. 18.

American Journal. 1995. Sept. 6.

Berlitz, Charles, and William L. Moore. 1980. *The Roswell Incident.* New York: Grosset and Dunlap.

Chittenden, Maurice. 1995. Film that "proves" aliens visited earth is a hoax. The *Sunday Times* of London, July 30.

Clark, Jerome. 1993. "UFO Hoaxes." In *Encyclopedia of Hoaxes,* ed. by Gordon Stein, 267–78. Detroit: Gale Research.

Jeffrey, Kent. 1995. Bulletin 2: The purported 1947 Roswell film, http://ds.dial.pipex.com/ritson/scispi/roswell/london.htm, May 26.

Kurtz, Paul. 1995. Quoted in CSICOP press release, "Alien Autopsy: Fact or Fiction?" film a hoax concludes scientific organization. April 25.

Stokes, Trey. 1995. Personal communication, Aug. 29–31.

Stringfield, Leonard, H. 1977. *Situation Red: The UFO Siege.* Garden City, N.Y.: Doubleday, 84, 177–79.

Thomas, Dave. 1995. The Roswell incident and Project Mogul. *Skeptical Inquirer* 19(4) (July–Aug.): 15–18.

Uthman, Ed. 1995. "Fox's 'Alien Autopsy': A Pathologist's View," http://www.neosoft.com/~uthman/rants/on_alien_autopsy.html, Sept. 15.

Wallace, Cliff. 1995. Letter to Union Pictures, Aug. 3, quoted in Wallace's letter to Graham Birdsall, *UFO Magazine*, Aug. 16, quoted on ParaNet newsgroup, Aug. 22.

Wecht, Cyril. 1995. Quoted on "Alien Autopsy: Fact or Fiction?" Fox Network, Aug. 28 and Sept. 4.

Chapter 42

Spirit Paintings

During the heyday of spiritualism, among the "physical phenomena" commonly manifested were so-called spirit paintings. These were portraits and other artworks, done in various media and produced under a variety of conditions but always ascribed to spirit entities. During 1998 and 1999, I was able to examine several of these at Lily Dale, the western New York spiritualist colony, and to thereby shed light on some century-old mysteries.

Full-fledged spirit paintings, often portraits of the dearly departed, were typically rather elaborate renderings in oils or pastels. Although looking for all the world like artworks done by professionals, they were produced under remarkable conditions: for example, during a short period of time, in complete or near darkness, etc. The most famous spirit-painting mediums were the Bangs sisters (discussed in the next chapter) and the Campbell brothers (discussed in this chapter).

Although there are myriad discussions of spirit painting (e.g., Coates 1911; Carrington 1920; Mulholland 1938), I have come across no real history of the alleged phenomenon and nothing to establish its origin or chronicle its development. The following few paragraphs are my attempt to fill this void.

Soon after modern spiritualism began in 1848 with the spirit rappings of the Fox sisters (who confessed their trickery four decades later), spirit pictures began to appear in a very simple form. The earliest ones of which I am aware were drawings produced as an extension of "automatic" writing, whereby messages were supposedly dictated by otherworldly entities or the medium's hand was allegedly guided by them. For example, in

1851 John Murray Spear (b. 1804) produced séance writings and "also geometrical drawings and strange unintelligible figures, of which no interpretation was vouchsafed" (Podmore 1902, 1:216). In the mid 1860s, a Glasgow cabinetmaker and spiritualist named David Duguid (1832–1907) began painting small landscapes while being observed, according to psychical investigator Frank Podmore (1902, II:130), "apparently in deep trance, and with his eyes apparently closed"—emphasis on the word *apparently*. Podmore (1902, II:131) was "disposed to regard Duguid's trance utterances as probably not involving conscious deception," but his later mediumistic demonstrations are another matter. Magician John Mulholland in his *Beware Familiar Spirits* (1938, 158), says Duguid was among the mediums who employed "simple substitution of painted for unpainted cards."

After the debut of slate writing—a phenomenon claimed to have been "discovered" by Dr. Henry Slade—spirit drawings also began to appear, sometimes accompanying writing, sometimes separately. Like the messages, these drawings could be made with a simple slate pencil, but more ornate ones were rendered with colored chalks or paints. The slate effects were created under conditions that supposedly precluded trickery, thereby seeming to prove they were authentic spirit productions. In fact, however, they were easily produced by a variety of conjuring techniques, and mediums were repeatedly caught faking the phenomena (Houdini 1924).

Although spirit painting is distinct from spirit photography, there was actually some overlap. Interestingly, early photographic techniques—daguerreotypes, ambrotypes, etc.—did not yield spirit portraits; those awaited the advent of glass-plate negatives, which facilitated double exposures. After spirit photography became established in 1862 (by Bostonian William H. Mumler), *painted* portraits or other artworks obviously served on occasion as the basis for photographed spirit "extras."[13] Some mediumistic photographers produced photo images with artistically added "veils," "shrouds," and other funereal trappings (see examples in Permut 1988). And David Duguid expanded his repertoire from spirit paintings to spirit photographs and even "psychographs" (supposedly noncamera spirit or psychic photos) (Coates 1911, 65). One way the latter were produced involved using seemingly unprepared paper that actually contained a chemically bleached-out image. At the appropriate time, the paper would be secretly pressed against a blotter dampened with a developing solution (Carrington 1920, 220–21).

At Lily Dale, I was able to examine several pictures by the Campbell brothers—or I should say, "brothers," since they were unrelated. (According to my sources at Lily Dale, they were a gay couple in a time when differences in sexual orientation were less tolerated.) They were Allan B. Campbell (1833–1919) and Charles "Campbell" (born Charles Shourds, who died August 23, 1926). They lived at Lily Dale but traveled widely, reportedly making twenty-two trips to Europe. Their mediumship involved slate writing and spirit typewriting (produced in a portable cabinet), but they are best known for their spirit portraits and paintings ("Campbell Brothers" n.d.).

The Campbells' "spirit" artists produced pastel and oil portraits. I inspected examples of both with an illuminated 10X loupe (a small magnifier used especially by jewelers and watchmakers) and found them indistinguishable from works produced by the human hand. Some writers claim the pictures "have no brush marks" (Jackson 1975). That is true of the pastels, which were of course done without brushes or paints and which in fact have the characteristics of pastel drawings. The oil paintings do indeed have brush marks, which may easily be found by the use of oblique light—a technique used to enhance surface irregularities (Nickell 1999).

One of the oils is a striking forty-by-sixty-inch painting of Allan Campbell's alleged spirit guide, Azur (figure 42.1). It was produced on June 15, 1898, in a single sitting lasting only an hour and a half. In a signed statement, six witnesses (all of them apparently spiritualists, some of them prominent) described the conditions under which the picture was produced:

> On the evening mentioned we met at the cottage of the Campbell Brothers on the hill and proceeded to their Egyptian séance room. Across the bay window at the end of the room was hung a large silk curtain, where stood a small table and a canvas 40" x 60." Each one in turn went up to the canvas and magnetized it by passing his hands over the surface. We then placed whatever marks we pleased on the back, some placing names, some numbers, some marks to suit their fancy. Mr. A. Campbell then invited one of the circle to sit with him in the impromptu cabinet and the silken curtain enclosing them; each member of the

Figure 42.1. "Spirit" painting, *Azur,* produced in stages during an 1898 séance (exhibited at the Maplewood Hotel, Lily Dale).

circle in turn sat within the cabinet with Mr. Campbell. Every time the curtain was withdrawn we saw the partly finished picture of Azur. During the entire séance there was light enough for us to see everything perfectly and note the gradual growth of the painting on the canvas. Mr. A. Campbell was entranced and Azur, using his organism, gave us some very beautiful words of welcome and lessons of a high order. He spoke of the stars and their significance, which we fully realized afterwards.

After some music, additional lights were brought, the curtain withdrawn, and lo! The picture was complete. It represented Azur with arms uplifted as in the act of speaking and fully life size. While we were admiring it, there came at the back of the head a six-pointed star, which is now distinctly seen (Prendergast et al. 1989).

One notes that the picture was only observed in stages, but how was it done under the conditions described (assuming them to be true) and in so short a time for a large oil painting? To begin an answer we turn to Hereward Carrington (1920, 222) who describes the two major techniques used for spirit paintings rendered in oils:

One method is for the medium to take an ordinary oil-painting, as fresh as possible (so long as the oil is quite dry), and over this lightly gum, around the edges, *another* piece of blank canvas, seeing to it that it looks neat at the edges. Now, as soon as the medium is alone in the cabinet, he carefully peels off this outside piece of canvas, secreting it about his person, and exposing the under canvas (the one upon which is the painting) to view. In order to produce the impression of the painting still being wet, he quickly rubs over the painting with poppy-oil, and there is your spirit painting!

The second method Carrington describes as a "chemical means," but that is something of a misnomer. As he explains: "The oil-painting in this case is first varnished, and, after this is thoroughly dry, it is covered with a solution of water and 'zinc white.' The canvas will now have the appearance of being blank, and may be inspected. All the medium has to do, in order to restore the painting, is to wash over the canvas with a wet sponge, when the painting will appear as before." In the second technique, the zinc white might be sponged off incrementally so that the picture seems to develop in stages. And it would be appropriately damp when brought forth (Gibson 1967). With either method employed, the sitters' placing their names and other identifying marks on the back of the canvas to prevent substitution—a common ploy of spirit-painting mediums (Gibson 1967)—was a disarming but irrelevant act since the main canvas on which the marks were placed was not switched.

In examining *Azur*, I detected no traces of zinc white residue that might be expected to remain. However, I did discover—in each of the four corners—evidence of surface damage, seemingly consistent with the first scenario Carrington described. Although unmistakable, the damage is much less apparent to the unaided eye than is seen in an oblique-light

Figure 42.2. Surface damage apparent in each of the four corners of *Azur*—a possible indication of trickery. (Photos by Joe Nickell)

photograph intended to reveal it (figure 42.2). In fact, the damage would no doubt generally go unnoticed, and indeed I had seen the painting on previous occasions without observing it. My eventual discovery reminds me of an exchange between Sherlock Holmes and Inspector Gregory, in "Silver Blaze" (Doyle 1894), concerning a clue, a "wax vesta [match], half burned":

"I cannot think how I came to overlook it," said the inspector with an expression of annoyance.

"It was invisible, buried in the mud [Holmes replied]. I only saw it because I was looking for it."

"What! You expected to find it?"

"I thought it not unlikely."

If my observation of surface damage in the four corners of *Azur* means what I think it does (no innocent, alternate explanation comes to mind), then Allan Campbell seems to have had a blank canvas covering the finished *Azur*, lightly glued at the corners. There may actually have been two or more overlays so that intermediate stages of the painting could have been prepared in advance. Or there could have been a partial rendering on the *back* of the blank canvas for the same purpose (although that would have required reattachment after reversal). Allan Campbell might even have had a brush and paints available so that he could have produced on the overlay the first several stages of the painting until ready to reveal the finished product. (These could have been kept in the drawer of the "small table" referred to.)

How do we explain the star-shaped halo that afterward appeared on the painting, as the sitters attested, "while we were admiring it?" I suggest that the star, which is not particularly bold, was not at first noticed. When the sitters' attention was called to it, and they then focused on it, they were deceived by the power of suggestion into thinking it had spontaneously materialized.

What about the members of the circle having taken turns sitting with the medium in the makeshift spirit cabinet (the curtained-off bay-window area)? Would not the presence of even a single observer have precluded trickery? Hardly. The painting may have had a covering placed over it, which was used to conceal the removal of the (hypothesized) canvas overlays. And Charles "Campbell" might have played an important role. It is curious that his involvement was not described; he might, for example, have been the first to sit with Allan Campbell, making removal (or reversal) of one overlay a cinch. He could have sat more than once, or one of the other sitters might have been a confederate. Again, we do not know that a sitter was *always* present or that the picture advanced to a new stage during each sitting. No doubt, whatever the actual conditions, they were insufficiently stringent to prevent deception.

Even if I am wrong about the implications of the surface damage in the corners, the hypothetical scenario I have sketched remains a valid explanation, since it would be possible to attach an overlay without such damage. (One version of the trick calls for tacks to be used to attach the blank sheet [Gibson 1967].) Given the evidence, the painting of "Azur"— indeed the entire body of spirit paintings, like other physical spiritualistic phenomena—can scarcely be taken as proof of a transcendent realm.

References

"Campbell Brothers." n.d., Album, Lily Dale Museum.

Carrington, Hereward. 1920. *The Physical Phenomena of Spiritualism.* New York: American Universities, 220–23.

Coates, James. 1911. *Photographing the Invisible.* n.p. [USA]: Advanced Thought.

Doyle, Arthur Conan. [1894] n.d. [1930]. "Silver Blaze," in *Memoirs of Sherlock Holmes,* reprinted in *The Complete Sherlock Holmes,* Garden City, N.Y.: Garden City Books.

Gibson, Walter. 1967. *Secrets of Magic: Ancient and Modern.* New York: Grosset & Dunlap, 138–39.

Houdini, Harry. [1924] 1972. *A Magician Among the Spirits.* Reprinted New York: Arno.

Jackson, Dorothy. 1975. Lily Dale-spiritualism center in Chautauqua County, unidentified clipping, dated Oct. 1, in "Campbell Brothers," n.d.

Mullholland, John. [1938] 1979. *Beware Familiar Spirits.* Reprinted New York: Charles Scribner's Sons.

Nickell, Joe. 1995. *Entities.* Amherst, N.Y.: Prometheus.

Nickell, Joe, and John F. Fischer. 1999. *Crime Science.* Lexington: Univ. Press of Kentucky, 177, 178.

Permutt, Cyril. 1988. *Photographing the Spirit World.* Wellingborough, England: Aquarian, 13–15, 22–23, 26, 29–30.

Podmore, Frank. 1902. *Modern Spiritualism.* London: Methuen.

Prendergast, Emma, et al. 1898. Text given in a brochure, *Spirit Painting: Azur.* Lily Dale, N.Y.: Lily Dale Historical Society, n.d. (Other signers were Abby Louise Pettengill, M. Sage, Sidney Kelsey, F. Corden White, and Helen White.)

Swann, Irene. 1969. *The Bangs Sisters and Their Precipitated Spirit Portraits.* Chesterfield, Ind.: Camp Chesterfield.

Chapter 43

Watching the Spirits Paint

In addition to the Campbell "brothers" (the subject of the previous chapter), the other major spiritualists whose mediumship produced "spirit" paintings were the Bangs sisters of Chicago. Sitters watched portraits of their deceased loved ones gradually appear before their eyes.

Misses Elizabeth S. and May E. Bangs were reportedly mediums since childhood, but their "gift" of spirit painting did not appear until the fall of 1894 (*Chesterfield* 1986). They offered clairvoyance, séance trumpet effects and spirit "materializations," "direct" (or so-called automatic) writing, spirit typewriting, and slate effects. But they were most famous for their allegedly ghost-rendered paintings. Their business card advertised, "Life Sized Spirit Portraits a Specialty" ("Bangs Sisters" n.d.; Swann 1969). Indeed, they appear to have made something of a racket of it, as indicated by an Associated Press story of 1908. A woman who alleged to be the wife of a Chicago millionaire accused May Bangs of enticing him into a bigamous relationship, the man having been, it was claimed, "inveigled into the marriage through the instrumentality of a 'spirit portrait' of his dead mother"—produced by the Bangs sisters ("Spirit" 1908).

The Bangses were exposed as tricksters many times. For example, a minister, the Reverend Stanley L. Krebs (1901) sat for one demonstration that involved producing a "spirit" reply to a multipaged letter that he had been instructed to bring, sealed in an envelope. At the beginning of the séance, it was placed between two bound slates. Careful observation, and the use of a small mirror that permitted viewing under the table, allowed Krebs to see how the bound slates were secretly wedged apart and the envelope dropped into Miss Bangs's lap, from whence it was transferred to a tray on the floor and drawn under a closed door. In time, after her accomplice/sister had done her work of steaming open the envelope and penning a reply, the seemingly impossible effect was completed.

The sisters used a variety of techniques for their spirit portraits. Typically, for reasons skeptics may well imagine, "their method was to have the sitter bring a photograph of the dead person to be painted, and the following day the spirits would paint the portrait" (Mulholland 1938, 158). For one-day service, the photograph was reportedly "concealed" from the sisters' view (Swann 1969, 4), but they may have gotten access to it in much the same way as they did the previously described letter.

According to a booklet published at the Indiana spiritualist colony Camp Chesterfield (where the Bangses had a cottage for a number of years), the sisters' earliest work involved "a locked cabinet or curtained off space" and "several 'sittings' were necessary." Later, the "canvas" (actually a paper-mounted panel) was placed before a window with light streaming through, and the sitter watched the picture progress over a period of up to forty minutes or so. Still later, the sisters were able to produce artworks in "as little as five minutes" (Swann 1969, 3).

Reportedly, the Bangs sisters' portraits were examined by unnamed "art experts" who concluded they were not done in any known artistic medium. Rather, the colored substance "could be compared to the dust on a butterflys [sic] wings" (Swann 1969, 3). That is, the particulate matter resembled pollen and would thus seem consistent with a pastel "painting" (i.e. a drawing done in pastel crayons, which consist of pigment mixed with gum).

In fact, at Lily Dale, where the sisters resided for many seasons, I was able to examine two of their "spirit" portraits, which were framed and mounted under glass (as would be expected for certain media, like watercolors or pastels, but not others—for example, oils). I used an illuminated 10X loupe for the inspection. Having myself done portraits in oils, pastels, watercolors, and numerous other media, I saw very familiar characteristics that I could not distinguish from ordinary pastel renderings (Woolwich 1996), including layering and blending of colors and even unmistakable crayon strokes (as in the hair). (See figure 43.1). Indeed, although claiming that for some pictures the spirits under the Bangses' mediumship furnished "their own colouring matter," one contemporary source stated that "for the usual portraiture, coloured French pastels are

Figure 43.1. A typical "spirit" portrait produced by the Bangs sisters.

placed in front of the canvas and these are used by the spirit artists—by a process called 'precipitation'" (Coates 1911, 294).

But how were the pictures actually produced? The evolution of their techniques would seem consistent with deception. The early cabinet method suggests the pictures were simply painted by the sisters out of patrons' view, and the latest productions (done in "five minutes") no doubt involved the substitution of a previously prepared picture. The 'window' technique is most interesting.

Explaining the technique is made difficult by the conflicting descriptions given by credulous observers who lacked knowledge of conjuring methods and who may have misperceived or misremembered exact details. Some accounts insist the effect was produced "in broad daylight" with the blank picture panel simply standing on a table before a window, but May Bangs herself admitted (1910), "The room is shaded sufficiently to cause all the light from the window to pass through the canvas." A more detailed explanation states:

> Two identical, paper-mounted canvases in wooden frames were held up, face to face, against the window, the lower edges resting on a table and the sides gripped by each medium with one hand. A short curtain was hung on either side and an opaque blind was drawn over the canvases. With the light streaming from behind[,] the canvases were translucent. After a quarter of an hour the outlines of shadows began to appear and disappear as if the invisible artist made a preliminary sketch, then the picture began to grow at a feverish rate and when the frames were separated the portrait was found on the paper surface of the canvas next to the sitter. Though the paint was greasy and stuck to the finger on being touched, it left no stain on the paper surface of the other canvas which closely covered it. [Fodor 1933]

The effect was reproduced by stage magicians who were probably inspired by the Bangs sisters' phenomenon. As described in Thayer's *Quality Magic Catalog* (1928), two canvasses were placed face to face in a frame before "a powerful light from the rear." Then, "With the house lights off and while all eyes are intent upon the white illuminated canvas, slowly and faintly at first, a dim shadow appears. Gradually this shadow grows larger and becomes more distinct. The outlines begin to take shape, colors appear, and in a few short moments, a perfect finished picture in all its brilliancy of color is before them."

Thayer's catalog did not, of course, explain how the trick worked, but—significantly—prepared "spirit" portraits were sold with the apparatus. Whatever the secret, it may have been virtually identical to the method used by the Bangses. One notes that, like theirs, the Thayer method employed two canvases, and I think therein lies the crux of the matter.

After considerable experimentation, I have found a way to produce what seems a very similar effect. Someone witnessing it might well write, as one of the Bangses' clients did (Payne 1905): "At first it was a faint shadow, then a wave appeared to sweep across the canvas, and the likeness became plainer. It was a good deal like a sunrise—got brighter until it was perfectly plain and every feature visible." The effect is of a picture seeming to slowly materialize and gradually coming into focus. Indeed, that is just what occurs in the method I came up with.

Briefly, here is my hypothetical reconstruction of a Bangses' spirit-picture séance. Prior to the client entering the room, the previously prepared picture (rolled up perhaps) is secreted in its hiding place (say a drawer on the back of the table). The sitter is invited inside, allowed to casually inspect the premises, and invited to take a seat. The two blank panels are placed face to face, stood up on the table, and held by a sister seated on either side. The aforementioned short curtains are drawn to each side and the opaque blind pulled down. The spirits are invoked, while under cover of the drawn blind, one sister uses her free hand to extract the picture from its hiding place and attach it to the face of the rearmost panel, which is laid on the table behind the other panel. All is now ready for the blind to be raised.

Light is seen streaming through the blank panel, which will function as a sort of screen on which the seemingly materializing image will be projected from the rear. At a suitable time, one of the sisters, using her free hand behind the curtain, stands the picture panel upright a few inches from the other, an action which creates a shadowy, clouded effect upon the "screen." Slowly, the picture panel is moved forward, and as it approaches the screen, colors appear, followed by a blurry face which eventually comes into focus and is recognized. Finally, the completed picture is revealed in full light at the end of the séance (figures 43.2–43.5).[14]

That the Bangses employed some technique such as I have hypothesized is consistent with the overall scenario described in various accounts (Coates 1911; Fodor 1933; "Bangs Sisters" n.d.).[15] It would certainly explain the otherwise puzzling use of *two* panels: the extra one serving both as a *shield* to hide the portrait panel from view and as a *screen* on which to permit rear projection of the image. The following account is also instructive: "A few minutes after they [the face and form] began to appear, the psychics (apparently under impression) lowered the canvas toward me until it touched my breast. May Bangs then got a message by Morse alphabet [supposed spirit-rappings] on the table: 'Your wife is more accustomed to see me in the other aspect.' Up went the canvas again and I saw the profile and bust, but turned round in the opposite direction; instead of the face looking to the right, it was looking to the left. The portrait then proceeded apace, until all the details were filled in"

Figure 43.2. Two paper panels are placed together before a window (or in this case a light box), with a hand showing that nothing is interjected.

[Moore 1910]. This is consistent with the methodology I have described, it having been merely necessary to "flop" (reverse) the picture panel as it was returned to its place on the table.

In some accounts, the picture behind the screen seemed to be manipulated in and out of focus. For example, one witness described how the developing image "disappeared, but came back very soon clearer than before" ("Bangs Sisters" n.d.). One case featured an illusion involving "three pairs of eyes" that "showed on the canvas at once in different poses and places" (an effect that could easily have been accomplished with a separate sheet of paper on which the sets of eyes were rendered).

Many times the spirit-picture production ended with a very interesting effect: the portrait's eyes—which up to that point had been closed—

Figures 43.3 (top left), 43.4 (top right), and 43.5 (right). In the transmitted light, a "cloudiness" forms (not shown), then colors and shapes gradually come into view. A face begins to be recognizable and eventually becomes even sharper. Finally, finished portrait on one panel (shown here in reflected light) is presented to the sitter. (Photos by Joe Nickell)

suddenly (or sometimes gradually) opened, "like a person awakening" (Payne 1905; Coates 294–331). Now, the same effect was actually a popular parlor diversion of the Bangses' time (the late nineteenth to early twentieth century) with advertising cards being specially printed for the purpose. One for Stafford's Ink, for instance, depicted a little girl with closed eyes, behind which—printed on the reverse with good registration—were a pair of heavily outlined, open eyes. In ordinary viewing (*reflected* light) the child slept, but when the card was held up to a window or lamp (i.e., viewed in *transmitted* light), the open eyes became dominant and she suddenly awoke. This effect may have been copied by the Bangs sisters, although it would have been accomplished differently, since the portrait-side of the finished picture would have required open eyes. Having closed eyes behind (as on an overlay) would not seem to work, since the open eyes (with their dark irises and pupils) would still dominate from the beginning. There may be several ways to solve the problem: the effect might simply have been produced by tipping the picture forward so that the eyes were brought into focus, coupled with the power of suggestion; or the finished, open eyes might actually have been drawn in, in a final stage, under some pretext of pulling down the opaque blind; or by some other method. (For example, it is possible to have a removable, opaque material applied on the back to the area behind the eyes so that in transmitted light there appear deep, shaded sockets, but when the material is peeled off the eyes open.) In any event, one sitter did report that before opening, the eyes of the spirit portrait were "*indistinct* and *apparently* closed" (emphasis added; Holland 1909).

Although, as indicated earlier, the Bangs sisters may not always have received a photograph of the deceased subject in advance of the séance, they could nevertheless proceed once they gained access (by some subterfuge) to the photo. One sister could then go off to produce the portrait while the other kept the patron distracted. For example, one wrote, "Entering the seance-room, and finding only three canvases, I selected two of them, took them out in the sunlight, in company with one of the Miss Bangs, exposed them for fifteen minutes to the strong rays of the noonday sun, examined the surface thoroughly to fully assure myself that they were not chemically prepared, at the same time to secretly mark them for identification." Subsequently, the identification marks would show that the "canvas" had not been switched (Thurston 1910). (If the panel was not marked—most accounts omit that detail—the procedure is simplified, since the portrait can be prepared on a panel that is switched for one of the selected ones, eliminating the need to surreptitiously affix the picture to a panel during the séance.)

One incident is particularly revealing: a couple who had sought a picture of their deceased son concluded that the resulting image resembled him only "in a general way" and "was not even a fairly good portrait." In rationalizing the failure, one writer pointed out (perhaps more wisely than he knew) that the couple "had no photograph of their departed son with them" (Coates 1911, 325). Thus the Bangs sisters were apparently left with few options. They could fish for a description (in the manner of a police artist eliciting an eyewitness's recollection) or opt to produce a generalized child's portrait that the credulous couple might accept. In contrast, when a photograph had been brought to the sitting, the "spirit" painting might be pronounced "a perfect enlargement of the original" ("Bangs Sisters" n.d.). Whatever techniques the sisters actually employed—and May Bangs (1910) acknowledged that "No two sittings" were "exactly alike"—they were obviously effective, given the many testimonials they elicited. Significantly, as *physical* mediumship has largely given way to *mental* phenomena (witness the rise of mediums like James Van Praagh, who limit themselves to readings [Nickell 1998]), "spirit" paintings have all but disappeared. A few historic examples remain as reminders of an earlier, though not necessarily more credulous, time.

References

"Bangs Sisters." n.d., Album, Lily Dale Museum (business card, clippings, photos, etc.)

Doerflinger, William. 1977. *The Magic Catalog.* New York: E.P. Dutton, 196.

Krebs, Rev. Stanley L. 1901. A description of some trick methods used by Miss Bangs, of Chicago. *Journal of Society for Psychical Research* 10.175 (Jan.): 5–16.

Moore, W. Usborne. 1910. Letter, quoted in Coates 1911.

Chapter 44

Stigmata

Of reputed miraculous powers, perhaps none is more popularly equated with saintliness than stigmata, the wounds of Christ's crucifixion allegedly duplicated spontaneously upon the body of a Christian. Indeed one historical survey indicated that about a fifth of all stigmatics are eventually beatified or canonized (Biot 1962, 23). The year 1999 brought renewed interest in the alleged phenomenon. Among the offerings were the movie *Stigmata* (which even contained a brief shot of my book, *Looking for a Miracle* [Radford 1999]); a Fox television pseudodocumentary, *Signs from God*, which featured a major segment on stigmata (Willesee 1999); and the Vatican's beatification of the Italian stigmatic Padre Pio (*CNN & Time* 1999). For a BBC documentary produced for the Discovery Channel, I took a new look at the subject.

Evolving Phenomenon

From the death of Jesus, about A.D. 29 or 30, nearly twelve centuries would pass before stigmata began to appear—unless one counts a cryptic reference by St. Paul. In Galatians 6:17 he wrote, "I bear in my body the marks of the Lord Jesus." Many scholars believe Paul was speaking figuratively, but in any case the statement may have been sufficient to prompt imitation.

St. Francis of Assisi (1182–1226) is credited with being the first stigmatic—or at least the first "true" one, his affliction occurring just two years after that of a man from Oxford who had exhibited the five crucifixion wounds in 1222. That man claimed to be the son of God and the redeemer of mankind, but he was arrested for imposture, his wounds presumed to have been self-inflicted. In 1224, St. Francis went with some of his "disciples" up Mount Alverno in the Apennines. After forty days of fasting and prayer, he had a vision of Christ on the cross, whereafter he received the four nail wounds and a pierced side. Francis appears to have sparked a copycat phenomenon, since publication of his reputed miracle was followed by occurrences of stigmata "even among people who were much lower than St. Francis in religious stature, and have continued to occur without intermission ever since," according to Catholic scholar Herbert Thurston (1952, 122–23). He continues: "What I infer is that the example of St. Francis created what I have called the 'crucifixion complex.' Once it had been brought home to contemplatives that it was possible to be physically conformed to the sufferings of Christ by bearing His wound-marks in the hands, feet and side, then the idea of this form of union with their Divine Master took shape in the minds of many. It became in fact a pious obsession; so much so that in a few exceptionally sensitive individuals the idea conceived in the mind was realized in the flesh." Thurston believed stigmatization was due to the effects of suggestion, but experimental attempts to duplicate the phenomenon, for example by using hypnosis, have been unsuccessful—except for one case which appears to have been a hoax. (The psychiatrist reported that bloody tears welled inside the subject's eyelids, but a photograph shows rivulets *originating outside* the eyes [see Wilson 1988].)

As the thirteenth century advanced, exhibitions of stigmata began to proliferate, one authority regarding it as "a sort of explosion" (Biot 1962, 18). Within a hundred years of St. Francis's death, over twenty cases had occurred. The trend continued in successive centuries, with no fewer than 321 stigmatics being recorded by 1908. Not only were they invariably Catholic, but more than a third had come from Italy and the rest mostly from France, Spain, and Portugal, demonstrating that "the Roman Catholic countries, mostly with a Latin and Mediterranean influence have dominated the history of stigmata" (Harrison 1994, 9; Wilson 1988, 10). The twentieth-century record of stigmata, however, "shows a change in pattern." Italy dominated somewhat less, and cases were reported from Great Britain, Australia, and the United States (Harrison 1994, 9). The latter included (in 1972) a ten-year-old African American girl named Cloretta Robinson, a Baptist and thus one of a very few non-

Catholic Christians to have exhibited the stigmata (including at least three Anglicans) (Harrison 1994, 9, 87).

Other evidence that stigmata represent an *evolving* phenomenon comes from the form of the wounds. Interestingly, those of St. Francis (except for the wound in his side) "were not wounds which bled but impressions of the heads of the nails, round and black and standing clear from the flesh" (Harrison 1994, 25). Since then, although bleeding wounds have been typical, they have been exceedingly varied, showing "no consistency even remotely suggesting them as replications of one single, original pattern" (Wilson 1988, 63). For example, some wounds have been tiny, straight slits, others simple crosses, multiple slash marks, or indentations—even, in the case of Therese Neumann, shifting from round to rectangular over time, presumably as she learned the true shape of Roman nails. In some instances, there were no apparent lesions beneath the seepages (or possibly fake applications!) of blood (Wilson 1988, 64; Harrison 1994, 70; Nickell 1999). Similarly, the wound in the side (representing the Roman soldier's lance [John 19:34]) has appeared at different locations in the right or left side, or has been variously shaped—as a lateral slit, crescent, cross, etc.—or has not appeared at all. Some stigmatics have exhibited wounds on the forehead (as if caused by a crown of thorns [John 19:2]), markings on the back (representing scourging [John 19:1]), or abrasions on the shoulder as from carrying a cross), and so on, while others have not exhibited these. There are even symbolic markings, such as "a vivid cross" that twice appeared on the forehead of stigmatist Heather Woods (a phenomenon previously experienced by seventeenth-century stigmatic Jeanne des Anges). And stigmata-like skin lettering—including the names of Joseph, Mary, and Jesus—appeared and reappeared on the left hand of Jeanne des Anges (1602–1665) (Wilson 1988, 64, 131–48; Harrison 1994, 2, 52).

Another trend in the evolving phenomenon—represented for example by Virginia priest James Bruse—is the location of nail wounds in the wrists. Others have tended to have them in the palms of the hands, so Bruse's wrist marks seem instructive. As Harrison observes (1994, 40), stigmata in the wrists have appeared only since photography "revealed the wounds so positioned in the Turin Shroud." Actually, while the hands of the figure on the shroud are folded so that a single exit wound shows, it seems to indicate the palm, although the flow of "blood" does extend to the wrist, thus giving the appearance of the wound being located there

278

(Nickell 1983). Those who believe the shroud authentic (despite definitive scientific proof to the contrary [Nickell 1998]) have an interest in promoting the wrist site. They point to experiments with cadavers that supposedly show nailed hands could not support the weight of a body and would therefore tear away (Barbet 1950). (Skeletal remains have been discovered of only a single first-century crucifixion victim, a man known as Jehohanan. A scratch on the lower end of the right radius suggests a nail had penetrated between the radius and ulna. Interestingly, a nail had been driven through the heel bones from the side, indicating that Jehohanan had been forced into "a sort of sidesaddle position," quite unlike the familiar depiction of Jesus in Christian art [Wilson 1979, 50, illus. fol. 128].)

In any event, if it is true that the wrist location is anatomically untenable—notwithstanding the gospels (John 20:25–27 and Luke 24:40)—the argument could be made that all stigmata in the hands are therefore false, a judgment that would exclude most reported instances. Certainly the shift of location to the wrists (in keeping with a modern view) is not surprising. Stigmatics in the middle ages likewise "produced wounds in themselves which corresponded to the pictures of Christ suffering around them" (Harrison 1994, 128). Similarly, the 1974 crucifixion vision of Ethel Chapman, during which her stigmata allegedly appeared, was "based on the images in an illustrated Bible which she'd been given" (Harrison 1994, 128; Wilson 1988, 147). Such strong connections between popular images and the nature of the stigmata are powerful evidence that the phenomenon is imitative.

Stigmatic Profile

A look at stigmata as an evolving phenomenon also sheds light on the people involved. The previously mentioned census of 321 stigmatics reveals "an interesting seven-to-one proportion of women to men." Not only were almost all Roman Catholics, but "a very high proportion were cloistered priests or nuns"—as was, of course, the first stigmatic, St. Francis, and such thirteenth-century stigmatics as the Blessed Helen of Veszprim (1237); St. Christina of Stommeln (1268); and others (Harrison 1994, 10, 27–28; Wilson 1988, 131–33). Indeed, of the 321 stigmatics, 109 came from the Dominican Order and 102 from the Franciscans—an overall percentage of 66 percent from religious orders versus 34 percent laypeople (Biot 1962, 20).

Many stigmatics seem—also like St. Francis—to have had an early life that might be characterized as notably "worldly" before coming to believe they had been called to serve God. As a youth, Francis—the son of a wealthy merchant—was "gay, adventurous, generous, and popular" (Coulson 1958) and spent his leisure time in "hedonistic extravagance" (Jones 1994), even being crowned by his friends "king of the revelers" ("Francis" 1960). He later claimed he heard Christ's voice asking him to rebuild a church, whereupon he plunged into religious service, adopting the life of a hermit and later forming the order of friars named for him (the Franciscans) (Coulson 1958). Others who were transformed from worldly to austere included the Blessed Angela of Foligno (1250–1309), who had married and had several children but lost them all after her husband's death; selling all her possessions she gave the proceeds to the poor and joined the Third Order of St. Francis (Wilson 1988, 132). Another example would be St. Catherine of Genoa (1447–1510), who married at sixteen, spent "ten years of a pleasure-seeking existence," then, with her husband, devoted her life to tending to the sick in a local hospital (Wilson 1988, 133). A more recent example is that of Father James Bruse (the Virginia priest with the wrist wounds mentioned earlier). Bruse's preordination life included finding his way into the *Guinness Book of World Records* in 1978 for riding a roller coaster for five straight days. He became a Roman Catholic priest the following year but subsequently found he had lapsed into a routine. Then came the "dramatic" events of 1991–1992 in which he not only experienced the stigmata but discovered statues weeping in his presence (Harrison 1994, 80–87).

Also characteristic of many, if not most, stigmatics is a variety of symptoms "ranging from what have been described as the 'mystical' to the 'hysterical'" (Harrison 1994, 31). Taking the hysterical first, Marguerite of the Blessed Sacrament (Marguerite Parigot, 1619–1648) was prey to "devastating apparent diabolic attacks," while Anna Maria Castreca (1670–1736) "would hurl herself violently around the room" and revert "to the speech and manner of a child," and in his early life, Padre Pio (1887–1968) was "emotionally disturbed." A few stigmatics were allegedly attended by "poltergeist phenomena" (disturbances attributed to "noisy spirits" but often found to be the pranks of adolescents); among them were Johann Jetzer (c. 1483–c. 1515) and Teresa Helena Higginson (1844–1905) (Wilson 1988, 131–48).

Illness is another frequent characteristic. René Biot, in his *The Enigma of the Stigmata* (1962, 57), exclaims with wonder at "how many stigmatics have been bedridden!" He notes that St. Lidwina (d. 1433) had so many alleged illnesses that she was "a sort of pathological museum," indeed a "museum of horrors." Similarly, Therese Neumann experienced alternate bouts of convulsions, blindness, deafness, mutism, paralysis, and so on—effects that appear to have been due to hysterical hypochondria or, more likely, outright fakery since the alleged conditions evaded diagnosis (Rogo 1982, 65–66; Nickell 1993, 227–28). Given such cases, one researcher noted the parallels between stigmata and Münchausen's syndrome, an emotional disorder involving feigned or inflicted illness (Schnabel 1993).

281

Still other stigmatics—like St. Veronica Giuliani (c. 1640–1727), Victoire Claire (c. 1808–1883), along with numerous others—often lapsed into states of ecstasy (i.e., apparent trance arising out of religious fervor). Following St. Francis, who supposedly received his stigmata during a vision of Jesus' crucifixion, came several emulators, including Passitea Crogi, who on Palm Sunday 1589, fell into an ecstasy and later described a vision of Christ bruised and bleeding. Other vision-delivered stigmata were claimed by Johann Jetzer, Therese Neumann (1898–1962), and James Bruse.

A great number of stigmatics were blessed, allegedly, with other supernatural phenomena, including the powers of prophecy and healing, levitation, bilocation (supposedly being in two places simultaneously), and inedia (the alleged ability to forgo nourishment). As an example of the latter, Angela of Foligno (1250–1309) reportedly went without food for twelve years. After death, the bodies of a few stigmatics were discovered to be "incorruptible" (i.e., able to withstand decay). Also, vials of blood preserved from the stigmatic wounds of Passitea Crogi purportedly reliquefy on occasion (Wilson 1988, 131–48). Needless to say, perhaps, such claims are unproved, and may be attributed to folklore, misperceptions and misunderstandings born of superstition, and pious fraud (Nickell 1993).

That many stigmatics were fakes is well established. For example, Magdalena de la Cruz, having become ill in 1543 and fearful of dying a sinner, confessed that her stigmata, inedia, and other phenomena were deliberate deceptions. Another, Maria de la Visitacion, known as the "holy nun of Lisbon," was accused by a sister nun who saw her painting a fake wound onto her hand. Although initially defended by doctors in 1587, she was brought before the Inquisition, whereupon her wounds were scrubbed and the coloration washed off, revealing "unblemished flesh" beneath (Wilson 1988, 26). Another fake was Palma Maria Matarelli, who not only exhibited the stigmata but also "miraculously" produced Communion wafers on her tongue. Pope Pius IX privately branded her a fraud, stating that he had the proof in his desk drawer and adding, "She has befooled a whole crowd of pious and credulous souls" (quoted in Wilson 1988, 42). A more public condemnation awaited Gigliola Giorgini (b. 1933): discredited by church authorities, in 1984 she was convicted of fraud by an Italian court (Wilson 1988, 42, 147).

The authenticity of some stigmata may be questioned in light of the mystic's character. For example, Teresa Helena Higginson (1844–1905), an English stigmatic, was dismissed as a teacher on accusations of theft, drunkenness, and unseemly conduct. And Berthe Mrazek, a Brussels-born circus performer turned stigmatic, was first regarded seriously, but doubts came in 1924 when she was arrested for theft by deception and committed to an insane asylum (Nickell 1993, 223). Still other stigmatics must be viewed in light of their propensity for self-punishment and -mutilation. These include the thirteenth-century masochist Lukardis of Oberweimar who, before exhibiting the stigmata "had the habit of driving her fingernails into her palms" (Wilson 1988, 132)!

Circumstances surrounding the twentieth century's two best-known stigmatics—Theresa Neumann and Padre Pio (both mentioned previously)—raise further doubts about the genuineness of the phenomenon. For example, a Professor Martini conducted a surveillance of Therese Neumann and observed that blood would flow from her wounds only on those occasions when he was persuaded to leave the room, as if something "needed to be hidden from observation." He added: "It was for the same reason that I disliked her frequent manipulations behind the raised [bed] coverings." (Similar suspicions also accompanied her professed demonstration of inedia.) (Wilson 1988, 53, 114–15) As to Padre Pio, the local Roman Catholic clergy accused his friary of putting him on display in order to make money. Certainly a cult grew up around him, and village hucksters sold his credulous disciples alleged relics in the form of pieces of cloth daubed with chicken blood. Some physicians believed his wounds superficial, but the determination was made difficult by their supposed painfulness and their being covered by "thick crusts" of supposed blood. A distinguished pathologist sent by the Holy See noted that beyond the scabs was a lack of "any sign of edema, of penetration, or of redness, even when examined with a good magnifying glass." Indeed, he concluded that the side "wound" had not penetrated the skin at all. And while in life Pio perpetually kept his "wounds" concealed (wearing fingerless gloves on his hands), at death there was only unblemished skin (Ruffin 1982, 146–54, 305).

Many Catholic scholars have expressed skepticism about the genuineness of stigmata. One was a neuropsychiatrist who had personally observed thirty stigmatization cases and in none of them "was able to eliminate, absolutely and decisively, every kind of artificial action" (quoted in Biot 1962, 102–03). Although attributing most instances to suggestion rather than hoaxing, Herbert Thurston (1952, 100) found "no satisfactory case of stigmatization since St. Francis of Assisi." Thurston and others defend Francis on grounds of his piety and character; however, his single-minded desire to imitate Jesus, his "immense capacity for self-sacrifice," and the fact that "he was a son of the church to the marrow of his bones" (Coulson 1958, 188) may have led him to foster a pious deception—something that many others have clearly been unable to resist.

A Recent Case

The Fox network's "Signs from God" heralded the Bolivian miracle claimant Katya Rivas, whose repertoire included not only stigmata but the production of an unusual "delta state" on an EEG, automatic writing in languages she allegedly did not know, and multicolored "glitter" on a print of the Image of Guadalupe in her home. (For a review, see Nickell 1999.) The show was hosted by Australian journalist Michael Willesee who, during an airplane accident in 1998, had "re-embraced his Roman Catholic faith in an instant conversion" (Randi 1999).

Rivas claimed she received a message from Jesus telling her that while she would not produce stigmata as hoped on Good Friday (the day Christians commemorate Jesus' crucifixion), patience would be rewarded. A later message announced that full stigmata would take place on the day following Corpus Christi (a Catholic festival honoring the Eucharist or Lord's Supper). The night before the stigmata were to appear, Rivas gave a sample of her blood as a control, since there was speculation that the blood from her stigmatic wounds might not be hers exclusively. Come the appointed time, unsuspecting viewers were treated to what had all the signs of a staged event. Rivas was abed, in a fashion reminiscent of

Therese Neumann, and the covers provided ample concealment if trickery were involved. No doctor was in attendance. Michael Willesee made a cursory examination of Rivas's hands and feet and referred to scars from previous stigmata. These appeared on her feet, but it was unclear whether there were prior marks on her hands also. (This is significant in light of developments, as we shall see.)

During real or pretended suffering, Rivas exhibited, first, pricklike marks and bleeding on the forehead (as from a crown of thorns)—though apparently not on the sides or back of the head, suggesting the marks were only for show. Then there was (possibly) a pink mark on the left palm, followed by a tiny cross on the back of the hand that was initially without blood. Later there were bloody "wounds" on both sides of the hands and feet. Willesee used swabs to obtain samples of the blood for analysis. No side wound or other crucifixion markings ever appeared. At the end of the experience—or demonstration—Rivas displayed paroxysms of a deathlike agony imitative of Jesus' crucifixion.

Rivas's wounds were never seen in the act of spontaneously issuing but instead were shown in incremental shots *after* each appearance—just as they would if self-inflicted during periods of concealment. Among other suspicious elements were the mismatching of "entrance" and "exit" wounds, those on the left foot being far out of alignment. Also, those on the palms and soles of the feet were, as far as could be seen, only smears of blood. Moreover, such wounds as could be distinguished were not puncturelike but rather consisted of multiple cuts, including the cross on the back of the left hand (figure 44.1) and an array of slashes atop each foot. The latter are curiously in pairs (figure 44.2) as if produced by a two-pronged implement, like the sharp-cornered, calyxlike ring Katya Rivas wore during the event.

Supposedly only twenty-four hours later, the camera recorded Willesee inspecting Rivas's wounds. Apparently those on the palms and soles had vanished completely (but were not specifically shown), and the markings that remained were seemingly in an advanced state of healing. Willesee treated this as remarkable, but another interpretation is that the vanishing of some "wounds" indicated they were never there in the first place and that most or all of the markings were old cuts from previously faked stigmata. A genuine element of the affair was the blood itself, which was shown by DNA analysis to be Katya Rivas's. Unfortunately for the miracle-mongering journalist Willesee—who made much of the possi-

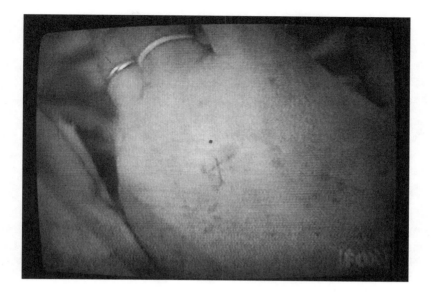

Figure 44.1. Cross-shaped wound on back of Katya Rivas's left hand.

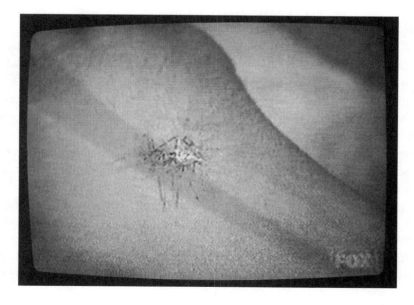

Figure 44.2. Post-stigmata marks on top of one of Rivas's feet, most or all of which are scars from previous "stigmata."

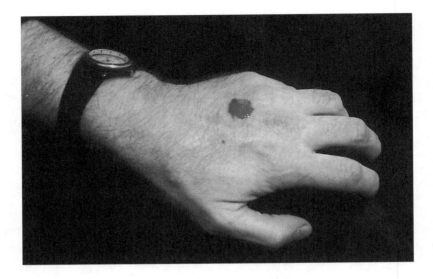

Figure 44.3. Small cuts on author's hand produce sufficient blood to simulate a sizeable wound.

bility that it might be Christ's blood in whole or in part—it proved to be Rivas's alone.

When I was asked to appear on a television documentary on stigmata and to discuss the Katya Rivas case, I decided to experiment beforehand by inflicting wounds on myself. I used a sharp blade to cut a cross on the back of my left hand. This shallow, superficial wound yielded enough blood to produce the effect of a larger wound (44.3) and even (by transfer) create a "wound" on the palm (figure 44.4). The next day, the latter had of course vanished and the cross had begun to heal. There are certain medicinal preparations that allegedly promote healing and, as I found, cosmetic creams that through their hiding power can seemingly advance the healing or eliminate the wound entirely.

My examination of the video showing Katya Rivas's alleged stigmatization and the simple experiments I performed persuaded me that not only could her stigmata not be authenticated, but, indeed—like other instances of the alleged phenomenon throughout history—they cannot be distinguished from a pious hoax.

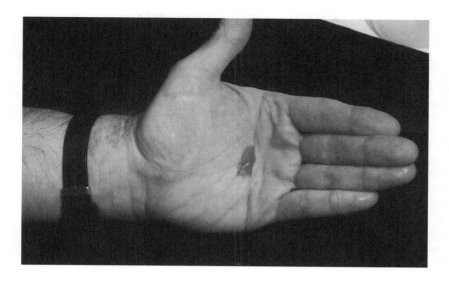

Figure 44.4. Transfer of blood from wound shown in figure 3 produced fake wound on palm.

References

Barbet, Pierre. 1950. *A Doctor at Calvary*, Fr. ed.; Eng. trans. Garden City, N.Y.: Image, 1963, 103–20.

Biot, René. 1962. *The Enigma of the Stigmata.* New York: Hawthorn.

CNN & Time. 1999. TV segment on CNN, August 8.

Coulson, John, ed. 1958. *The Saints: A Concise Biographical Dictionary.* New York: Hawthorn, 187–88.

"Francis of Assisi, St." 1960. *Encyclopaedia Britannica.*

Harrison, Ted. 1994. *Stigmata: A Medieval Phenomenon in a Modern Age.* New York: St. Martin's.

Jones, Alison. 1994. *The Wordsworth Dictionary of Saints.* Ware, England: Wordsworth Editions, 116–18.

Nickell, Joe. 1993. *Looking for a Miracle.* Amherst, N.Y.: Prometheus.

———. 1998. *Inquest on the Shroud of Turin.* Buffalo, N.Y.: Prometheus, 61–63.

———. 1999. Thumbs down on Fox's "Signs from God." *Skeptical Inquirer* 23.6 (Nov./Dec.): 61.

Radford, Ben. 1999. Movie review: *Stigmata. Corrales (New Mexico) Comment,* Sept. 25.

Randi, James. 1999. Randi's Archive, James Randi Educational Foundation,http://www.randi.org/jr/7-30-1999.html, July 30.

Rogo, D. Scott. 1982. *Miracles. A Parascientific Inquiry into Wondrous Phenomena.* New York: Dial.

Ruffin, C. Bernard. 1982. *Padre Pio: The True Story.* Huntington, Ind.: Our Sunday Visitor.

Thurston, Herbert. 1952. *The Physical Phenomena of Mysticism.* Chicago: H. Regnery.

Schnabel, Jim. 1993. The Münch bunch. *Fortean Times* 70 (Aug./Sept.), 23–29.

Willesee, Michael (exec. prod.) 1999. *Signs from God,* Fox TV, July 28.

Wilson, Ian. 1979. *The Shroud of Turin,* rev. ed. Garden City, N.Y.: Image.

———. 1988. *The Bleeding Mind.* London: Weidenfeld and Nicolson.

Chapter 45

Haunted Inns

If testimonials in countless books and articles are to be believed, spending the night in a quaint old hotel might provide an encounter with an extra, ethereal visitor. In the course of thirty years of paranormal investigation, I have had the opportunity to experience many "haunted" sites. These have included burial places, like England's West Kennet Long Barrow (where I failed to see the specter of a "Druid priest" that allegedly attends the ancient tomb); religious sanctuaries, such as Christ Church Cathedral in Fredericton, New Brunswick, Canada (where the apparition of the first bishop's wife did not materialize); theaters, including the Lancaster (New York) Opera House (where a spectral "Lady in Lavender" was a no-show); houses, like the historic residence of William Lyon Mackenzie in Toronto (where ghostly footfalls on the stairs were actually those of real people on a staircase next door); and other sites, notably inns—the subject of this investigative roundup. (Most of the inns cited— all personally investigated—included an overnight stay, staff interviews, background research, etc. [Nickell 1972–2000]).

Why haunted inns? Obviously, places open to the public have more numerous and varied visitors, and hence more opportunities for ghostly experiences, than do private dwellings and out-of-the-way sites. And inns—meaning hotels, motels, guesthouses, bed-and-breakfasts, and other places that provide overnight lodging—offer much more. They not only allow extended time periods for visitors to have unusual experiences but also insure that the guests will be there during a range of states from alertness through sleep. Almost predictably, sooner or later, someone will awaken to an apparition at his or her bedside.

Appearances of the Dead

The experience is a common type of hallucination, known popularly as a "waking dream," which takes place between being fully asleep and fully awake. Such experiences typically include bizarre imagery (bright lights or apparitions of demons, ghosts, aliens, etc.) and/or auditory hallucinations. "Sleep paralysis" may also occur, whereby there is an inability to move because the body is still in the sleep mode (Nickell 1995).

A good example of an obvious waking dream is reported by "A.C." She was asleep on board the *Queen Mary*, the former ocean liner that since 1971 has been permanently docked at Long Beach, California. As the woman relates: "I awoke from a deep sleep around midnight. I saw a figure walking near my daughter's sleeping bag toward the door. Thinking it was my sister, I called out. There was no answer. It was then that I noticed my sister was lying next to me. I sat up in bed and watched the person in white walk through the door! Another example reported at the Hotel Queen Mary is credited to "H.V.":

> I was awakened from my sleep and observed the image of a person standing in front of my bed. There were no apparent physical features, but it appeared to be holding a flashlight, with a light shining out of it that was brighter than the form itself. I watched as the image swayed back and forth. When I called my roommate the image backed up. I called again and the vision backed up even further, toward the door. I reached for the light switch and tried to turn it on. The light switch seemed to spark and wouldn't turn on all the way. Finally, my roommate woke up; the light came on, and whatever it was, was gone. We slept with the TV on the rest of the night. It was a great experience, and I had a lot of fun! (Wlodarski et al. 1995, 33, 35)

To be sure, not all sightings of ghostly figures are of the waking-dream variety, many in fact occurring during normal activity. Some are like the report of "J.M.," who was at the *Queen Mary's* Purser's Desk when, he stated, "I caught a brief glimpse out of the corner of my eye, of someone or something moving," or like that of "P.T.," who said, "I saw something move out of the corner of my eye . . . a brief glimpse of someone or something" (Wlodarski 1995, 32, 36). Actually, the illusion that something is moving in the peripheral vision is quite common. The typical cause may be a "floater," a bit of drifting material in the eye's vitreous humor, although a twitching eyelid or other occurrence is also possible.

Such an illusion or a different stimulus—a noise, a subjective feeling, etc.—might trigger, as in one person who had such an experience aboard the *Queen Mary,* a "mental image." In that case it was of a man "wearing a blue mechanic's uniform"—a "feeling" that left after a few moments (Wlodarski et al. 1995, 32). In certain especially imaginative individuals, the mental image might be superimposed upon the visual scene, thus creating a seemingly apparitional event.

This may be the explanation for a frequently reported type of apparition that is seen momentarily and then vanishes when the percipient looks away for an instant. For example, a New Mexico hotel, La Posada de Santa Fe—which is allegedly haunted by the spirit of Julie Staab (1844–1896), wife of the original builder—offers no fewer than three sightings of this type. One was reported in 1979 by an employee who was cleaning one night. Although the place was deserted, he looked up to see a translucent woman standing near a fireplace. Inexplicably, he "returned to his cleaning," an act that one writer noted showed "remarkable composure." Then, "when he looked up again the figure had vanished." On another occasion a security guard showed less reserve when, seeing what he thought was Julie Staab, "He turned and ran, and when he looked back, the figure had vanished." Yet again, a "beautifully dressed" Julie, reposing in an armchair, was seen by the hotel phone operator. However, "When she looked back at the chair a few seconds later, the ghost had vanished" (Mead 1995, 157–58). Such reports suggest that the apparition is only a mental image that occurs in a kind of reverie.

Indeed, personal experience as well as research data demonstrates that ghostly perceptions often derive from daydreams or other altered states of consciousness. Haraldsson (1988), for instance, specifically determined that apparitional sightings were linked to periods of reverie. As well, Andrew MacKenzie (1982) demonstrated that a third of the hallucinatory cases he studied occurred either just before or after sleep, or while the percipient was in a relaxed state or concentrating on some activity like reading, or was performing routine work. The association of apparitional experiences with a dreamlike state was also reported by G.N.M. Terrell (1973). He observed that apparitions of people invariably appear fully clothed and are frequently accompanied by objects, just as they are in dreams, because the clothing and other objects are required by the apparitional drama. The three La Posada encounters are consistent with all of these research observations. That the apparitions vanish when the observer's gaze is shifted could be explained by the hypothesis that the reverie is merely broken.

Whereas "waking-dream" type encounters are obviously more likely to be experienced by hotel guests rather than employees, the reverie or daydream type is often reported by the latter—as in all three of the La Posada examples, as well as some of the instances from the *Queen Mary* (Wlodarski et al. 1995, 48, 49) and elsewhere. Hotel staff performing routine chores may be particularly susceptible to this type of apparitional experience.

Selling Ghosts

The power of suggestion can help trigger ghostly encounters. According to noted psychologist and fellow ghostbuster Robert A. Baker, "We tend to see and hear those things we believe in" (Baker and Nickell 1992, 129). Even without the prompting that comes from an inn's reputation for being haunted, the mere *ambiance* of places with antique architecture and quaint decor can set the stage for spirits to debut. An example is Belhurst Castle (figure 45.1), a turreted stone inn in Geneva, New York, whose high-ceilinged lobby is graced with wood paneling, a large fireplace, and a suit of armor to help conjure up romantic notions. Historic sites like Maine's Kennebunk Inn (expanded from a home built in 1799); Gettysburg, Pennsylvania's Farnsworth House (constructed in 1810 and its south side pockmarked with bullet holes from the Battle of Gettysburg); and even the more recent Hotel Boulderado in Boulder, Colorado (which opened on New Year's Day 1909 and boasts among its former guests Bat Masterson), offer the impress of history and legend. So does the Bardstown, Kentucky, Jailer's Inn, a bed-and-breakfast converted from the old Nelson County Jail (built in 1819), and in Santa Fe, the historic, adobe La Fonda Inn.

The influence of setting and mood on reports of phantoms is sometimes acknowledged even by those who approach the subject with great credulity, although they may interpret the linkage differently. Broadcaster Andrew Green, for example, in his treatise *Haunted Inns and Taverns* (1995), says of some copies of English pubs in Europe, the United States, and elsewhere: "A few have reproduced the ambiance so successfully that ghostly manifestations, such as might be associated with a genuine article, have occurred there." Green opines that the "genial atmosphere" of

Figure 45.1. Belhurst Castle, an inn in Western New York, is the subject of haunting tales and other legends.

such taverns attracts authentic English ghosts. He seems not to consider the possibility that the setting merely influences the imaginations of those making the reports.

In contrast is the knowing statement of ghost hunter Mason Winfield (1997, 176)—referring to the allegedly haunted Holiday Inn at Grand Island, New York—that "The environment of the Inn is not the gloomy, historic sort that puts people in mind of spooks." As one who has spent an uneventful night in that resort hotel, indeed in its reputedly most haunted room 422, I quite agree. But apparitions can occur anywhere. The Holiday Inn's child ghost "Tanya" apparently originated with an impressionable maid who was cleaning the fourth-floor room shortly after the hotel opened in 1973. The housekeeper suddenly glimpsed a little girl standing in the doorway and, startled, dropped a couple of drinking glasses. When she looked up again, the child was gone. As the maid tried to flee, it was reported, "somehow her cart trapped her in the room. She screamed" (Winfield 1997, 176). Her apparitional encounter seems consistent with the typical conditions we have already discussed: at the time, she was performing routine chores. As to the cart, most likely, flustered, she merely encountered it where she had left it, blocking her flight, and panicked.

Other sightings there—like that of a Canadian man who awoke to see a little girl at the foot of his bed (Safiuddin 1994)—were of the waking-dream variety. But why is it often a little girl (even if varyingly identified as age "five or six" or "about age 10" [Winfield 1997, 176; Safiuddin 1994])? Those knowing about "Tanya" before their sighting may thus be influenced, while those who do not may, in light of subsequent statements or leading questions from those to whom they report an incident, reinterpret a vague sense of presence or a shadowy form as the expected ghost child. To compound the problem, many of the reports are at second- or third-hand, or an even greater remove.

Researching tales like that of the Holiday Inn's child specter can be illuminating. In that case, there is no evidence to support claims of "a little girl who was burned to death in a house that formerly stood on the site" (Hauck 1996, 291). The Grand Island historian was unable to document any deadly fire at that locale. The only known blaze at the site occurred in 1963, at which time the historic John Nice mansion had been transformed into a restaurant, and there was not a single fatality (Klingel 2000). My search of the nearby Whitehaven Cemetery, where the Nice family is buried, failed to turn up any credible candidate for the role of ghost girl, least of all one named "Tanya"—which, as census and cemetery records show, was not the name of any of John Nice's ten daughters (Linenfelser 2000).

A similar lack of substantiation characterizes many other haunting tales. Consider, for instance, the previously mentioned Belhurst Castle, located in New York's scenic Finger Lakes region. Its colorful brochure announces: "Tales persist of the romantic past, of secret tunnels, hidden treasures buried in the walls and on the grounds, of ghosts and hauntings. Fact or Fancy? No one knows." Actually the tales originated with the old mansion that previously stood on the site. No tunnel was ever found, and the stories apparently derive from a "small blind cellar" discovered beneath the old house when it was razed in 1888 to build the present "castle." There was merely speculation that it might have served as a hidden vault for the securing of valuables. Prior to this, the dilapidated mansion "was a favorite playground of Geneva's adventure-seeking youth, who were enticed by its reputation of being haunted," according to a knowledgeable source, who adds, "However, there is no record that any 'spooks' were ever encountered there, or ghostly manifestations of any sort whatsoever" (Emmons 1959). Nevertheless, citing some other Belhurst tales, Robin Mead states in his *Haunted Hotels* (1995), "a property such as Belhurst Castle ought to be surrounded by legends like this, for they complement the atmosphere of romance and add a touch of mystery."

295

Several inns I have investigated have featured ghosts in their promotional materials. In addition to Belhurst Castle, they include the Hotel Boulderado, the Hollywood Roosevelt Hotel, and Gettysburg's Historic Farnsworth House Inn. The latter advertises that it is "open for tours and ghost stories": "Descend the staircase into the darkness of the stone cellar. Hear, by candlelight, tales of phantom spectres whom [*sic*] are still believed to haunt the town and its battlefield." These storybook ghosts may be the only ones to inhabit the inn. The owner told me emphatically that he had never seen a ghost—there or anywhere else. "I don't believe in that stuff," he said. However, his daughter, who manages the inn, is not so skeptical, having "felt" a "presence" there. She related to me the experience of one guest who had seen a spectral figure after having gone to bed—very likely a common waking dream (Nickell 1995, 55).

The effect of new ownership has seemingly launched many hotel hauntings. Stories of ghostly events on the *Queen Mary* did not surface until after the ship became a tourist attraction in 1967 (Wlodarski et al. 1995, 13). At many other hotels, alleged paranormal events have seemed to wax and wane with changes in management. At the Holiday Inn on Grand Island, for example, the ghost tales—beginning soon after the initial opening—were happily related by one manager. He told a ghost hunter (Myers 1986, 291), "Our housekeepers have stories about Tanya that could fill a book." But a successor was "concerned with trying to improve the reputation of his hotel and dispel the rumors surrounding it," refusing "to acknowledge any paranormal happenings" (Gibson 1999).

Ghost tales may indeed be good for business. Explained an owner of one restaurant with bar, which "had a reputation for having ghosts" (Myers 1986, 228), "It was good conversation for the kind of business we're in. I never tried to dissuade anyone." Other proprietors may go even further. An alleged ghost at the Kennebunk Inn in Kennebunk, Maine, may have originated with the purchase of the inn by one of its earlier owners. He reportedly told a bartender one night that he was "going to make up a story about a ghost," presumably to promote the inn. Years later the former bartender related the story to the current owner, who in turn told me (Martin 1999). A hoax could well explain the "ghostly activity" at the Kennebunk Inn, which included "moving and flying crystal goblets, exploding wineglasses behind the bar, disarrayed silverware, and moving chairs" (Hauck 1996, 198). In fact, prior to the particular change of ownership that seemed to spark the poltergeist effects, apparently "all was quiet" at the historic inn (Sit 1991). Apparently the ghost moved away when, after about fifteen years, the business was sold again. Still later owners John and Kristen Martin reopened the inn in mid-1997 and along with a tenant who had lived there for twenty years, reported no experiences (Martin 1999).

Hoaxes do occur. For example, I caught one pranking "ghost" fla-grante delicto. In 1999, I accompanied a teacher and ten high school stu-dents from Denver's Colorado Academy on an overnight stay in a "haunted" hotel. Located in the Rocky Mountains, in the old mining town of Fairplay (where an art teacher conducts "ghost tours"), the Hand Hotel was built in 1931 (figure 45.2). In the early evening, as we gathered in the lobby beneath mounted elk heads and bear skins, the lights of the chandelier flickered mysteriously. But the teacher and I both spied the surreptitious action of the desk clerk, whose sheepish smile acknowl-edged that one brief hotel mystery had been solved.

Other signs of pranking there included a "ghost" photo (displayed in a lobby album), which the clerk confided to me was staged, and some pennies placed on the back of a men's room toilet, which from time to time would secretly become rearranged to form messages—like the word "WHY?" that I encountered. This obvious running prank invited other mischief makers (like one student) to join in.

Enter "Psychics"

Ghostly presences are hyped at many inns when "psychics" visit the pre-mises. One session at the Farnsworth House was part of a television pro-duction for Halloween, an indication of how much credibility should be afforded it. Brookdale Lodge, near Santa Cruz, California (which I inves-tigated for a Discovery Channel documentary that aired May 24, 1998), once invited Sylvia Browne. A regular on the *Montel Williams* TV show, the self-claimed clairvoyant and medium envisioned a ghost girl who

Figure 45.2. Does this corridor view in Colorado's Hand Hotel show spectral entities, or just silhouetted students? You decide. (Photos by Joe Nickell)

she named "Sara" (Gerbracht 1998), helping to bring the total number of entities thus far "detected" at Brookdale to forty-nine—and counting (Hauck 1996, 38). Such psychics typically offer unsubstantiated, even unverifiable claims, or information that is already known. This may be gleaned in advance from research sources or obtained by the "psychic" from persons who have such knowledge through the technique of "cold reading" (an artful method of fishing for information employed by shrewd fortune-tellers). Alternatively, the psychic may make numerous pronouncements, trusting that others will count the apparent hits and ignore, or interpret appropriately, the misses.

This is not to say that all such pronouncements are insincere. Those who fancy themselves psychics may exhibit the traits associated with a "fantasy-prone" personality—a designation for an otherwise normal person with an unusual ability to fantasize. As a child, he or she may have an imaginary playmate and live much of the time in make-believe worlds. As an adult, the person continues to spend much time fantasizing, and may report apparitional, out-of-body, or near-death experiences; claim psychic or healing powers; receive special messages from higher beings; be easily hypnotized; and/or exhibit other traits (Wilson and Barber 1983). Anyone may have some of these traits, but fantasizers have them in profusion. Sylvia Browne, for example, as a child had what her parents called "made-up friends," particularly a "spirit guide"—still with her—that she named "Francine." Browne undergoes "trances" in which "Francine" provides alleged information from "Akashic records, individual spirit guides, and messages from the Godhead." Browne also claims to see apparitions, talk to ghosts, have clairvoyant visions, make psychic medical diagnoses, divine past lives, etc. She has even started her own religion, Novus Spiritus ("New Spirit") (Browne and May 1998; Browne 1999).

The use of psychics is a stock in trade of many so-called parapsychologists. Among them is Hans Holzer, one of whose many books bills him as "the world's leading expert on haunted houses" (1991), while another avows that his "cases" were "carefully investigated under scientifically stringent conditions" (1993). Unfortunately, these claims are belied by Holzer's credulous acceptance of "spirit" photos, anecdotal reports, and other doubtful evidence. For example, he "investigated" a former stagecoach inn at Thousand Oaks, California, by relying on self-styled "witch" Sybil Leek (1922–1982). In one room, Leek "complained of being cold all over" and "felt" that a man had been murdered there. No verification was provided, and Holzer admits that Leek "did not connect" with a female ghost whose "presence" had been "sensed" by the inn's owners. Nevertheless, Holzer casually opines that "Like inns in general, this one may have more undiscovered ghosts hanging on the spot" (Holzer 1991, 192).

298

Fantasy Quotient

Professional "psychics" like Sybil Leek and Sylvia Browne aside, we may wonder whether ordinary "ghost" percipients also have similar tendencies toward fantasizing. During three decades of ghost investigating I have noticed a pattern. In interviewing residents or staff of an allegedly haunted site, I would usually find a few who had no ghostly experiences—for example, a bell captain at La Fonda Inn in Santa Fe who had spent forty-three years there. Others might have moderate experiences—like hearing a strange noise or witnessing some unexplained physical occurrence such as a door mysteriously opening—that they attributed to a ghost. Often, those interviewed would direct me to one or more persons whom they indicated had had intensive haunting encounters, including seeing apparitions. In short, I usually found a spectrum that ranged from outright skepticism to mediumistic experiences. I also sensed a difference in the people: some appeared down-to-earth and level-headed, while others seemed more imaginative and impulsive, recounting with dramatic flair their phantomesque adventures. I had no immediate way of objectively measuring what I thought I was observing, but I gave it much reflection.

At length I developed a questionnaire that on the one hand measures the number and intensity of ghostly experiences, and on the other counts the number of exhibited traits associated with fantasy-proneness. Tabulation of a limited number of questionnaires administered thus far shows a strong correlation between these two areas—that, as the level of haunting experiences rises, the fantasy scale tends to show a similarly high score. As this and other evidence indicates, to date there is no credible scientific evidence that inns—or any other sites—are inhabited by spirits of the dead. As Robert A. Baker often remarks, "There are no haunted places, only haunted people."

References

Baker, Robert A., and Joe Nickell. 1992. *Missing Pieces.* Buffalo, N.Y.: Prometheus.
Browne, Sylvia, with Lindsay Harrison. 1999. *The Other Side and Back.* New York: Dutton.

Browne, Sylvia, and Antoinette May. 1998. *Adventures of a Psychic.* Carlsbad, Calif.: Hay House.

Emmons, E. Thayles. 1959. History of Belhurst Castle. *The Geneva (New York) Times,* Nov. 11.

Gerbracht, Molly. 1997. Pre-interview notes for Discovery Channel special, "America's Haunted Houses" (in Nickell 1972–2000).

Gibson, Benjamin S. 1999. Report on interview with then-current manager, March 29, (in Nickell 1972–2000).

Green, Andrew. 1995. *Haunted Inns and Taverns.* Princes Risborough, Buckinghamshire, U.K.: Shire.

Haraldsson, E. 1998. Survey of claimed encounters with the dead. *Omega: Journal of Death and Dying* 19: 103–13.

Hauck, Dennis William. 1996. *Haunted Places: The National Directory.* New York: Penguin.

Holzer, Hans. 1991. *America's Haunted Houses.* Stamford, Ct.: Longmeadow.

————. 1993. *America's Restless Ghosts.* Stamford, Ct.: Longmeadow.

Klingel, Marion. 2000. Interview by author, May 3. (Also cited in Safiuddin 1994.)

Linenfelser, Teddy. 2000. Current Grand Island historian, interview by author, May 8.

MacKenzie, Andrew. 1982. *Hauntings and Apparitions.* London: Heinemann.

Martin, John. 1999. Interview by author, June 25.

Mason, John. 1999. *Haunted Heritage.* London: Collins and Brown, 60.

Mead, Robin. 1995. *Haunted Hotels: A Guide to American and Canadian Inns and Their Ghosts.* Nashville, Tenn.: Rutledge Hill.

Myers, Arthur. 1986. *The Ghostly Register.* Chicago: Contemporary.

Nickell, Joe. 1972–2000. Case files for sites named in text. Except as otherwise noted, this is the source for information in this article.

————. 1995. *Entities: Angels, Spirits, Demons and Other Alien Beings.* Amherst, N.Y.: Prometheus.

Safiuddin, Farrah. 1994. Ghostly guest refuses to check out of Grand Island haunt. *Buffalo (New York) News,* Oct. 30.

Sit, Mary. 1991. Maine's friendly ghost. *Boston Sunday Globe* (Travel section), Oct. 27.

Tyrrell, G.N.M. 1973. *Apparitions.* London: The Society for Psychical Research.

Wilson, Sheryl C., and Theodore X. Barber. 1983. "The Fantasy-Prone Personality," in A.A. Sheikh, ed., *Imagery: Current Theory, Research and Application.* New York: John Wiley & Sons.

Winfield, Mason. 1997. *Shadows of the Western Door.* Buffalo, N.Y.: Western New York Wares.

Wlodarski, Robert, Anne Nathan-Wlodarski, and Richard Senate. 1995. *A Guide to the Haunted Queen Mary.* Calabasas, Calif.: G-Host.

Chapter 46

The Flatwoods UFO Monster

In modern police parlance, a long-unsolved homicide or other crime may be known as a "cold case," a term we might borrow for such paranormal mysteries as that of the Flatwoods Monster, which was launched on September 12, 1952, and never completely explained.

About 7:15 p.m. on that day, at Flatwoods, a little village in the hills of West Virginia, some youngsters were playing football on the school playground. Suddenly they saw a fiery UFO streak across the sky and apparently land on a hilltop of the nearby Bailey Fisher farm. The youths ran to the home of Mrs. Kathleen May, who provided a flashlight and accompanied them up the hill. In addition to Mrs. May, a local beautician, the group included her two sons, Eddie, 13, and Freddie, 14; Neil Nunley, 14; Gene Lemon, 17; and Tommy Hyer and Ronnie Shaver, both 10; along with Lemon's dog.

There are myriad, often contradictory versions of what happened next, but UFO writer Gray Barker was soon on the scene and wrote an account for *Fate* magazine based on tape-recorded interviews. He found that the least emotional account was provided by Neil Nunley, one of two youths who were in the lead as the group hastened to the crest of the hill. Some distance ahead was a pulsing red light. Then suddenly, Gene Lemon saw a pair of shining, animal-like eyes and aimed the flashlight in their direction. The light revealed a towering "man-like" figure with a round, red "face" surrounded by a "pointed, hood-like shape." The body was dark and seemingly colorless, but some would later say it was green, and Mrs. May reported drapelike folds. The monster was observed only momentarily, as suddenly it emitted a hissing sound and glided toward the group. Lemon responded by screaming and dropping his flashlight, whereupon everyone fled.

The group had noticed a pungent mist at the scene, and afterward some were nauseous. A few locals, then later the sheriff and a deputy (who came from investigating a reported airplane crash), searched the site but "saw, heard and smelled nothing." The following day, A. Lee Stewart Jr., from the *Braxton Democrat*, discovered "skid marks" in the roadside field, along with an "odd, gummy deposit"—traces attributed to the landed "saucer" (Barker 1953).

In his article, Barker (1953) noted that "numerous people in a 20-mile radius saw the illuminated objects in the sky at the same time," evidently seeing different objects or a single one "making a circuit of the area." Barker believed the Flatwoods incident was consistent with other reports of "flying saucers or similar craft" and that "such a vehicle landed on the hillside, either from necessity or to make observations." (At this time in ufological history, the developing mythology had not yet involved alien "abductions.")

In addition to Barker's article (1953) and later his book (1956), accounts of the Flatwoods incident were related by another on-site investigator, paranormal writer Ivan T. Sanderson (1952, 1967), as well as the early ufologist Major Donald E. Keyhoe (1953). More recent accounts have garbled details, with Brookesmith (1995), for example, incorrectly reporting five of the children as belonging to Mrs. May, and Ritchie (1994) referring to the monster's hoodlike feature as a "halo," which he compared with those in Japanese Buddhist art. However, Jerome Clark's *UFO Encyclopedia* (1998) has a generally factual, sensible account of the affair, appropriately termed "one of the most bizarre UFO encounters of all time."

The UFO

On June 1, 2000, while on a trip that took me through Flatwoods, I was able to stop off for an afternoon of on-site investigating. I was amused to be greeted by a sign announcing, "Welcome to Flatwoods / Home of the Green Monster." Although the village has no local library, I found something even better: a real-estate business, Country Properties, whose co-owners Betty Hallman and Laura Green generously photocopied articles for me and telephoned residents to set up interviews.

Johnny Lockard, 95, told me that virtually everyone who had seen the alleged flying saucer in 1952 recognized it for what it was—a meteor. He, his daughter Betty Jean, and her husband Bill Sumpter said that the fireball had been seen on a relatively horizontal trajectory in various states. In fact, according to a former local newspaper editor, "There is no doubt that a meteor of considerable proportion flashed across the heavens that Friday night since it was visible in at least three states—Maryland, Pennsylvania and West Virginia" (Byrne 1966). The meteor explanation contrasts with the fanciful notions of Sanderson (1967). He cites several persons who each saw a *single* glowing object. Although observing that "All of the objects were traveling in the same direction and apparently at the same speed and at exactly the same time," he fails to draw the obvious conclusion: that there was one object, albeit variously described. (For example, one report said the object landed on a nearby knoll, while another described it as "disintegrating in the air with a rain of ashes.") Instead of suspecting that people were mistaken or that they saw a meteor that broke apart, Sanderson asserts that "to be logical" we should believe that "a flight of aerial machines" were "maneuvering in formation." For some reason, the craft went out of control, with one *landing* rather than crashing at Flatwoods, and its pilot emerged "in a space suit." Observed, it headed back to the spaceship, which—like two others that "crashed"— soon "vaporized" (Sanderson 1967).

Such airy speculations aside, according to Major Keyhoe (1953), Air Force Intelligence reportedly sent two men in civilian clothes to Flatwoods, posing as magazine writers, and they determined that the UFO had been a meteor that "merely appeared to be landing when it disappeared over the hill." That illusion also deceived a man approximately ten miles southwest of Flatwoods, who reported that an aircraft had gone down in flames on the side of a wooded hill. (That was the report the sheriff had investigated, without success, before arriving at the Flatwoods site.) Keyhoe's sources told him that "several astronomers" had concluded that the UFO was indeed a meteor. As well, a staff member of the Maryland Academy of Sciences announced that a meteor had passed over Baltimore at 7:00 P.M. on September 12, "traveling at a height of from 60 to 70 miles" (Reese 1952). It was on a trajectory toward West Virginia, where the "saucer" was sighted minutes later.

Spaceship Aground?

If the UFO was not a spaceship but a meteor, then how do we explain the other elements—the pulsating light, the landing traces, the noxious smell, and above all, the frightening creature? Let us consider each in turn.

As the group had proceeded up the roadway that led to the hilltop, they saw "a reddish light pulsating from dim to bright." It was described as a "globe" and as "a big ball of fire" (Barker 1953), but Sanderson (1967) says they "disagreed violently on their interpretation of this object." We should keep in mind that it was a distance away—an unknown distance—and that there was no trustworthy frame of reference from which to estimate size (reported to Sanderson as over twenty feet across). Significantly, at the time of the incident, a local school teacher called attention to "the light from a nearby plane beacon," and Sanderson (1952) conceded that there were three such beacons "in sight all the time on the hilltop." However, he dismissed the obvious possibility that one of these was the source of the pulsing light, because he was advocating an extraterrestrial explanation.

But if a UFO had not landed at the site, how do we explain the supposed landing traces? They were found at 7:00 the morning after the incident by A. Lee Stewart Jr., editor of the *Braxton Democrat,* who had visited the site the night before. Stewart discovered two parallel "skid marks" in the tall meadow grass, between the spot where the monster was seen and the area where the red pulsating light was sighted. He also saw traces of "oil" or "an odd, gummy deposit" (Barker 1953). Johnny Lockard's son, Max, describes Stewart in a word: "windy." Max had tried to explain to him and others the nature of the unidentified object that left the skid marks and oily/greasy deposit—namely, Max's black 1942 Chevrolet pickup truck. Soon after news of the incident had spread around Flatwoods that evening, Max drove up the hillside to have a look around. He told me he left the dirt road and circled through the field but saw nothing—no monster and no landing traces in the meadow grass. At the time of the incident, a few locals who had been skeptical that a flying saucer had landed on the hill attributed the skid marks and oil to a farm tractor. When several others told Gray Barker that the traces had actually been left by Max Lockard, he recalled his old high school chum and decided to telephone him. They had a proverbial failure to communicate and Barker—who admitted to seeing "an opportunity to get my name in print again"—concluded that Max's truck had not been at the exact spot where the alleged UFO markings were found.

Reading Barker (1956), one senses his impulse to dismiss the tractor and pickup hypotheses and never even to consider the possibility of some other vehicle. It is not clear that Barker ever saw the traces. He arrived one week after the incident, and rain had obliterated evidence during the interval. He could find "no trace of the oil reported to have been on the ground," and although he saw "marks and a huge area of grass trampled down," he conceded that could be due to the "multitudes" that had "visited and walked over the location" (Barker 1953, 1956). Max Lockard took me to the site (figure 46.1) in his modern pickup. A locked gate across the road prompted him to shift into four-wheel drive and take us on a cross-country shortcut through a field, much as he had done in his search for the reported UFO and monster nearly a half century before. He has convinced me that he indeed left the supposedly unexplained traces. With a twinkle in my eye, I posed a question: "Max, had you ever piloted a UFO before?" His smile answered that he had not.

As to the reported nauseating odor, it has been variously described as a sulfurous smell, "metallic stench," gaslike mist, or simply a "sickening, irritating" odor. Investigators first on the scene noticed no such smell, except for Lee Stewart, who detected it when he bent close to the ground. The effect on three of the youths, particularly Lemon, was later to cause nausea and complaints of irritated throats (Barker 1953, 1956; Sanderson 1967; Keyhoe 1953). This element of the story may be overstated. Ivan Sanderson (1967), scarcely a militant skeptic, also noticed the "strange smell in the grass" but said that it was "almost surely derived from a kind of grass that abounds in the area." He added, "We found this grass growing all over the county and it always smelt the same, though not perhaps as strongly." Keyhoe (1953) reported that the Air Force investigators had concluded that "the boys' illness was a physical effect brought on by their fright." Indeed Gene Lemon, the worst affected, had seemed the most frightened; he had "shrieked with terror" and fallen backward, dropping the flashlight, and later "appeared too greatly terrified to talk coherently" (Barker 1956). As to the strange "mist" that had accompanied the odor (Barker 1953), that seems easily explained. Obviously it was the beginning stage of what the sheriff subsequently noticed on his arrival, a fog that was "settling over the hillside" (Keyhoe 1953).

Figure 46.1. Flatwoods, West Virginia, resident Max Lockard identifies site of 1952 "monster" sighting.

The Creature

Finally, and most significantly, there remains to be explained "the Flatwoods Monster," a.k.a. "the Phantom of Flatwoods," "the Braxton County Monster," "the Visitor from Outer Space," and other appellations (Byrne 1966). Many candidates have been proposed, but considering that the UFO became an IFO, namely a meteor, the least likely one is some extraterrestrial entity. I think we can also dismiss the notion, among the hypotheses put forward by a local paper, that it was the effect of "vapor from a falling meteorite that took the form of a man" ("Monster" 1952). Also unlikely in the extreme was the eventual explanation of Mrs. May that what she had seen "wasn't a monster" but rather "a secret plane the government was working on" (Marchal 1966). (Both she and her son Fred declined to be interviewed for my investigation.)

I agree with most previous investigators that the monster sighting was not a hoax; the fact that the witnesses *did* see a meteor and assembled

Figure 46.2. Split-image illustration compares fanciful
Flatwoods Monster (left) with the real-world creature it most
resembles—the common barn owl (right). (Photo and drawing
by Joe Nickell)

on the spur of the moment to investigate makes that unlikely. So does
the fact that everyone who talked to them afterward insisted—as Max
Lockard did to me—that the eyewitnesses were genuinely frightened.
Clearly, they saw something that frightened them, but what? The group
described shining "animal eyes," and Mrs. May at first thought they belonged to "an opossum or raccoon in the tree" (Barker 1956, Sanderson
1967). Locals continued to suggest some such local animal, including "a

buck deer" (Barker 1956), but a much more credible candidate was put forth by the unnamed Air Force investigators. According to Keyhoe (1953), they concluded the "monster" was probably "a large owl perched on a limb" with underbrush beneath it having "given the impression of a giant figure" and the excited witnesses having "imagined the rest."

I believe this generic solution is correct, except that the owl was not from the family of "typical owls" (*Strigidae*) that includes the familiar great horned owl, but from the other family (*Tytonidae*), which comprises the barn owls. Several elements in the witnesses' descriptions help identify the Flatwoods creature specifically as *Tyto alba*, the common barn owl, known almost worldwide (Collins 1959). Consider the following evidence: The "monster" reportedly had a "man-like shape" and stood some ten feet tall, although Barker (1953) noted that "descriptions from the waist down are vague; most of the seven said this part of the figure was not under view." These perceptions are consistent with an owl perched on a limb (figure 46.2).

Also suggestive of an owl is the description of the creature's "face" as "round" with "two eye-like openings" and a dark, "hood-like shape" around it (if not the "pointed" appearance of the latter) (Barker 1953). The barn owl has a large head with a "ghastly," roundishly heart-shaped face, resembling "that of a toothless, hook-nosed old woman, shrouded in a closely fitting hood" and with an expression "that gives it a mysterious air" (Jordan 1952, Blanchan 1925).

Very evidential in the case of the Flatwoods Monster is the description of its cry as "something between a hiss and a high-pitched squeal" (Barker 1953). This tallies with the startling "wild, peevish scream" or "shrill rasping hiss or snore" of the barn owl. Indeed its "shrill, strangled scream is a most unbirdlike noise." Its "weird calls" include "hissing notes, screams," and "guttural grunts" (Blanchan 1925, Peterson 1980, Bull and Farrand 1977, Cloudsley-Thompson et al. 1983). The latter might explain the monster's accompanying "thumping or throbbing noise" (Barker 1953), if those sounds were not from the flapping of wings.

Descriptions of the creature's movement varied, being characterized as "bobbing up and down, jumping toward the witnesses" or as moving "evenly," indeed "describing an arc, coming toward them, but circling at the same time" (Barker 1956). Again, it had "a gliding motion as if afloat in midair." These movements are strongly suggestive of a bird's flight. When accidentally disturbed, the barn owl "makes a bewildered and erratic getaway" (Jordan 1952)—while hissing (Blanchan 1925)—but its flight is generally characterized with "slow, flapping wing beats and long glides" (Cloudsley-Thompson et al. 1983).

According to Barker (1953), "Not all agreed that the 'monster' had arms," but "Mrs. May described it with terrible claws." Sanderson (1967) cites the witnesses' observation that "the creature had small, claw-like hands that extended in front of it," a description consistent with a raptor (a predatory bird). The barn owl is relatively long-legged and knock-kneed, sporting sizable claws with sharp, curved talons that may be prominently extended (Peterson 1980, Forshaw 1998).

It is important to note that the youths and Mrs. May only glimpsed the creature briefly—an estimated "one or a few more seconds," and even that was while they were frightened. Barker (1956) asks, "If Lemon dropped the flashlight, as he claimed, how did they get an apparently longer look at the 'monster'?" Some said the being was lighted from within (probably only the effect of its "shining" eyes), while Nunley stated that it was illuminated by the pulsing red light (ostensibly from the supposed UFO but probably from one of the beacons mentioned earlier). This might also explain the "fiery orange color" of the creature's head (Sanderson 1967), but an alternative explanation, while the barn owl is typically described as having a white facial disc and underparts, in the case of the female those parts "have some darker buff or tawny color" ("Barn Owl" 2000).

For this reason, as well as the fact that in this species (a medium-sized owl, measuring about fourteen to twenty inches [Peterson 1980]), the male is typically the smaller (Blanchan 1925), I suspect the Flatwoods creature was a female. It is also interesting to speculate that it may not have been too late in the year for a female to have been brooding young. That could explain why "she" did not fly away at the first warning of intruders (given barn owls' "excellent low-light vision and exceptional hearing ability" ["Barn Owl" 2000]); instead, probably hoping not to be noticed, she stood her ground until invaders confronted her with a flashlight, a threatening act that provoked her hissing, attacklike swoop toward them.

Significantly, the locale where the Flatwoods Monster made its appearance—near a large oak tree on a partially wooded hilltop overlooking a farm on the outskirts of town—tallies with the habitat of the barn owl. Indeed, it is "the best known of farmland owls" (Cloudsley-Thompson 1983). It builds no nest but takes as its "favorite home" a "hollow tree" (Blanchan 1925). It "does not mind the neighborhood of man" (Jordan 1952), in fact seeking out mice and rats from its residence in "woodlands, groves, farms, barns, towns, cliffs" (Peterson 1980).

Considering all of the characteristics of the described monster, and making small allowances for misperceptions and other distorting factors, we may conclude (adapting an old adage) that if it looked like a barn owl, acted like a barn owl, and hissed like a barn owl, then it was most likely a barn owl.

How "Monsters" Appear

It may be wondered, however, why the creature was not immediately recognized for what it was. The answer is that, first, the witnesses were led to *expect* an alien being by their sighting of a UFO that appeared to land and by the pulsating red light and strange smell that seemed to confirm the landing. Therefore, when they then encountered a strange creature acting aggressively, their fears seemed to be confirmed and they panicked.

Moreover, the group had probably never seen a barn owl up close (after all, such birds are nocturnal) and almost certainly not under the adverse conditions that prevailed. The brief glimpse, at night, of a being that suddenly swept at them—coupled with its strange "ghastly" appearance and shrill frightening cry—would have been disconcerting to virtually anyone at any time. But under the circumstances, involving an inexperienced group primed with expectations of extraterrestrials, the situation was a recipe for terror.

And so a spooked barn owl in turn spooked the interlopers, and a monster was born. A "windy" newspaperman and pro-paranormal writers hyped the incident, favoring sensational explanations for more prosaic ones. Such is often the case with paranormal claims.

References

Barker, Gray. 1953. The monster and the saucer. *Fate*, Jan., 12–17.
———. 1956. *They Knew Too Much About Flying Saucers.* New York: Tower.
"Barn Owl." 2000. http://www.vetmed.auburn.edu/raptor/history/barnowl.htm
Blanchan, Neltje. 1925. *Birds Worth Knowing.* Garden City, N.Y.: Nelson Doubleday, 180–82.

Brookesmith, Peter. 1995. *UFO: The Complete Sightings.* New York: Barnes & Noble, 54.

Bull, John, and John Farrand Jr. 1977. *The Audubon Society Field Guide to North American Birds: Eastern Region.* New York: Knopf, 500.

Byrne, Holt. 1966. The phantom of Flatwoods. *Sunday Gazette-Mail State Magazine* (Charleston, W. Va.), March 6.

Clark, Jerome. 1998. *The UFO Encyclopedia*, second edition. Detroit: Omnigraphics, I: 409–12.

Cloudsley-Thompson, John, et al. 1983. *Nightwatch: The Natural World from Dusk to Dawn.* New York: Facts on File.

Collins, Henry Hill, Jr. 1959. *Complete Guide to American Wildlife: East, Central and North.* New York: Harper & Row.

Forshaw, Joseph. 1998. *Encyclopedia of Birds.* San Diego: Academic Press.

Jordan, E.L. 1952. *Hammond's Nature Atlas of America.* Maplewood, N.J.: C.S. Hammond.

Keyhoe, Donald E. 1953. *Flying Saucers from Outer Space.* New York: Henry Holt.

Marchal, Terry. 1966. Flatwoods revisited. *Sunday Gazette-Mail State Magazine* (Charleston, W. Va.), March 6.

"Monster" held illusion created by meteor's gas. 1952. *Charleston Gazette* (Charleston, W. Va.), Sept. 23.

Peterson, Roger Tory. 1980. *A Field Guide to the Birds.* Boston: Houghton Mifflin, 174–75.

Reese, P.M. 1952. Cited in Sanderson 1967.

Ritchie, David. 1994. *UFO: The Definitive Guide to Unidentified Flying Objects and Related Phenomena.* New York: MJF Books, 83, 96.

Sanderson, Ivan T. 1952. Typewritten report quoted in Byrne 1966.

———. 1967. *Uninvited Visitors: A Biologist Looks at UFOs.* New York: Cowles, 37–52.

Chapter 47

Milk-Drinking Idols

Throughout the Hindu world on September 21, 1995, statues of Indian deities sipped spoonfuls of milk in supposed fulfillment of a devotee's dream.

As the phenomenon progressed, it spread from the deity Lord Ganesh, the elephant-headed, multihanded, Hindu god, to other idols, including Nandi the Bull, and statues of Lord Shiva, who is often depicted in human form with a serpent around his neck. Spreading across India, the milk-sipping phenomenon soon extended to other parts of the Asian continent as well as to Europe and North America where it was duly noted on television and in newspapers.

An Indian psychiatrist explained: "All people are vulnerable to such credulousness. Hindus were especially susceptible because this was the season of *pitr baksh,* when the devout offered milk for the souls of their ancestors" (Nickell 1996). So many Hindus were caught up in the excitment that milk supplies were depleted and prices soared—even for canned and powdered milk, although only "Kachcha," unboiled milk, was supposed to be accepted by the deities.

Skeptics pointed out that many of the statues were made of baked clay, which absorbs liquids prodigiously by capillary attraction. States Julia Higgins, professor of polymer chemistry at London's Imperial College, "Break a flowerpot, dip it in water, and the water disappears like mad." With glazed statues, only a bit of the glaze need be absent, say from a tooth (as indeed seemed the case in one statue), for capillary attraction to work.

But what about relatively nonporous materials like marble or even nonporous ones such as brass and other metals? Some people noticed milk pooling at the bottoms of such statues but could not explain how it was getting there. The secret was discovered by the federal Department of Science and Technology in New Delhi. Researchers there offered a statue milk mixed with a red dye and observed that while the milk quickly disappeared from the spoon, it soon coated the statue due to surface tension. Explained the secretary of the Indian Rationalists' Society, Sanal Edamaruku: When a spoonful of milk is offered to a "wet idol" (many of the idols had been ritually washed) the spoon is naturally tilted a bit and the milk imperceptibly drains over the idol. In such a thin layer it is virtually transparent, especially on marble or other white or light-colored surfaces. "The basic principle behind it," says Edamaruku, "is that when two drops of a liquid are brought together it leads to the formation of one drop."

Hoaxing was apparently responsible in a few cases. For example, *India Abroad* reported (September 29, 1995): "At a temple in the Bengali Market area of the capital, canisters with pipes running into them were found in the backyard. The canisters had gathered the milk fed by the devotees." And at a temple in Toronto investigated by CSICOP Fellow Henry Gordon, a well-known magician and author in Canada, the attendants refused to allow him to lift the small, thirsty idol from its large base. (He was also refused the opportunity to give the idol water and thus test the claim that it drank only milk.)

Although the widespread phenomenon reportedly ceased after one day, possibly due to official expectations, it continued in some homes in New York City for a time. Reported the *Miami Herald*, "It took 'the miracle' exactly eight days to reach Miami from India." On the other hand, at certain sites, such as the Ganesh temple in Toronto's Richmond Hill suburb, nothing ever happened.

Nature magazine (September 28, 1995) reported that "science took a hammering from religion" over the affair, but it did so only on the propaganda level. *Nature* seemed heartened by the statement signed by prominent scientists in Madras. It called on educated Indians to help ensure "that primitive obscurantism and superstition did not hold sway over a society on the threshold of the 21st century."

My own involvement with the phenomenon was initially to monitor developments and answer news queries, as well as write a short article about the events for *Skeptical Inquirer* magazine. At the end of May 2001, however, I had an opportunity to study the phenomenon with Indian skeptic Vikas Gora. He was visiting the Center for Inquiry, where I have

Figure 47.1. Indian skeptic Vikas Gora demonstrates the milk-drinking-idol effect in the author's lab.

315

Figure 47.2. Statue of Ganesh appears to drink a spoonful of milk as it is drawn—seemingly mysteriously—onto the figurine.

my office and paranormal-investigation lab, and we spent an entertaining and illuminating afternoon replicating and discussing the milk-drinking effect. Vikas had witnessed the original "miracle" and had considerable first-hand knowledge about the entire matter.

Our experiments confirmed that it is not important what effigy is used, although white is best if milk is the beverage of choice. (A Casper the Friendly Ghost figure proved as thirsty as any other, for example.) When a colored figurine is used, water may be substituted for the milk. The statue does need to be wet for the first demonstration, but thereafter each successive dribbling sets up the next apparent sipping. Also the effect works best if the spoon is brimful of liquid.

References

Nickell, Joe. 1996. Milk-drinking idols, *Skeptical Inquirer* 20:2 (March/April 1996), 7. (See this for additional news sources.)

Notes

Chapter 3. Magicians Among the Spirits

1. I used principles and evidence detailed in my books *Pen, Ink and Evidence* (1990), *Detecting Forgery* (1996), and *Crime Science* (1999). The scrapbook consists of fifty-six leaves (112 pages) of unwatermarked, machine-made "wove" paper about 6 $^5/_8$ by 15 $^1/_4$ inches high, bearing ledger-style vertical rulings; it is bound with pasteboard covers (having marbled-paper exteriors and leather spine and corners) in the manner of many mid-nineteenth-century "blank books" (see Nickell 1990, 164). The dated clippings and writings are consistent with their time periods, ranging from 1856 to 1910.

2. Another clipping—annotated "1861/Adrian, Mich."—notes that on January 26, Ira E. Davenport wed "Miss Augusta Green of this city."

Chapter 8. A Study in Clairvoyance

3. Mr. B gave readings for three women, offering about a dozen assertions for each in a rambling style but scoring only one or two "hits" with each. Even those were dubious: for example, he told one woman, "I'm getting some sickness vibes with you, as if you had been in the hospital not too long ago, had been through something that came close to being an operation." He also said he saw a brother. She credited him with success by switching the focus from herself, saying (to applause), "I've a brother who had an operation, and I've been in his hospitals lately."

4. Dahmer's grisly crimes came to light with his arrest on July 22, 1991; he was sentenced February 17, 1992 (see Croteau and Worcester 1993).

Chapter 9. The Kennedy Curse

5. This contrast in approaches is illustrated with regard to the Shroud of Turin in my "Science vs. 'Shroud Science,'" *Skeptical Inquirer* 22.4 (July/August 1998): 20–22.

Chapter 13. The Silver Lake Serpent

6. A native American named John John was cited as relating how, long before, two members of his tribe who had camped on the lake shore were frightened by the appearance of a monstrous serpent. The Senecas have a legend of *Djo-nih-gwa-donh* or the Great Horned Serpent. (See Jesse J. Cornplanter, *Legends of the Longhouse*, New York: J.B. Lippincott, 1938, 73–80.)

7. "Boniface" refers to the landlord in Irish dramatist George Farquhar's comedy, *The Beaux' Strategem* (1707). The term has come to mean "a hotel proprietor; innkeeper." (See *Webster's New Universal Unabridged Dictionary*, 2nd ed. New York: Dorset & Baber, 1983.)

8. This appears to be a variant of "nigger in the woodpile," an offensive expression referring to some hidden factor that has an adverse effect on something. (See E. M. Kirkpatrick and C. M. Schwarz, eds., *The Wordsworth Dictionary of Idioms*, Ware, U.K.: Wordsworth Reference, 1993, 240.)

Chapter 15. Paranormal Lincoln

9. Among other implicitly paranormal claims relating to Lincoln are the "mysterious coincidences" that are often claimed between him and President John F. Kennedy. See Martin Gardner, *The Magic Numbers of Dr. Matrix* (Buffalo, N.Y.: Prometheus, 1985) and Bruce Martin, "Coincidence: Remarkable or Random?" *Skeptical Inquirer* 22(5) (September/October 1998): 23–28.

Chapter 28. The Gypsies' "Great Trick"

10. Other sources suggest the term may derive from *hokey-pokey*, an alteration of *hocus-pocus*.

Chapter 31. The Cryptic Stone

11. The carved grooves also contain metallic scrape marks and traces of what appears to be black paint.

Chapter 37. The Secrets of Oak Island

12. Although the presence of coconut fiber on the island is unexplained, similar fiber has been reported on Sable Island, some two hundred miles to the east and the site of numerous shipwrecks.

Chapter 42. Spirit Paintings

13. Spirit photography was reportedly "discovered" by Boston photographer William H. Mumler, who noticed "extras" on recycled glass plates from which previous images had not been entirely removed. In 1862, Mumler began producing spirit photographs for credulous sitters but was later exposed when some of the entities were recognized as living city residents (Nickell 1995, 31).

Chapter 43. Watching the Spirits Paint

14. If it is true, as earlier stated, that the picture seemingly appeared on the "canvas" nearest the sitter, all that would have been needed was for the pair of panels to have been casually reversed as they were taken down from the frame and carried to the sitter.

15. I have wondered whether the Bangses might have produced a picture in "real time," working on the rearmost panel (reversed for the purpose) while the sitter viewed the progress. Such a scenario (too lengthy to detail here) would present many difficulties, and one would think even a credulous sitter would catch on. But it might still be possible.

Chapter 44. Stigmata

16. I also discovered that one could produce the opposite effect, renewing the bleeding of a cut that was many hours old, by applying hydrogen peroxide. This has implications to cases of stigmata in which bleeding was reported over an extended time, although there are many ways of accomplishing such an effect.

Index